Visions of New England

 Visit www.viewfromthepier.com

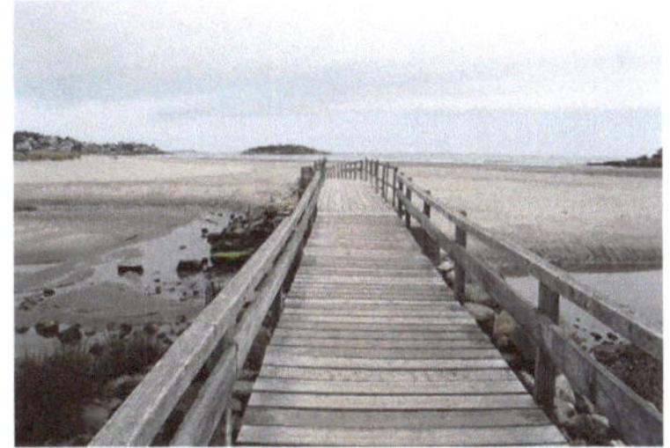

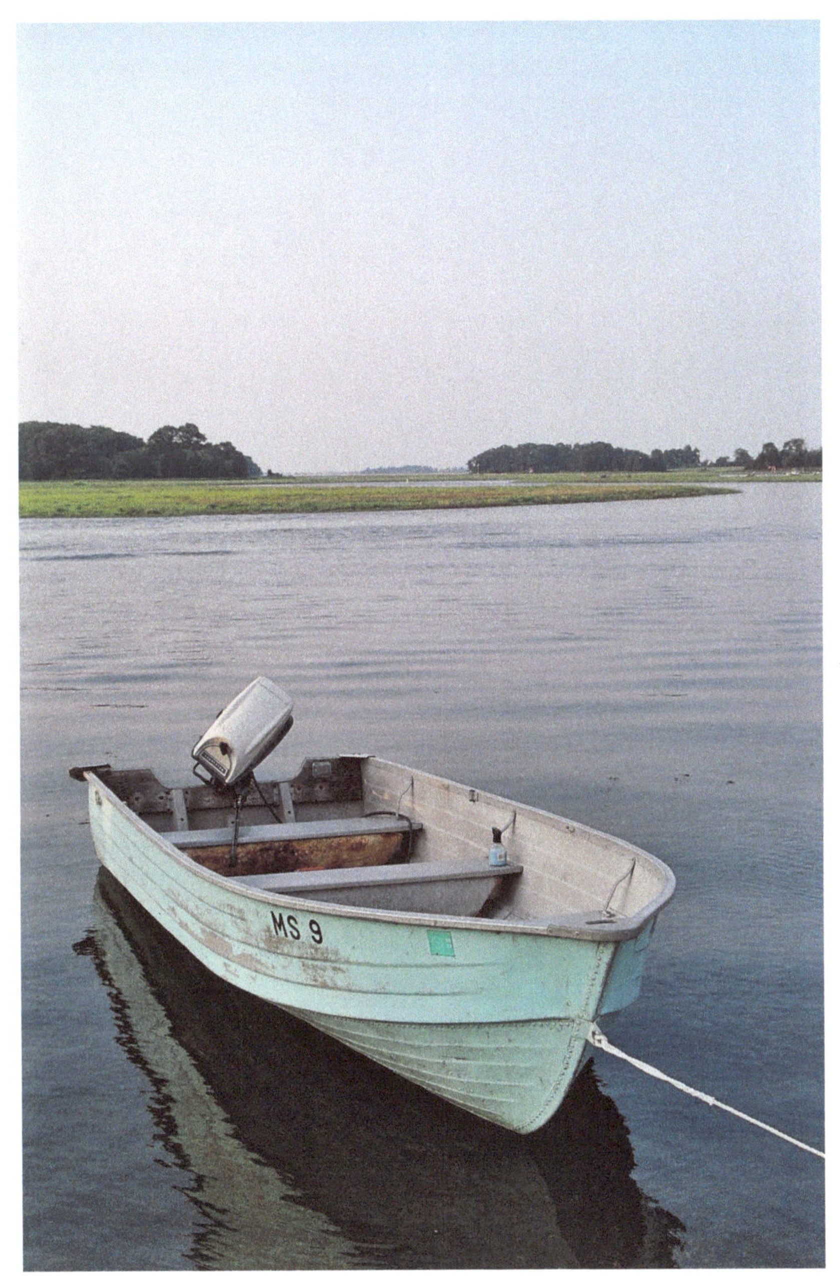

Essex, Massachusetts

I have often been adrift, but I have always stayed afloat.

--David Berry

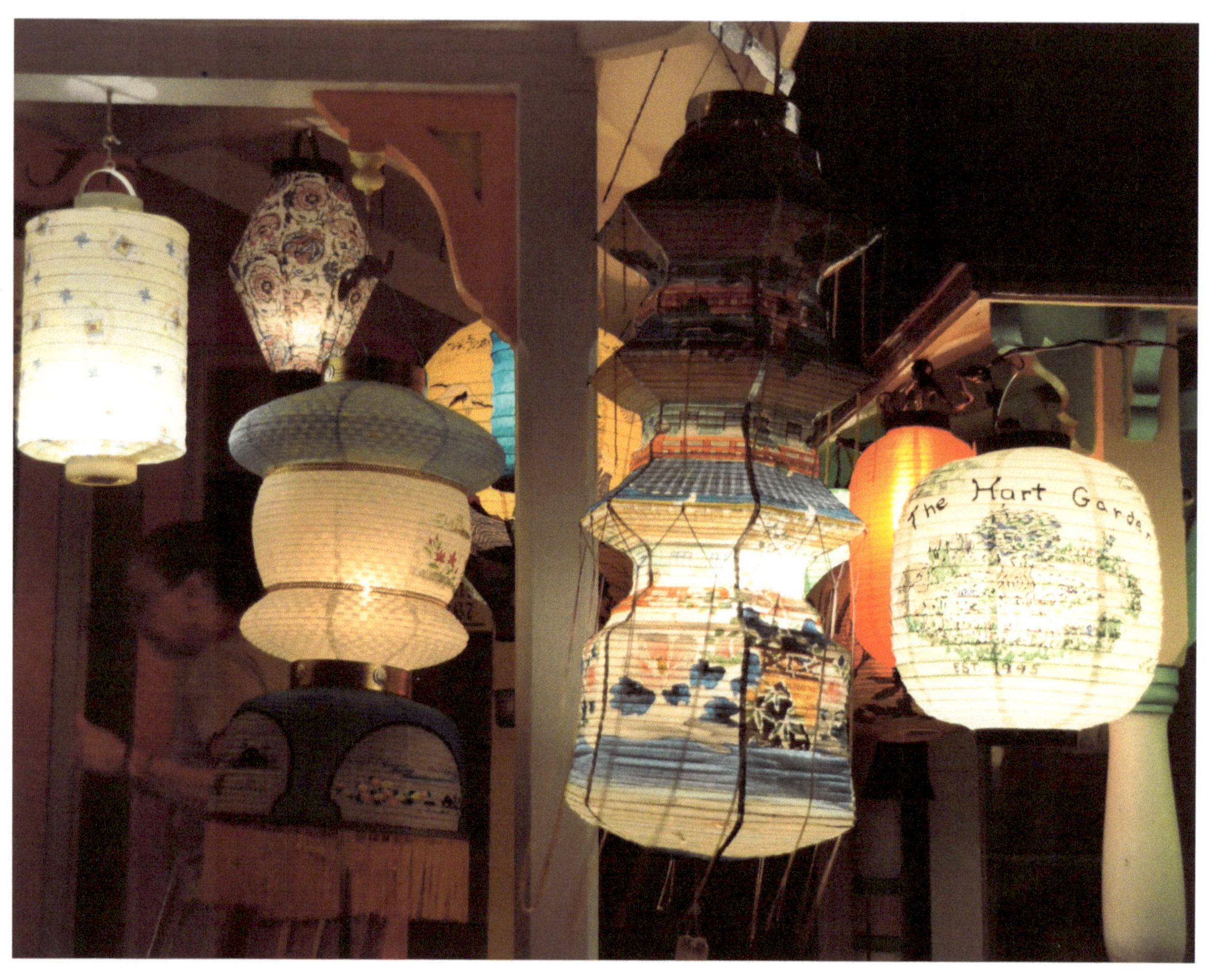

Oak Bluffs, Massachusetts

Every person has an ideal, a hope, a dream,
which represents the soul. We must give to it
the warmth of love, the light of understanding and
the essence of encouragement.
--Colby Dorr Dan

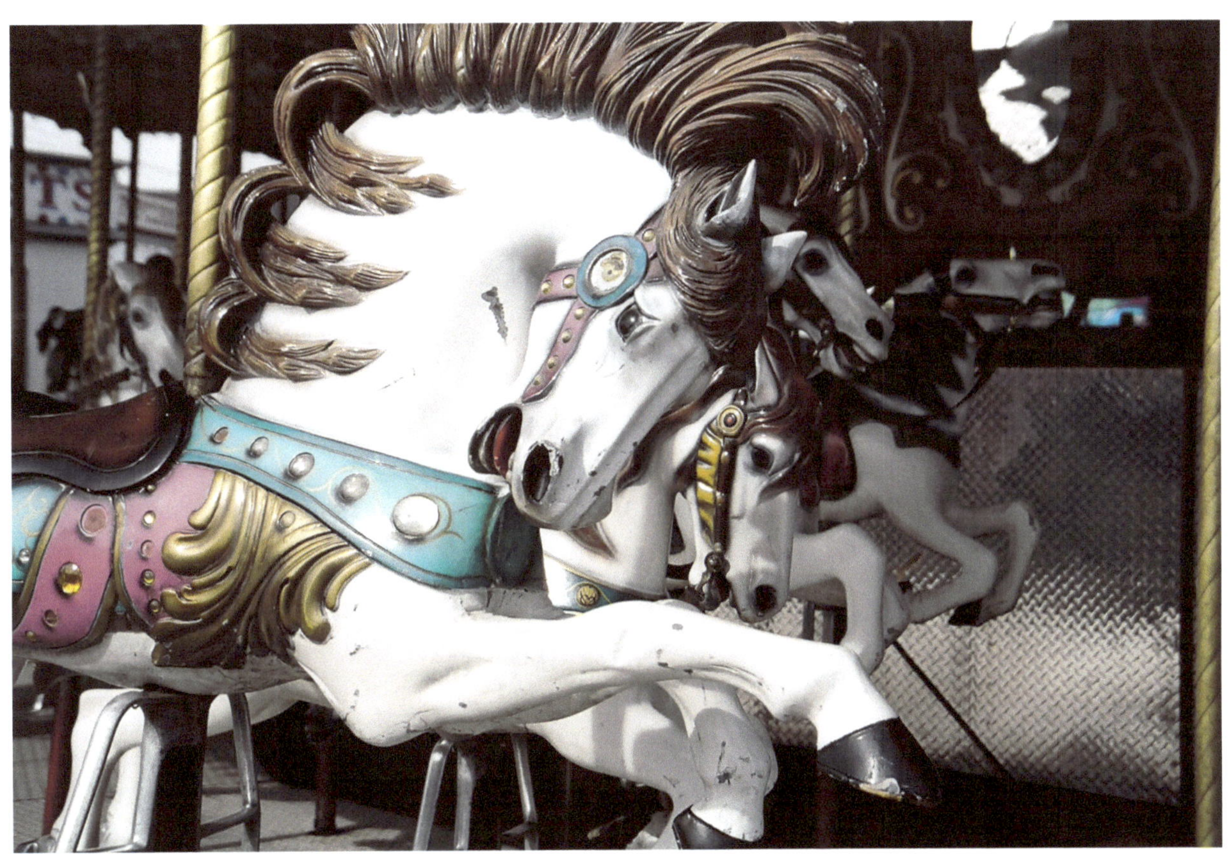

Topsfield, Massachusetts

Never forget that you are one of a kind.
Never forget that if there weren't any need for you
in all your uniqueness to be on earth,
you wouldn't be here in the first place.

--R. Buckminster Fuller, 1893 - 1983

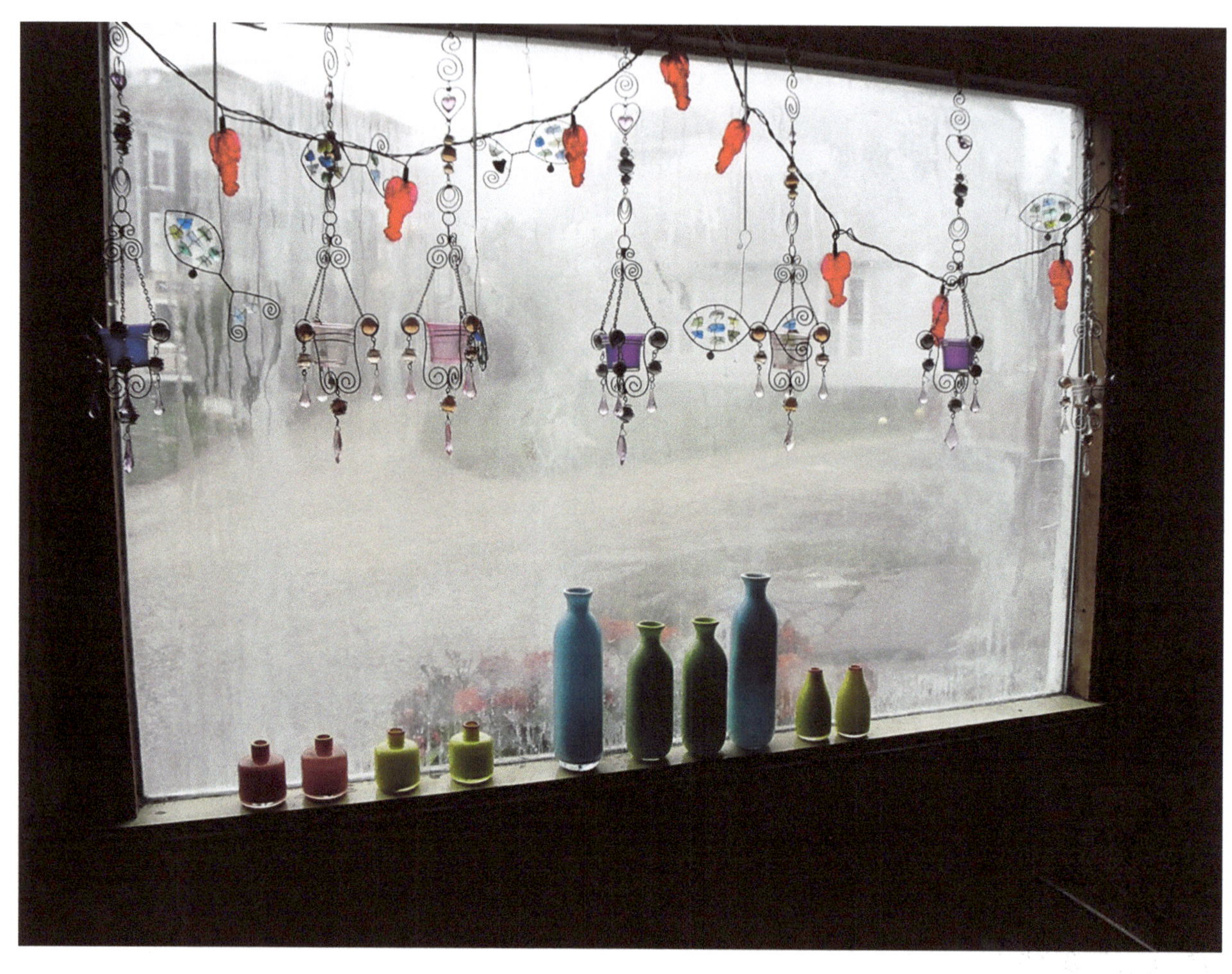

Monhegan Island, Maine

Poetry often enters through the window of irrelevance.

– Mary Caroline Richards, 1916 - 1999

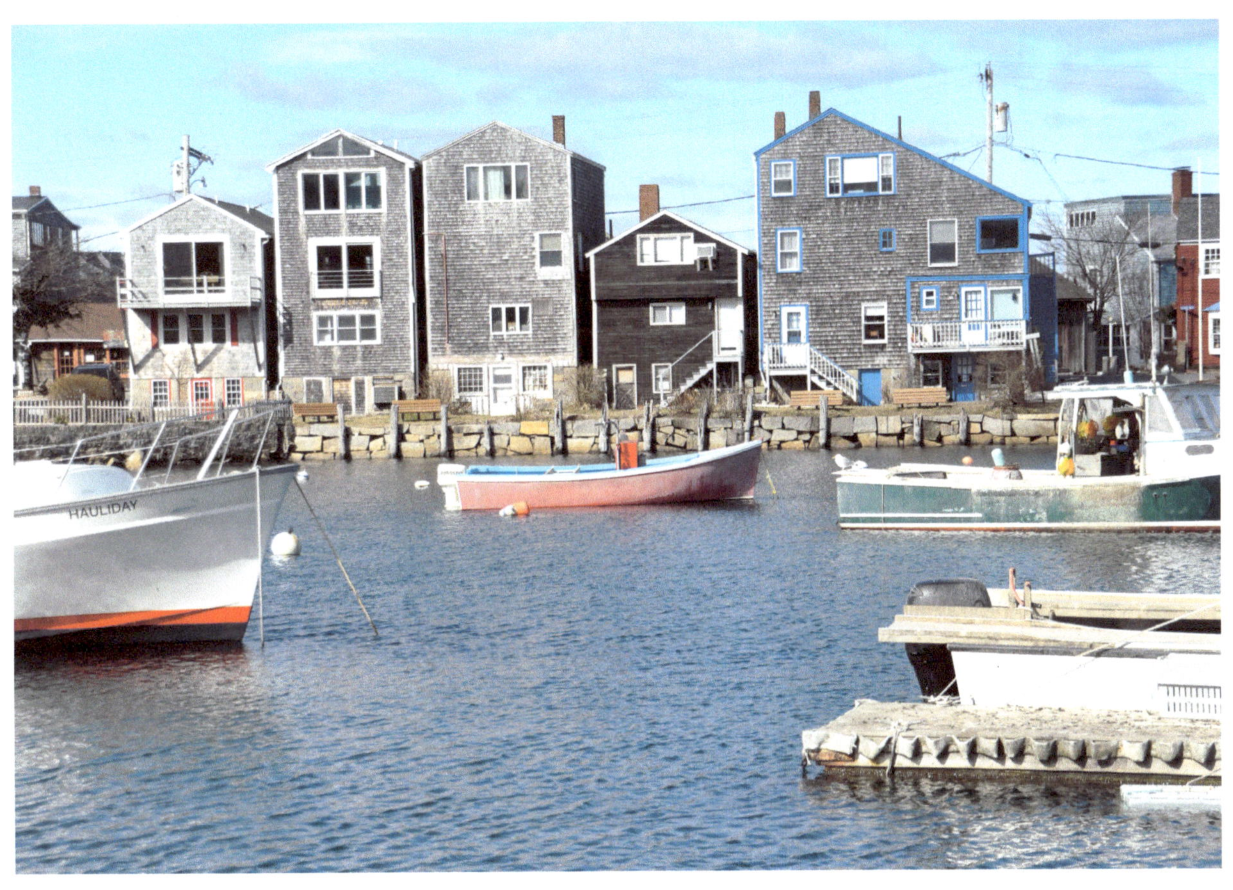

Rockport, Massachusetts

A harbor, even if it is a little harbor, is a good thing...

It takes something from the world, and has something to give in return.

--Sarah Orne Jewett, 1849 - 1909

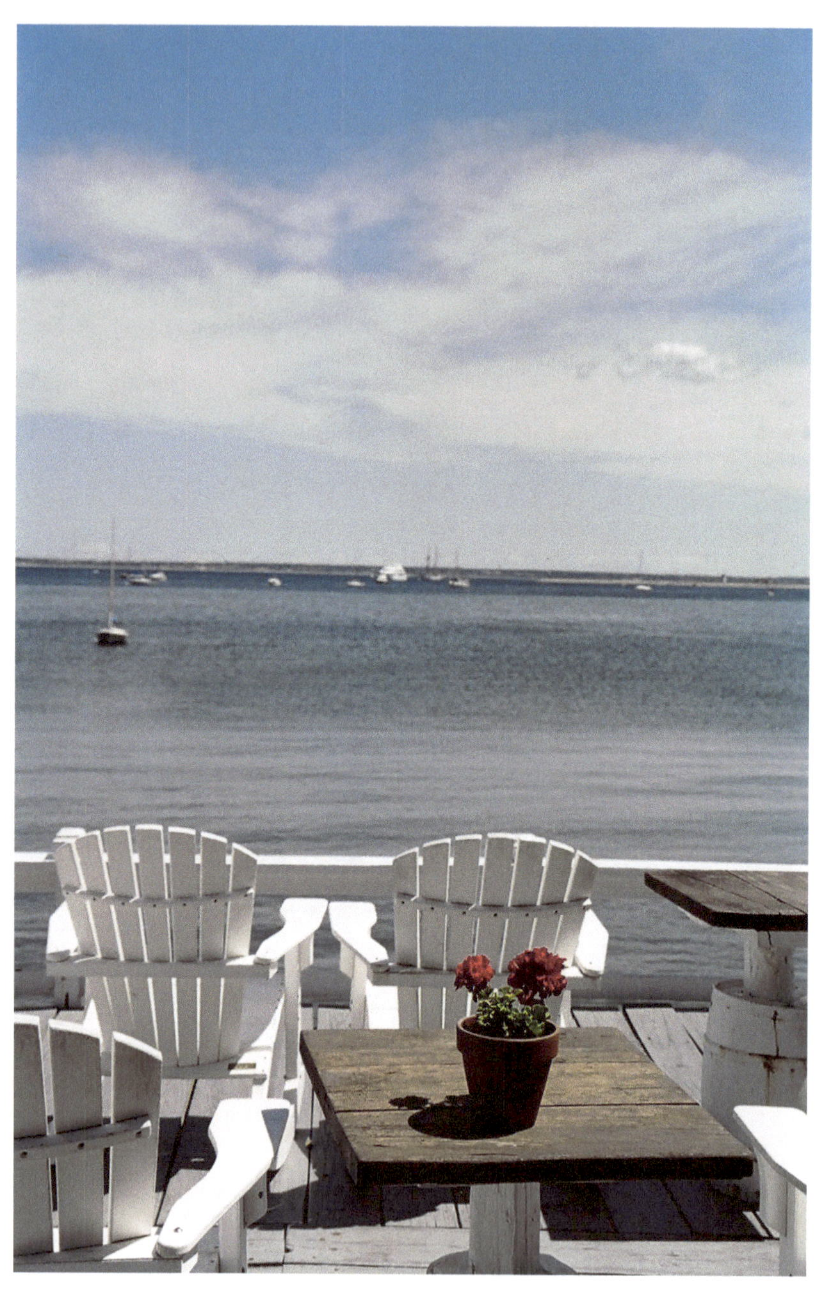

Provincetown, Massachusetts

You pray in your distress and in your need;
would that you might also in the fullness of your joy and in your days of abundance.
--Kahlil Gibran, 1883 - 1931

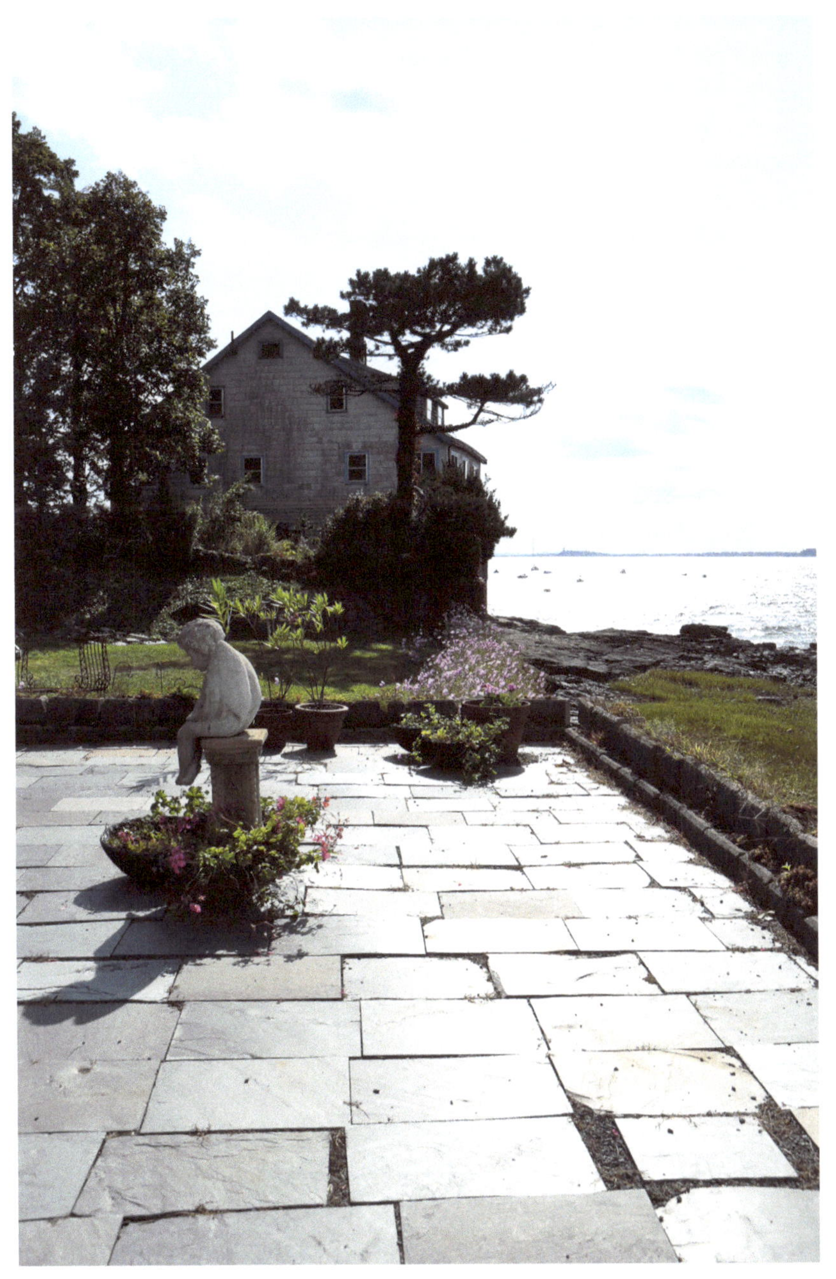

Nahant, Massachusetts

We look too much to museums.

The sun coming up in the morning is enough.

--Ralph Ellison, 1914 - 1994

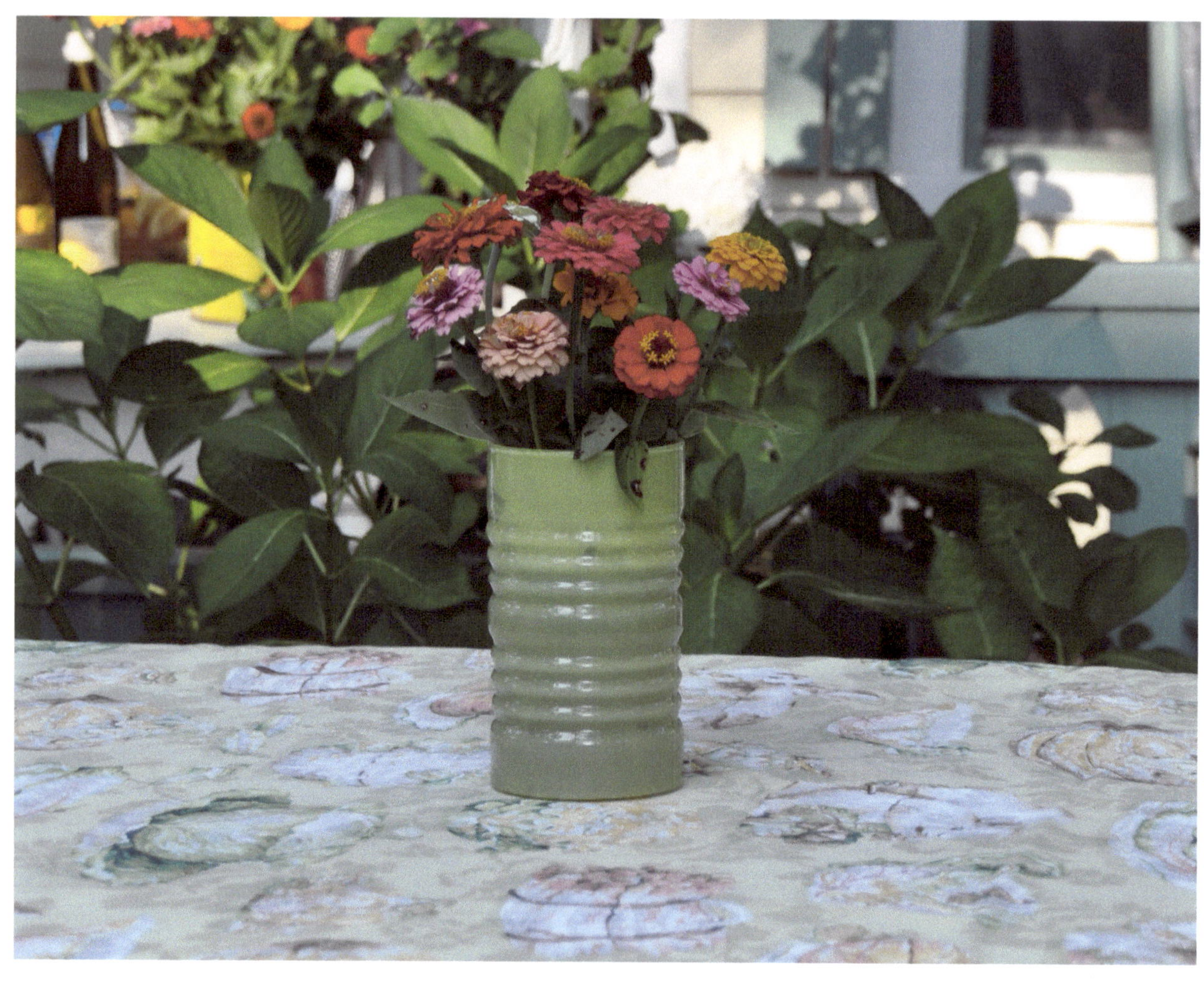

Oak Bluffs, Massachusetts

Arranging a bowl of flowers in the morning can give a sense of quiet in a crowded day - like writing a poem, or saying a prayer.

--Anne Morrow Lindbergh, 1906 - 2001

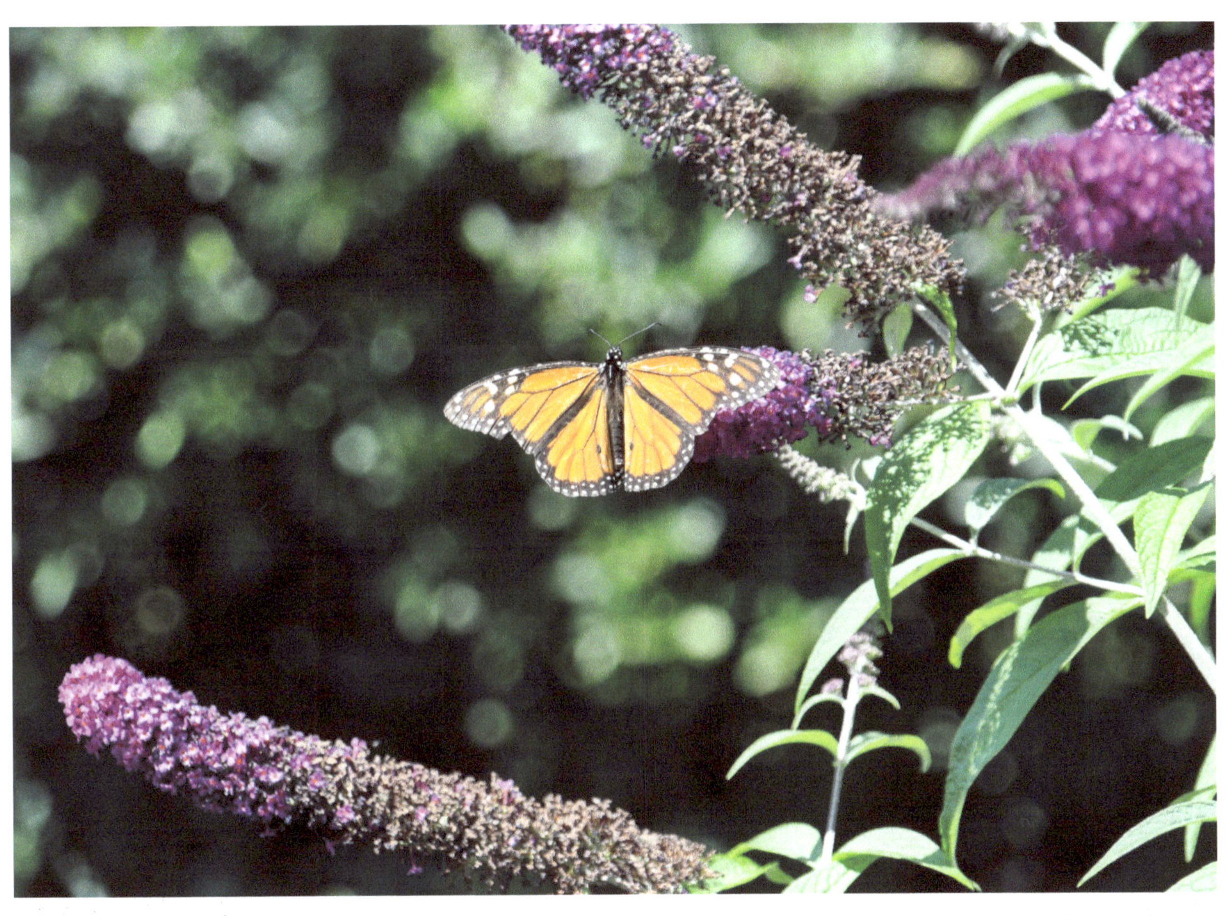

Nahant, Massachusetts

Happiness is as a butterfly which, when pursued, is always beyond our grasp,

but which if you will sit down quietly, may alight upon you.

--Nathaniel Hawthorne, 1804 - 1864

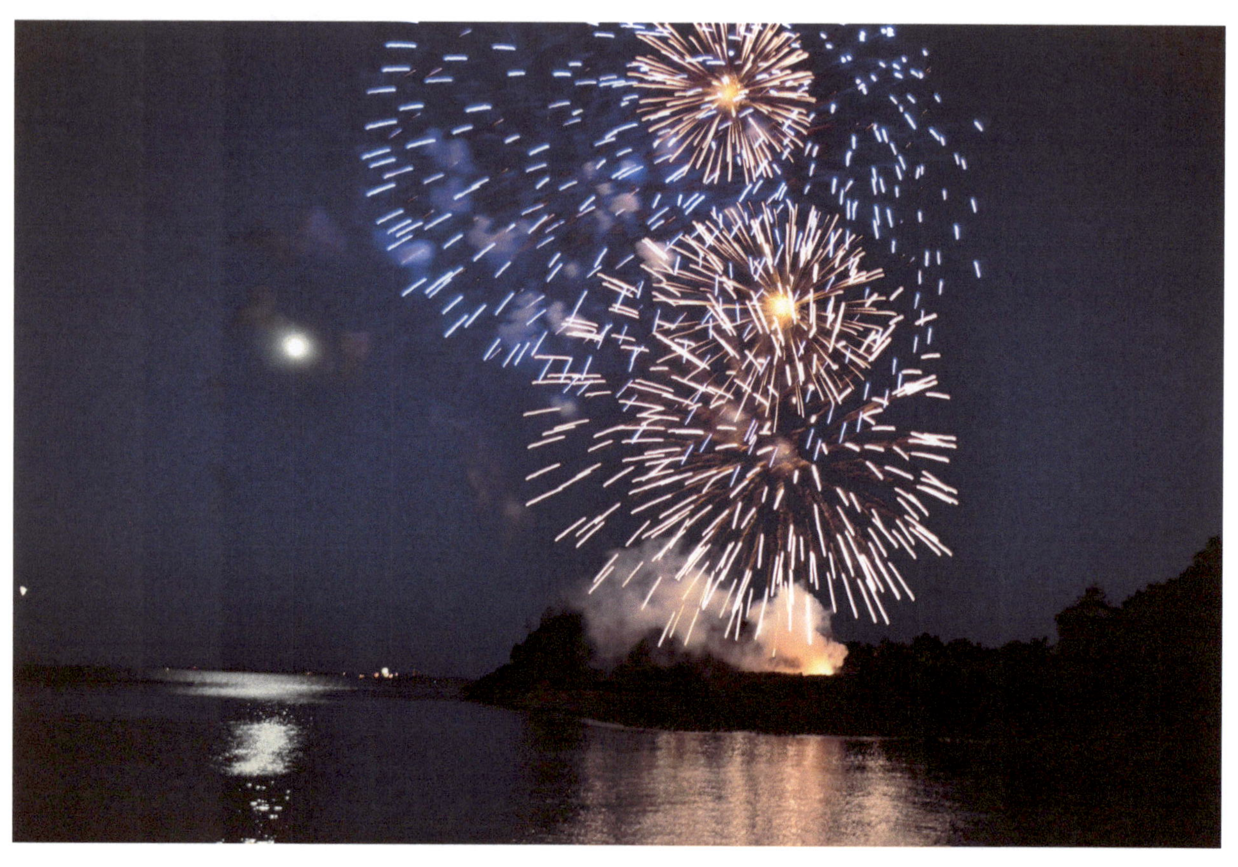

Nahant, Massachusetts

Without inspiration, the best powers of the mind remain dormant,
they is a fuel in us which needs to be ignited with sparks.
--Johann Gottfried Von Herder, 1744 - 1803

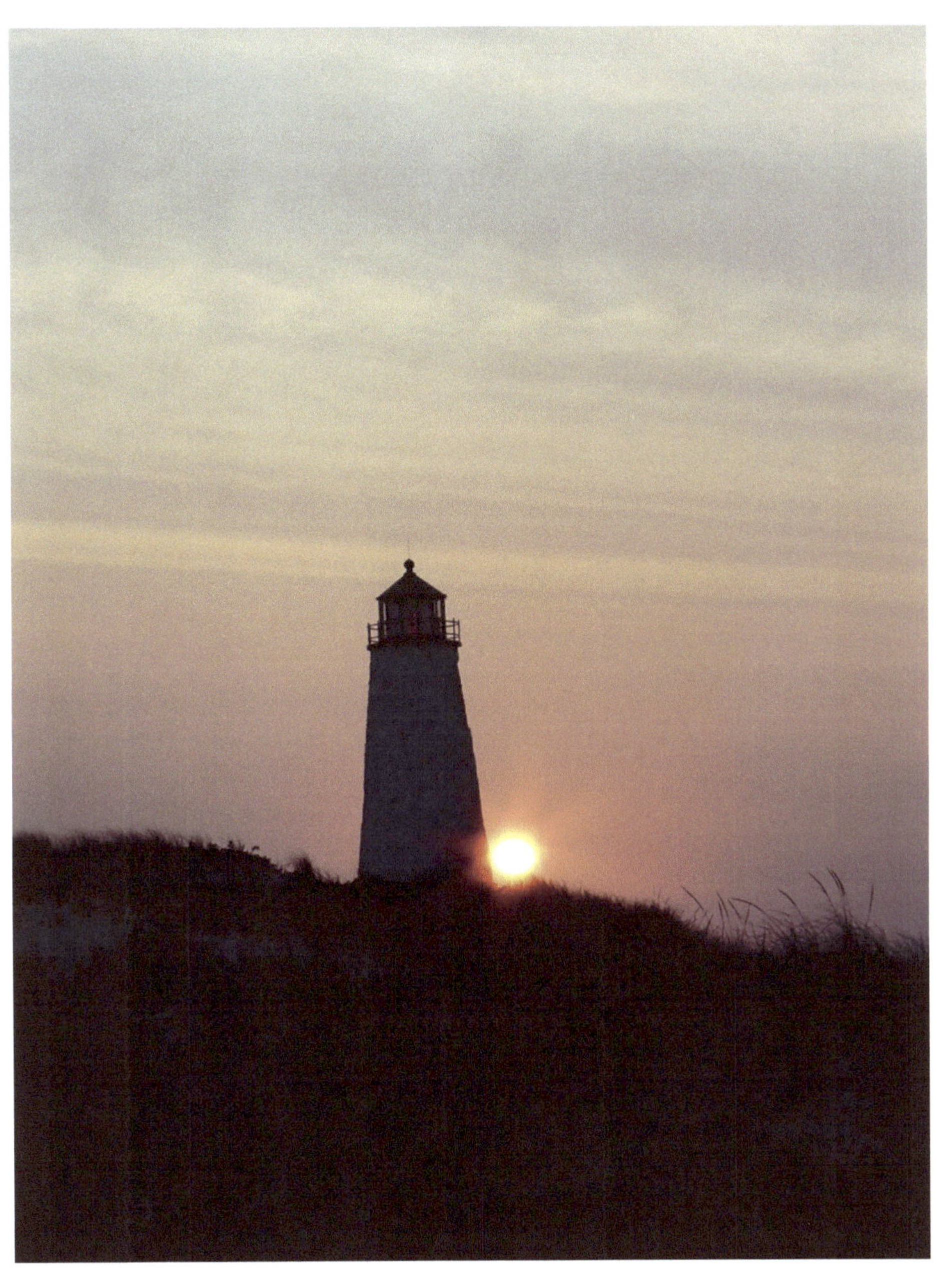

Great Point, Massachusetts

And o'er them the lighthouse looked lovely as hope,
That star of life's tremulous ocean.
--Paul Moon James, 1780 - 1854

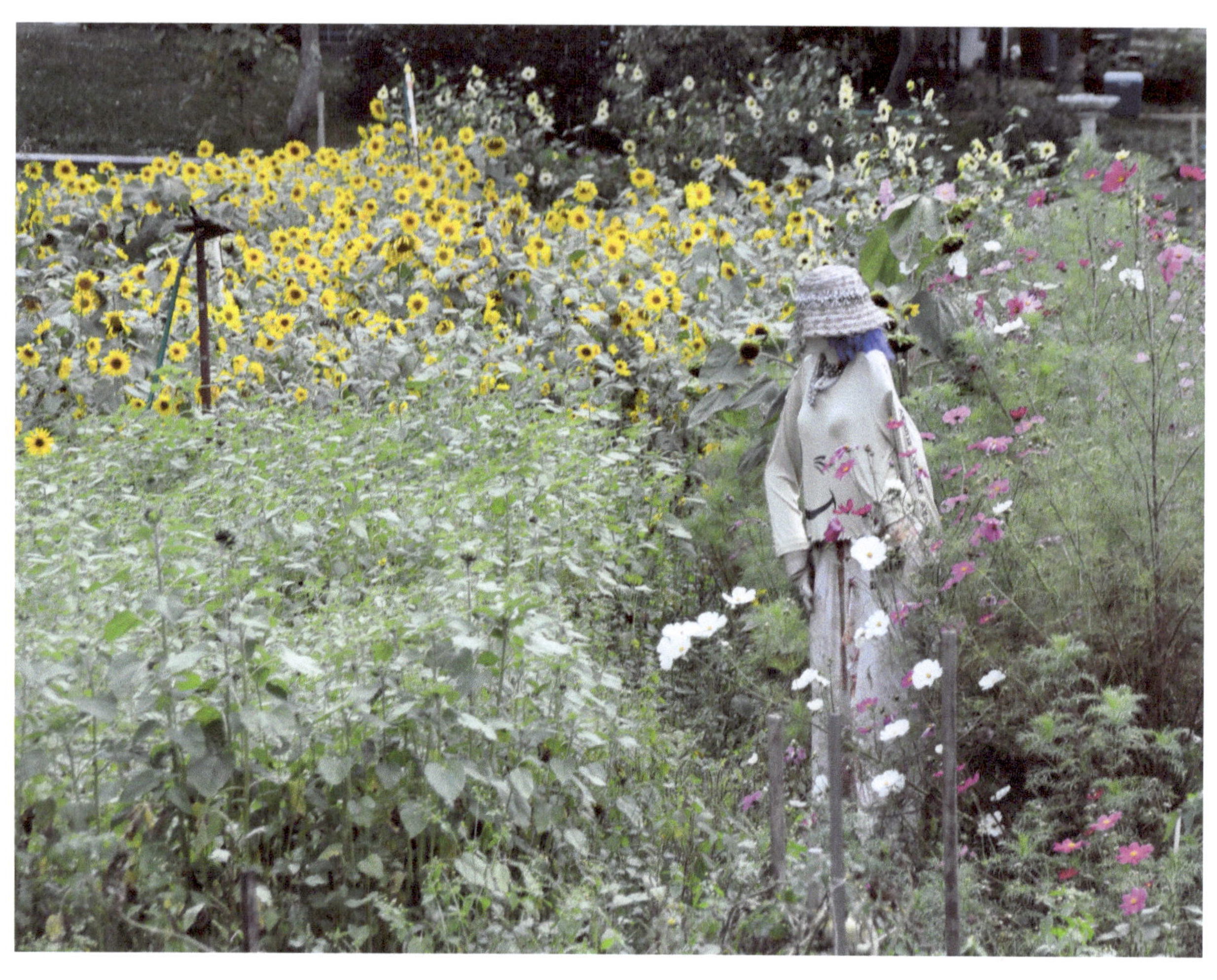

Truro, Massachusetts

Let us be grateful to people who make us happy:
They are the charming gardeners who make our souls blossom.
--Marcel Proust, 1871 - 1922

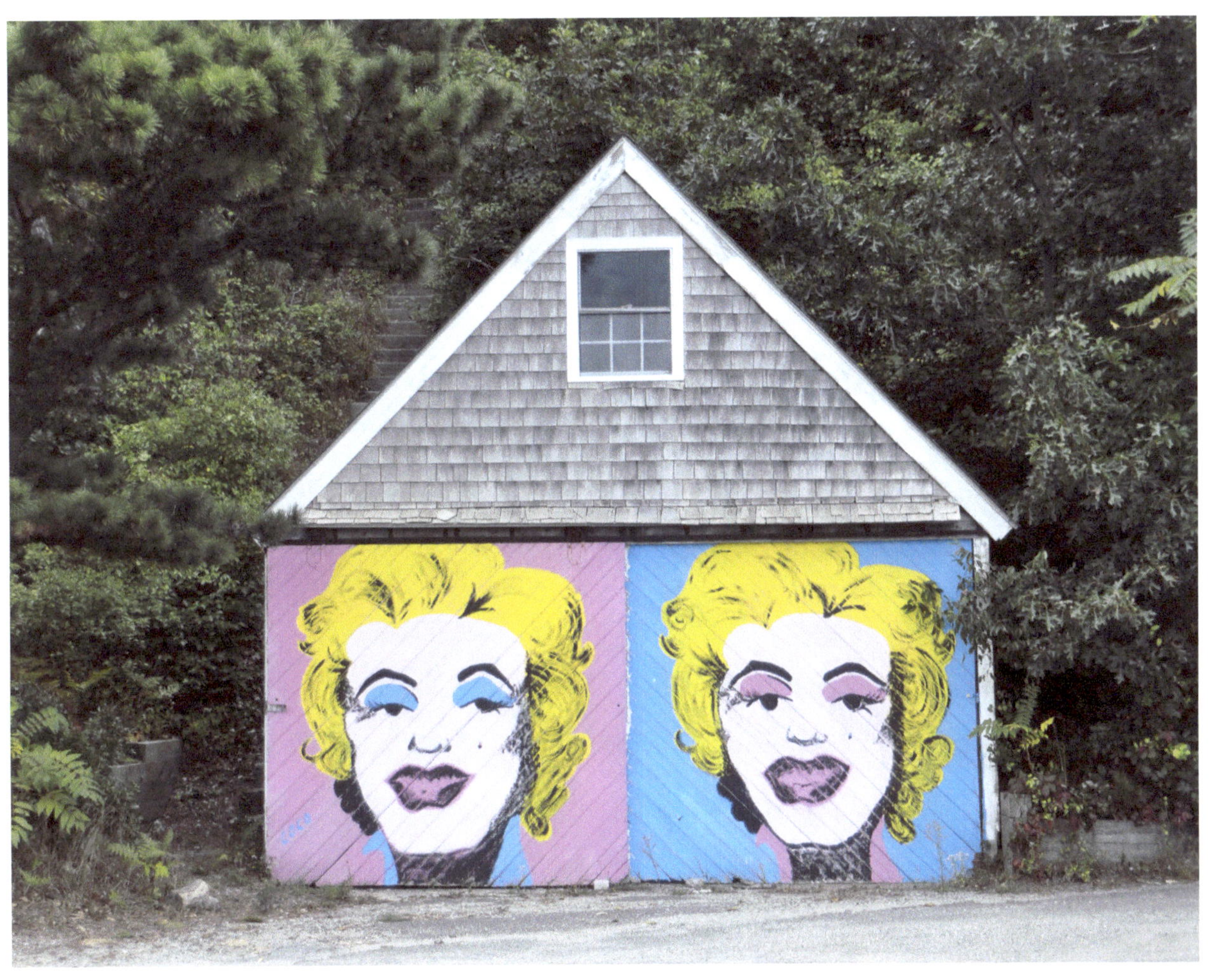

Truro, Massachusetts

One's life is not as fixed as one believes.

Surprises may lie in store for you, the unexpected often tends to happen,

sometimes bringing in its train the most delightful change in one's life or circumstance.

—Elizabeth Aston

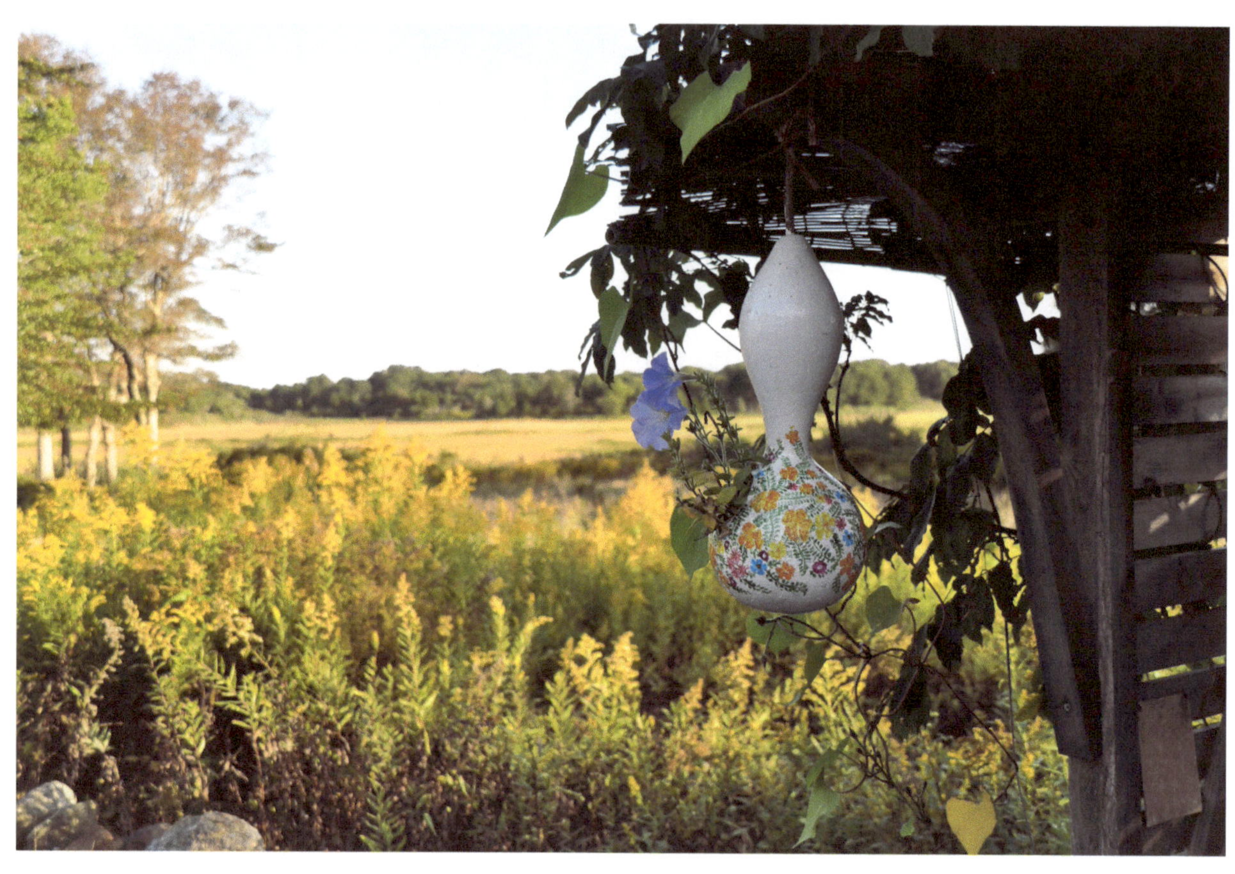

Dennis, Massachusetts

Every moment is a golden one for him who has the vision to recognize it as such.

--Henry Miller, 1891 - 1980

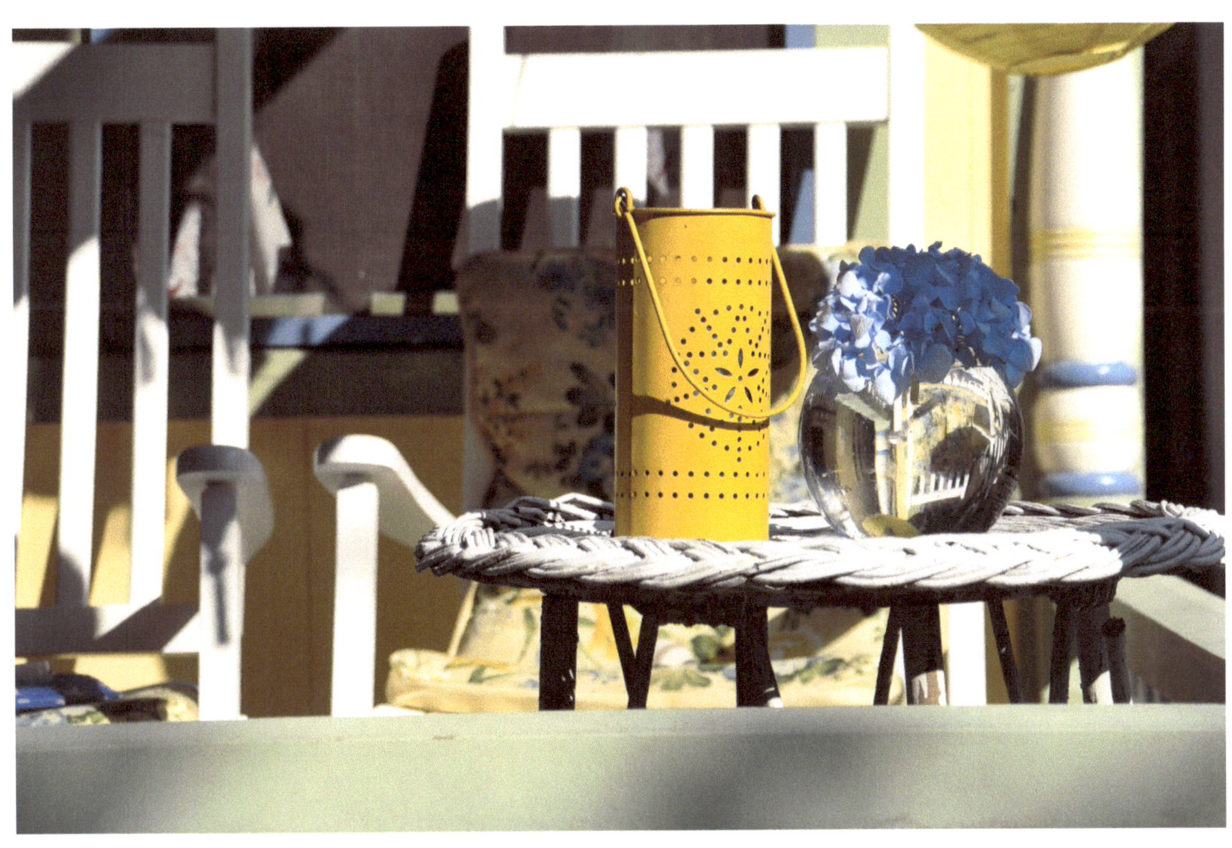

Oak Bluffs, Massachusetts

In the right light, at the right time, everything is extraordinary.

--Aaron Rose, 1969 -

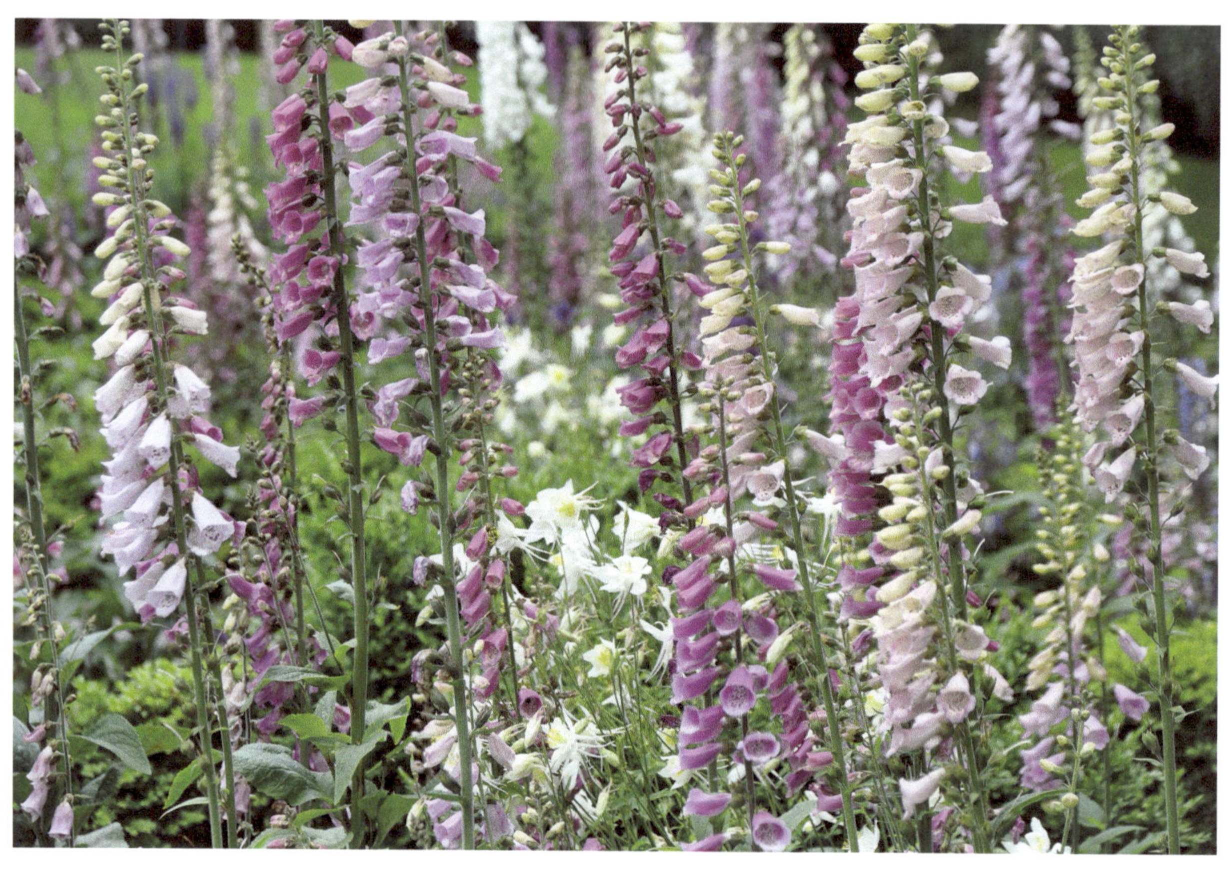

Portsmouth, Rhode Island

The most precious gift we can offer others is our presence.
When mindfulness embraces those we love, they will bloom like flowers.
--Thich Nhat Hanh, 1926 -

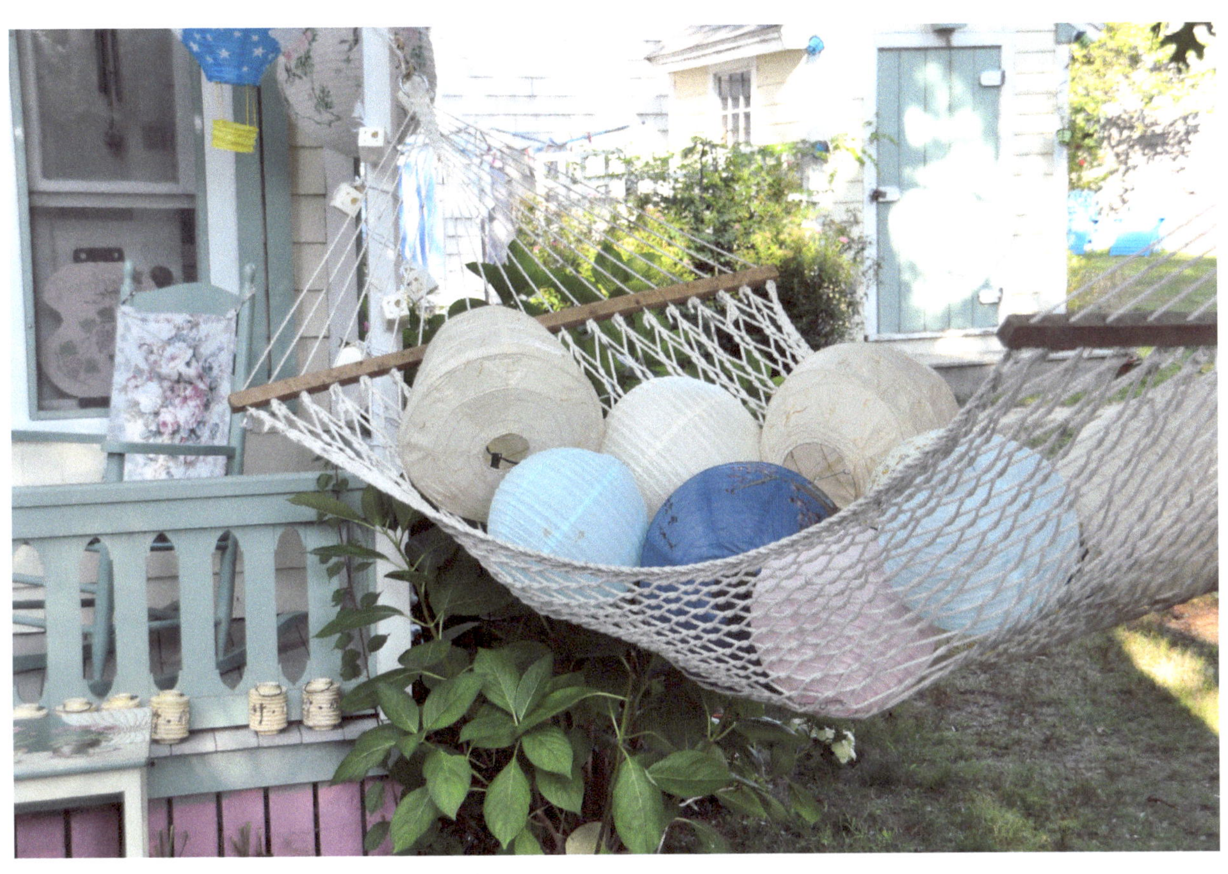

Oak Bluffs, Massachusetts

Light be the earth upon you, lightly rest.

--Euripides, 484 - 406 BC

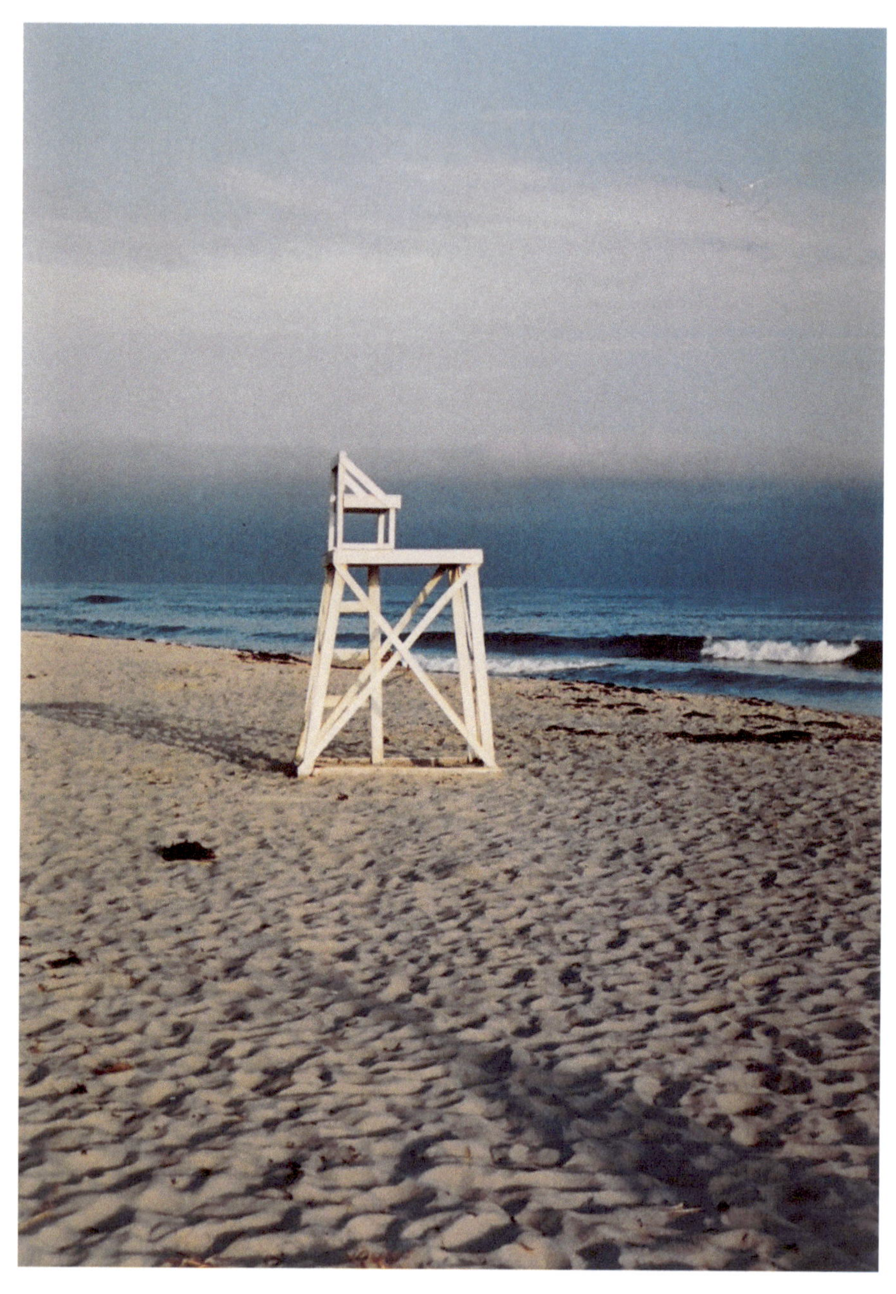

Nantucket, Massachusetts

Chance is perhaps the pseudonym of God
when he does not wish to sign his work.
-- Anatole Frank, 1844 - 1924

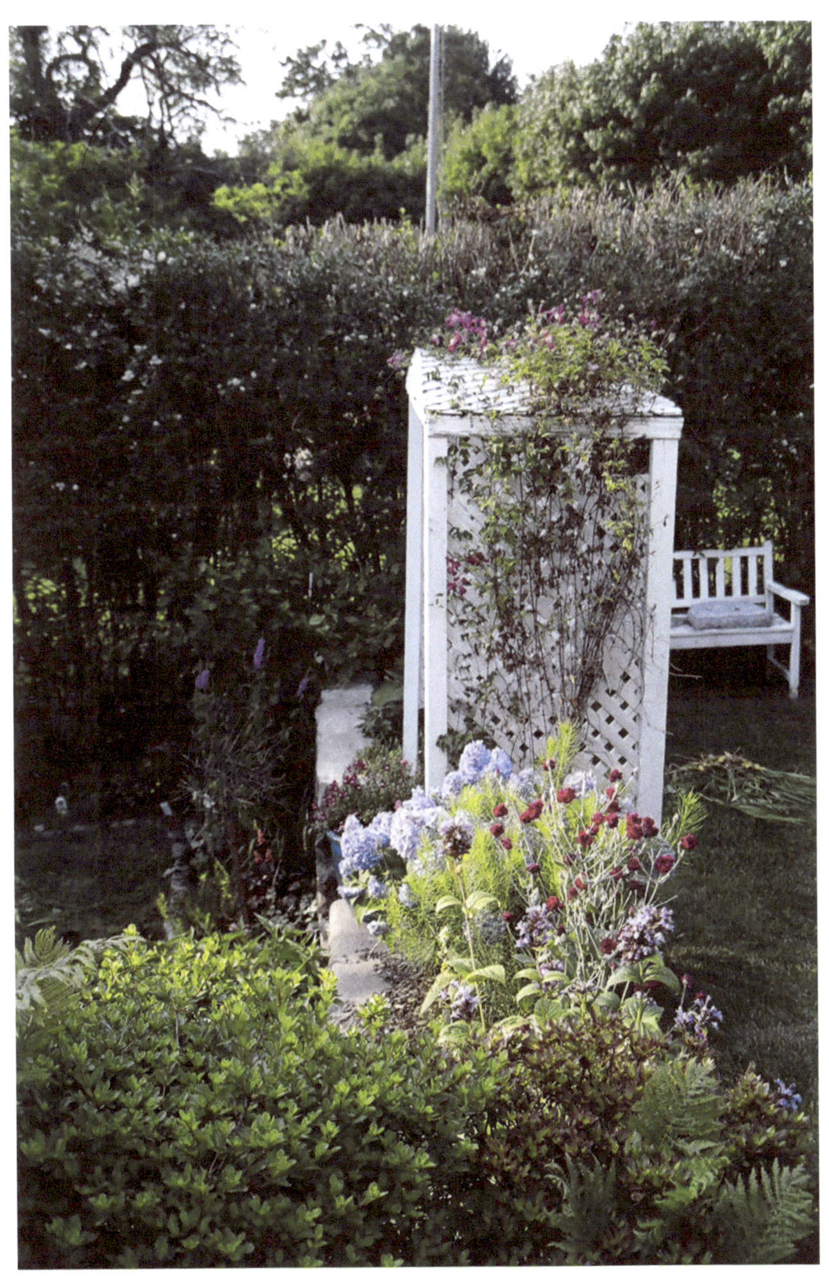

Nahant, Massachusetts

There is no need to go to India or anywhere else to find peace.
You will find that deep place of silence right in your room, your garden or even your bathtub.
-- Elisabeth Kubler-Ross, 1926 - 2004

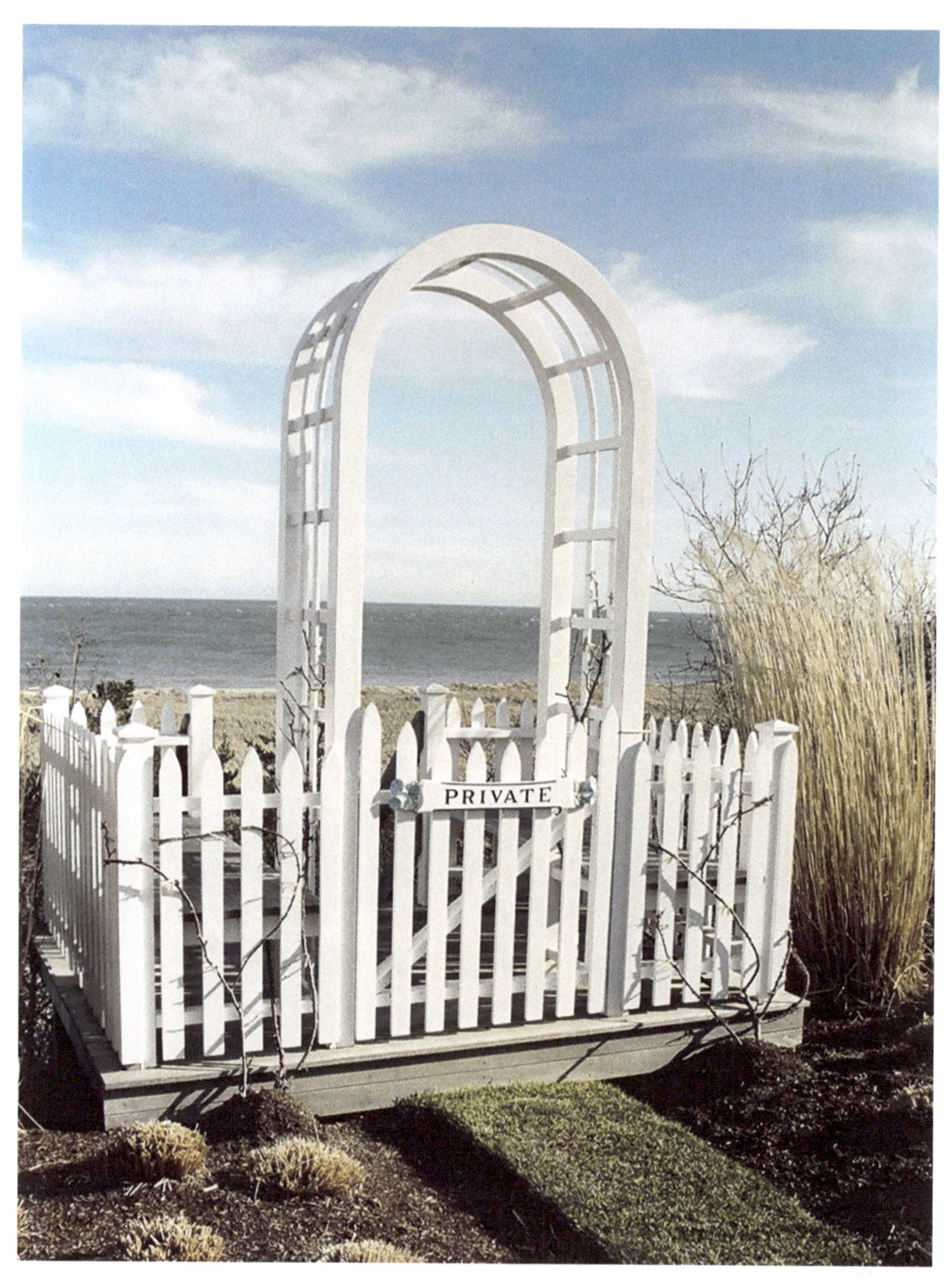

Nantucket, Massachusetts

In all affairs it is a healthy thing now and then
to hang a question mark on the things you have long taken for granted.
--Bertrand Russell, 1872 - 1970

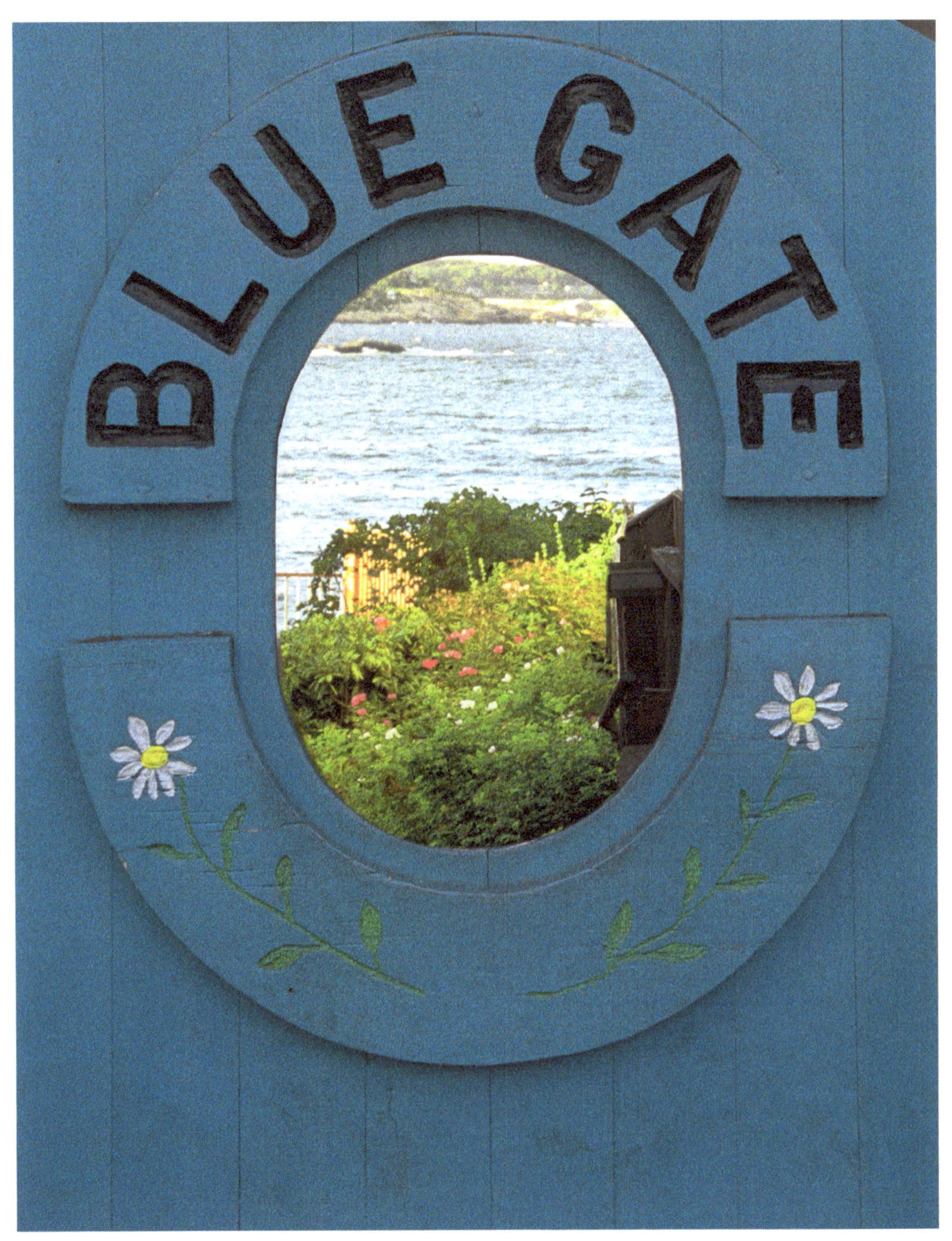

Rockport, Massachusetts

Still round the corner there may wait
A new road, or a secret gate.
--J.R.R. Tolkien, 1892 - 1973

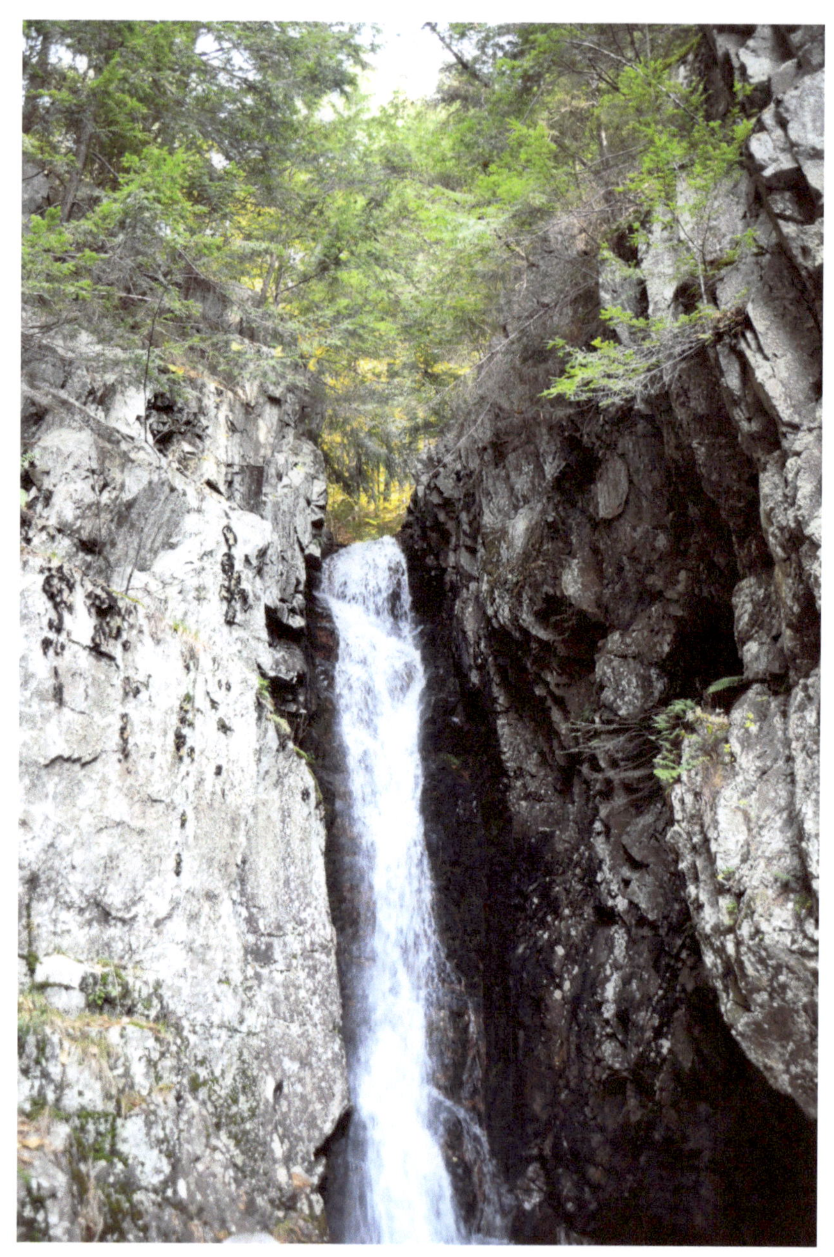

Moultonborough, New Hampshire

Nature has been for me, for as long as I remember, a source of solace, inspiration, adventure, and delight; a home, a teacher, a companion.

—Lorraine Anderson

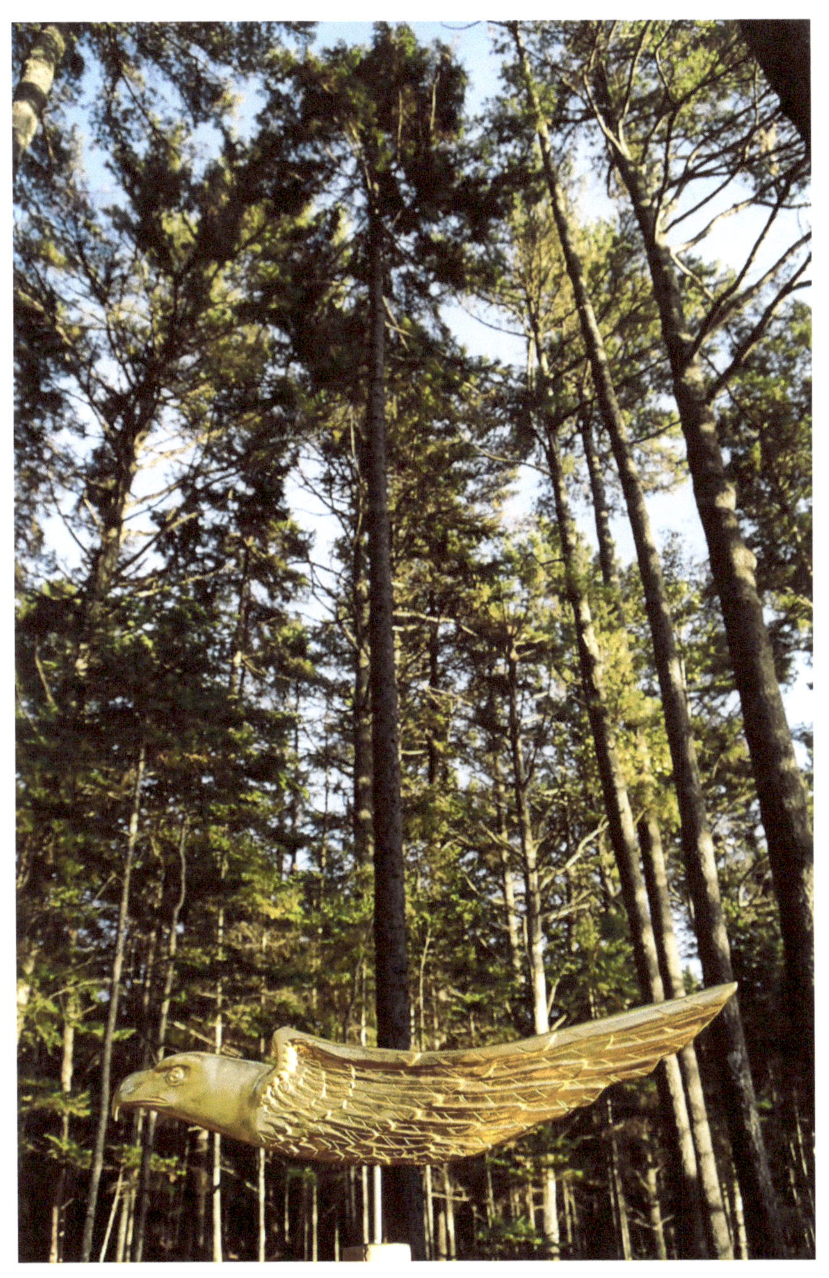

Boothbay, Maine

I know for sure that what we dwell on is who we become.

-- Oprah Winfrey, 1954 -

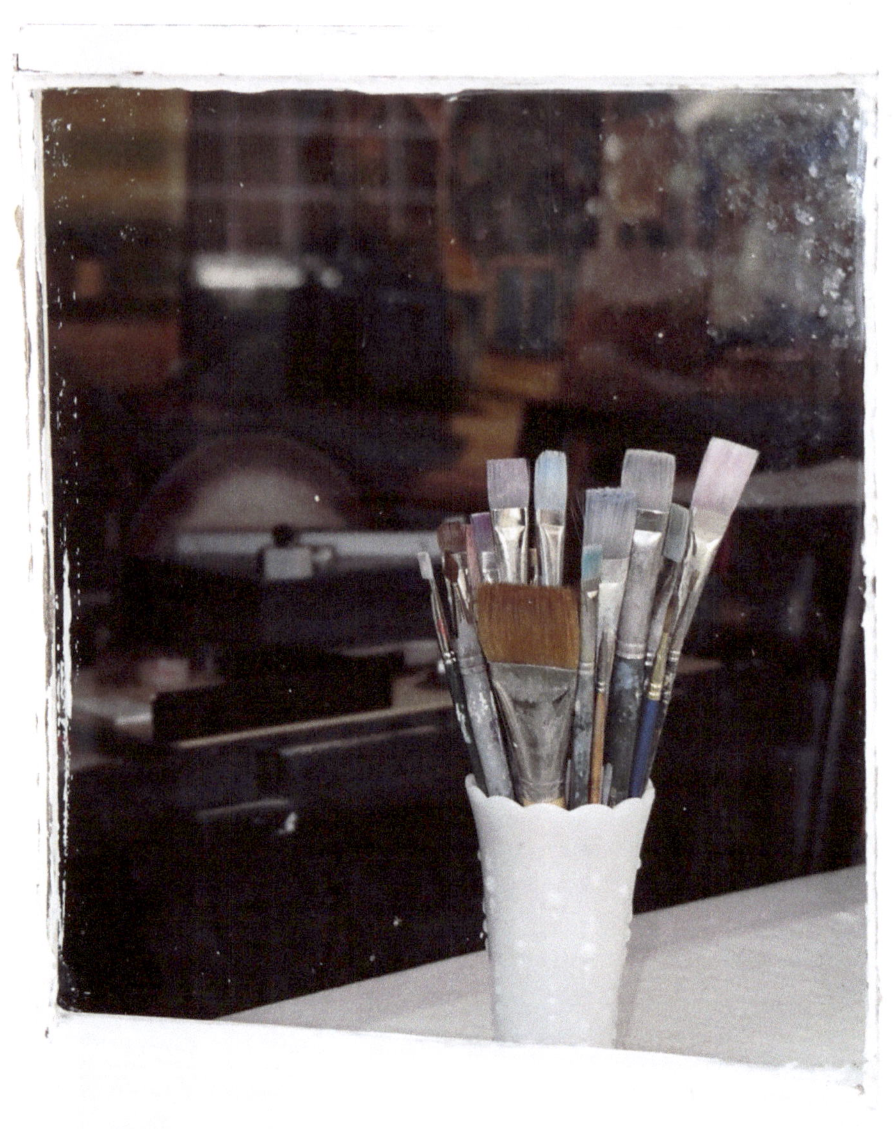

Provincetown, Massachusetts

Art is the window to a man's soul.
Without it, he would never be able to see beyond his immediate world;
nor could the world see the man within.
-- Lady Bird Johnson, 1912 - 2007

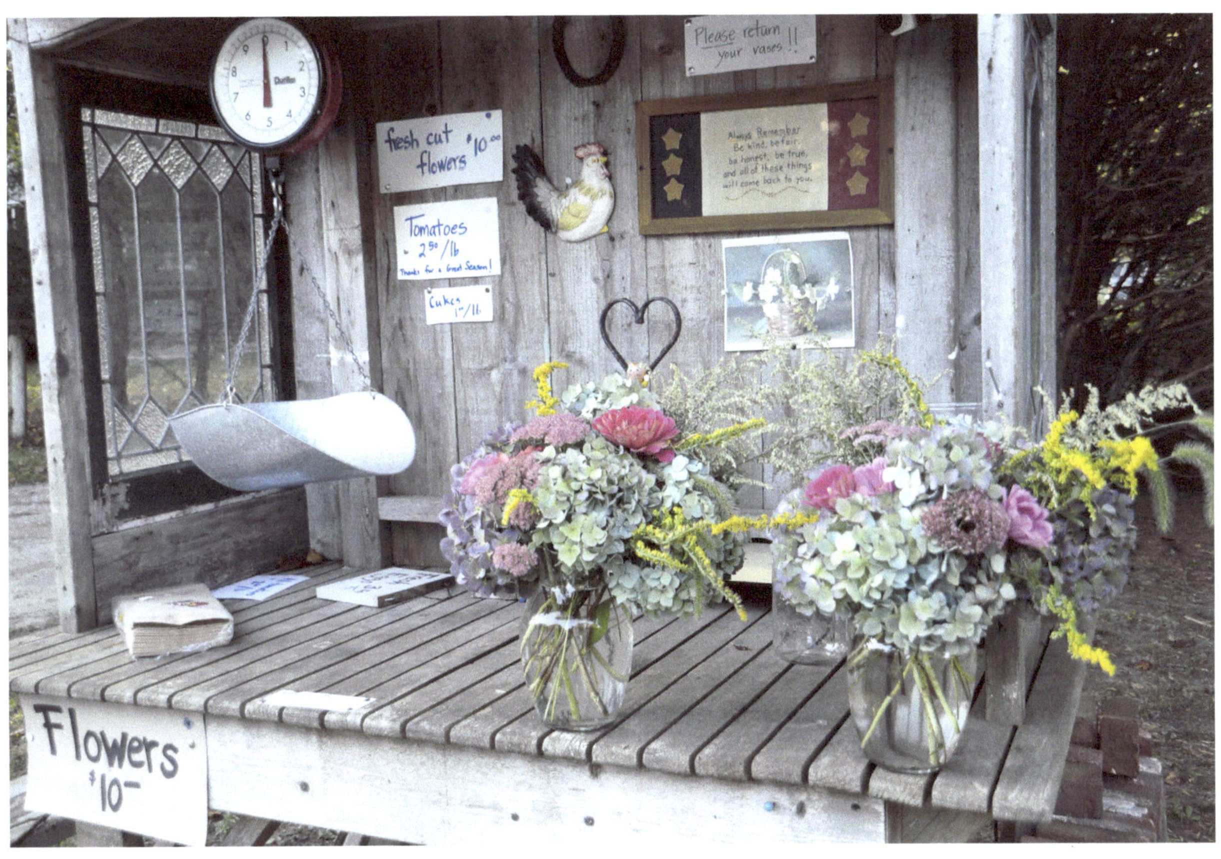

Dennis, Massachusetts

To finish the moment, to find the journey's end in every step of the road,
to live the greatest number of good hours, is wisdom.
--Ralph Waldo Emerson, 1803 - 1882

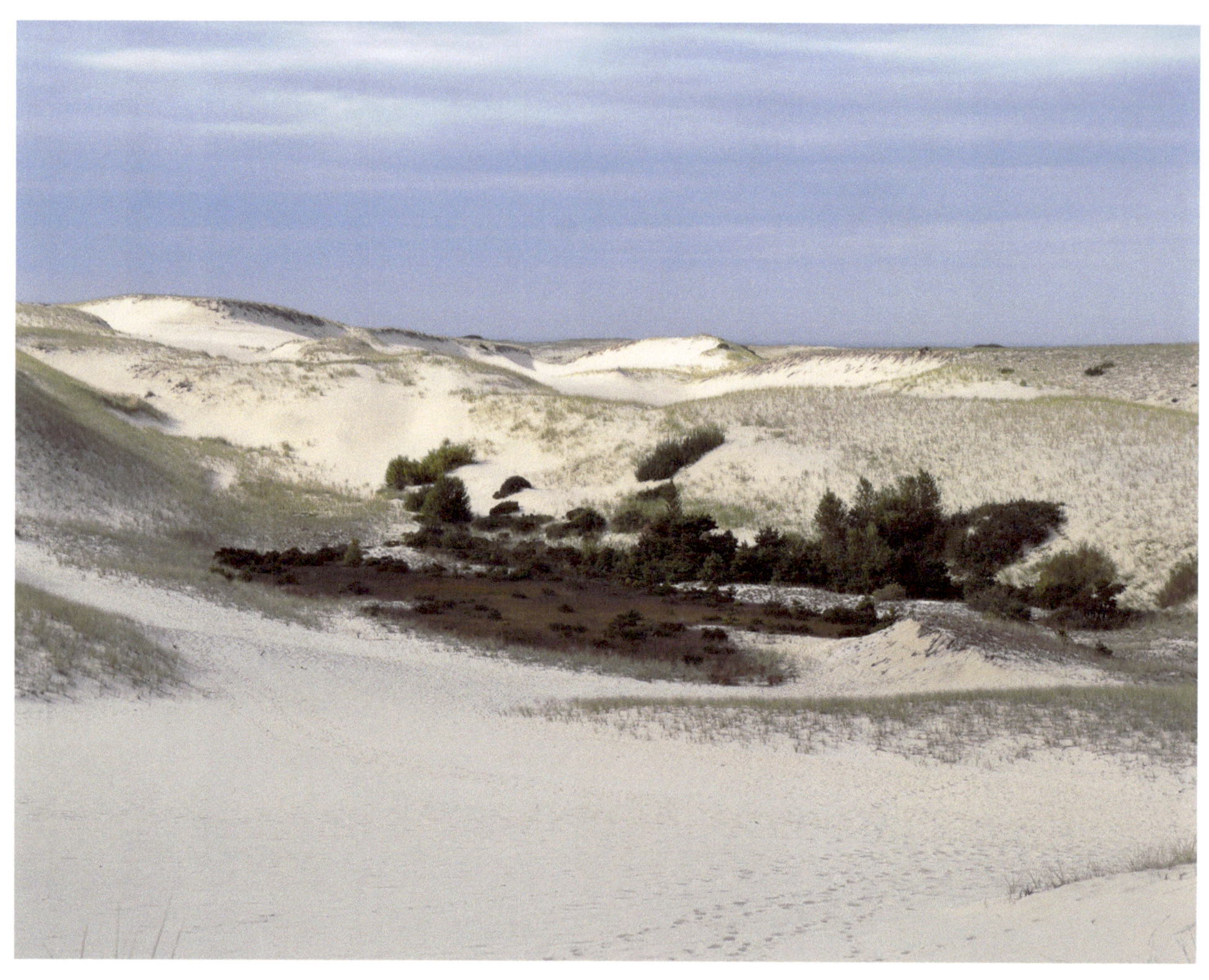

Truro, Massachusetts

Faith is an oasis in the heart which can never be reached by the caravan of thinking.
– Kahlil Gibran, 1883 - 1931

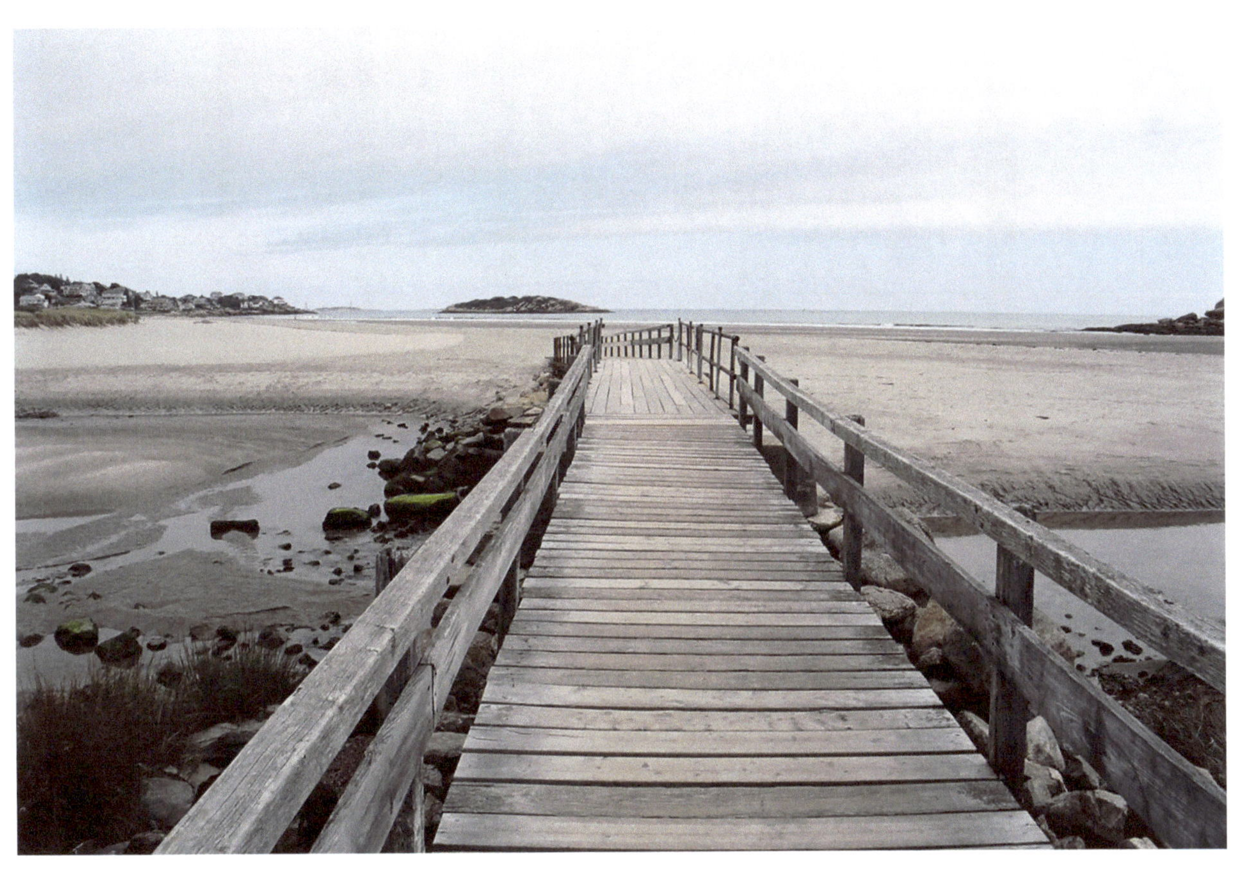

Gloucester, Massachusetts

One meets his destiny often on the road he takes to avoid it.

--French proverb

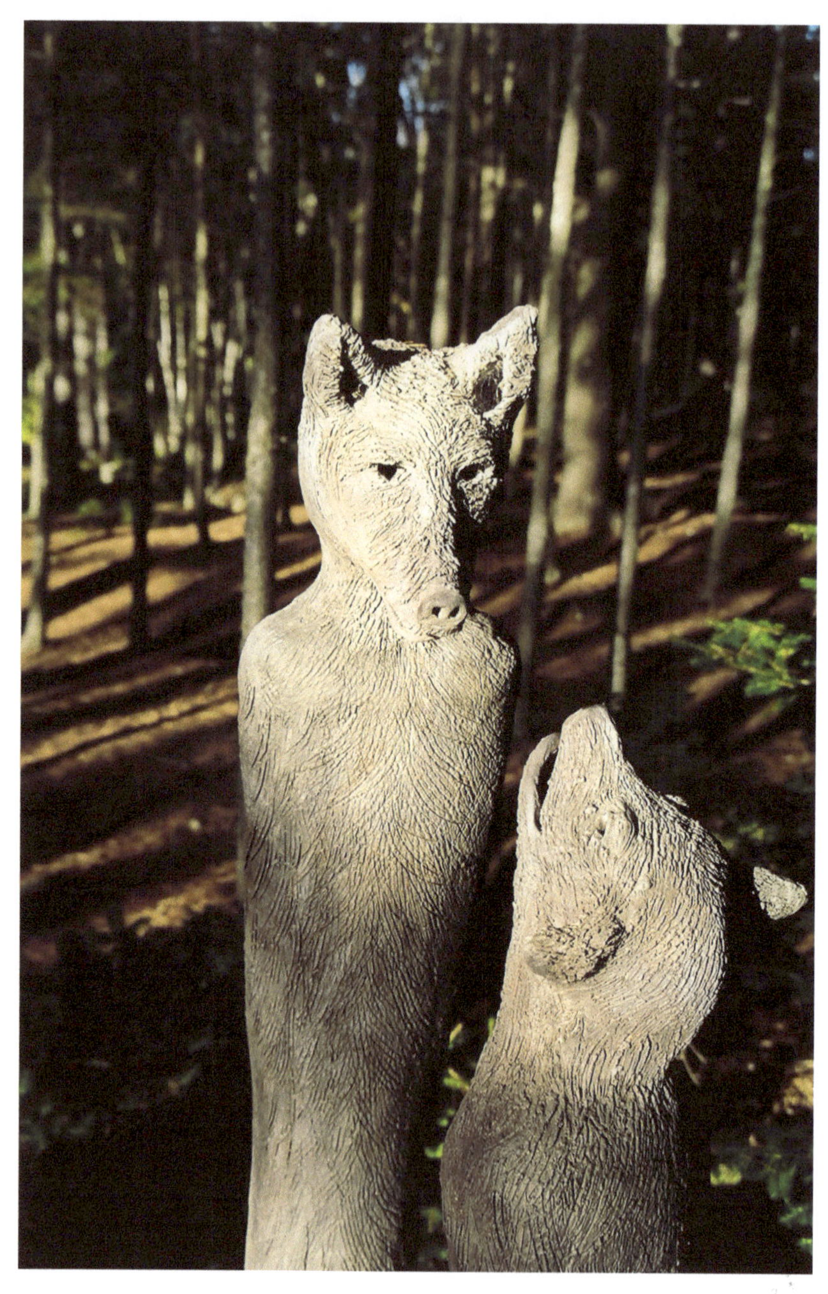

Boothbay, Maine

For the most part, fear is nothing but an illusion.
When you share it with someone else, it tends to disappear.
--Marilyn C. Barrick

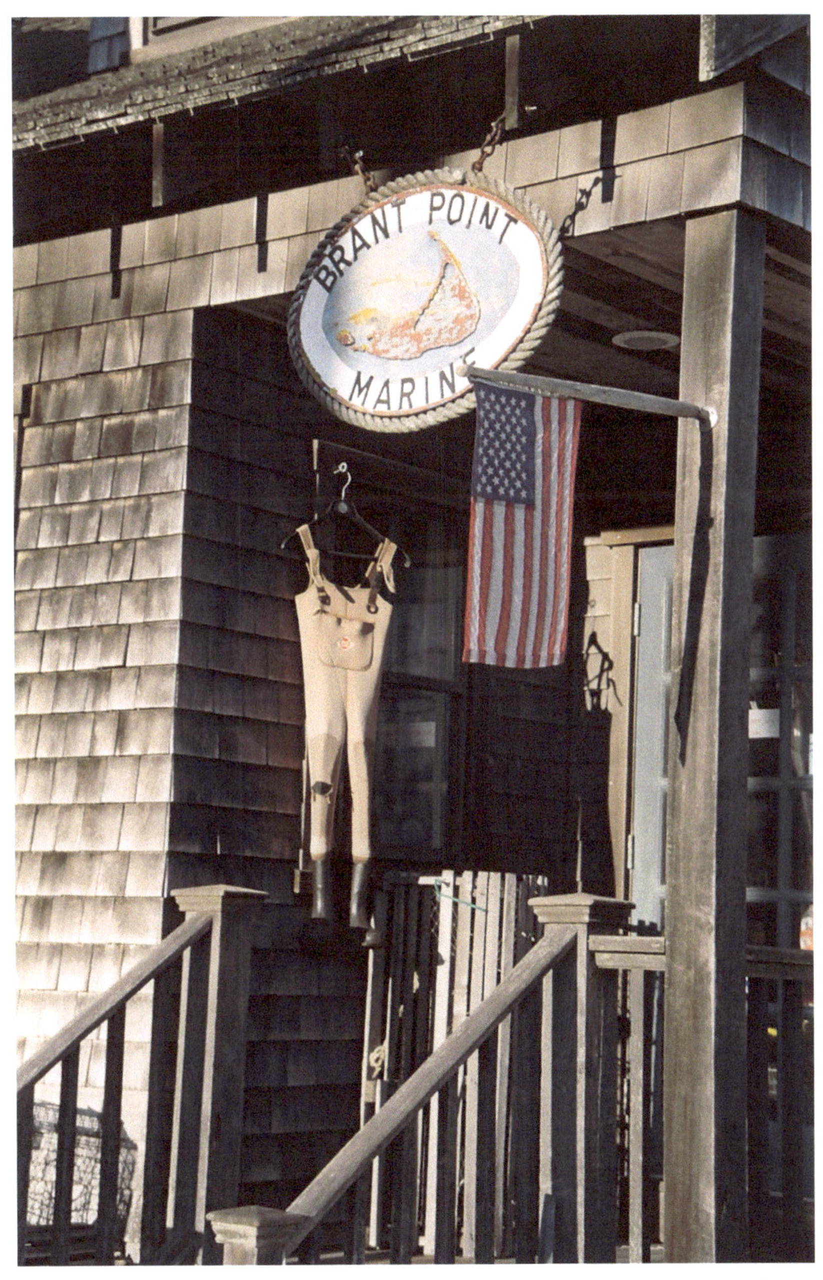

Nantucket, Massachusetts

The particular human chain we're part of is central to our individual identity.
—Elizabeth Stone, 1803 - 1881

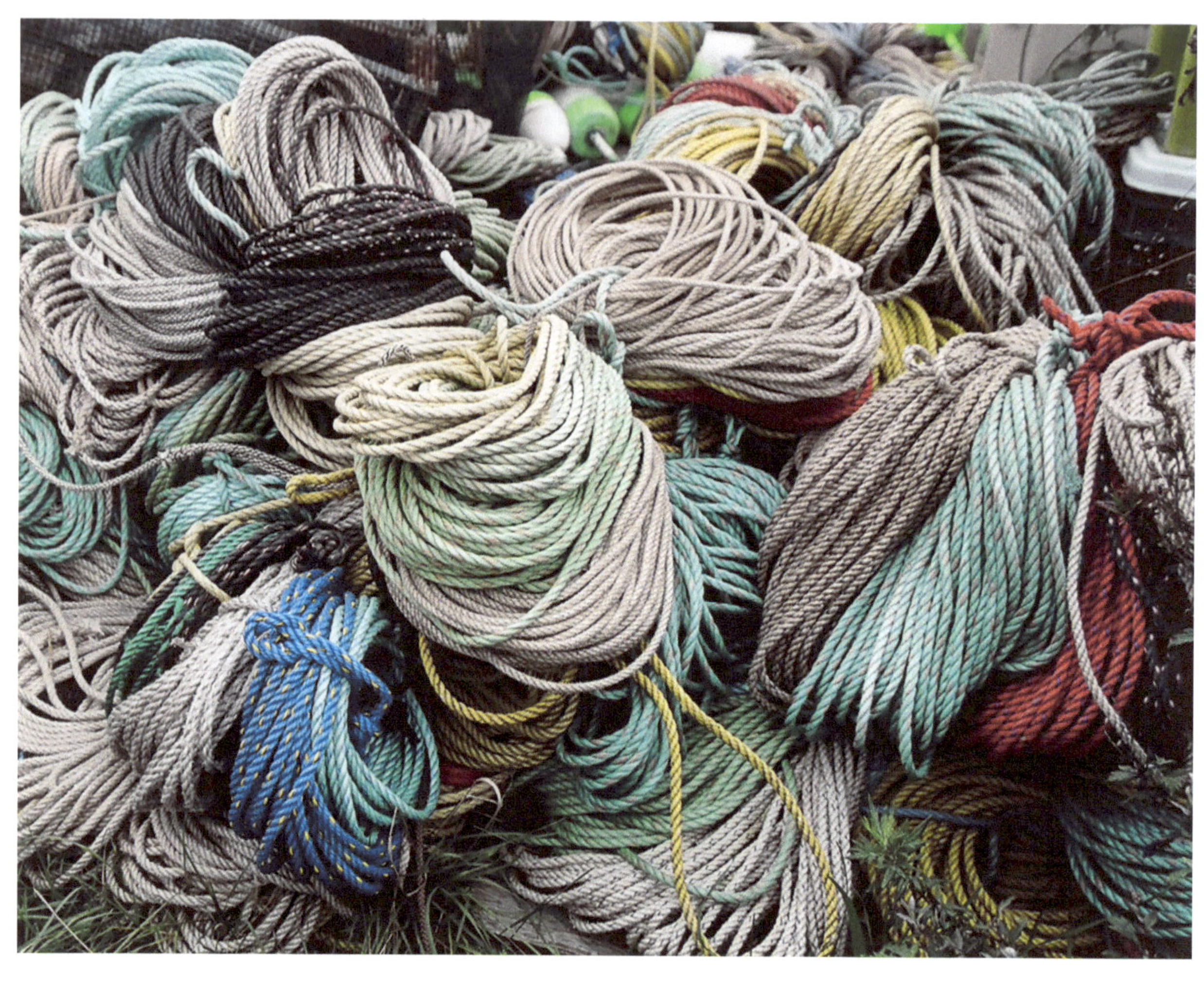

Monhegan Island, Maine

When you get to the end of your rope,
tie a knot and hang on.
-- Franklin D. Roosevelt, 1882-1945

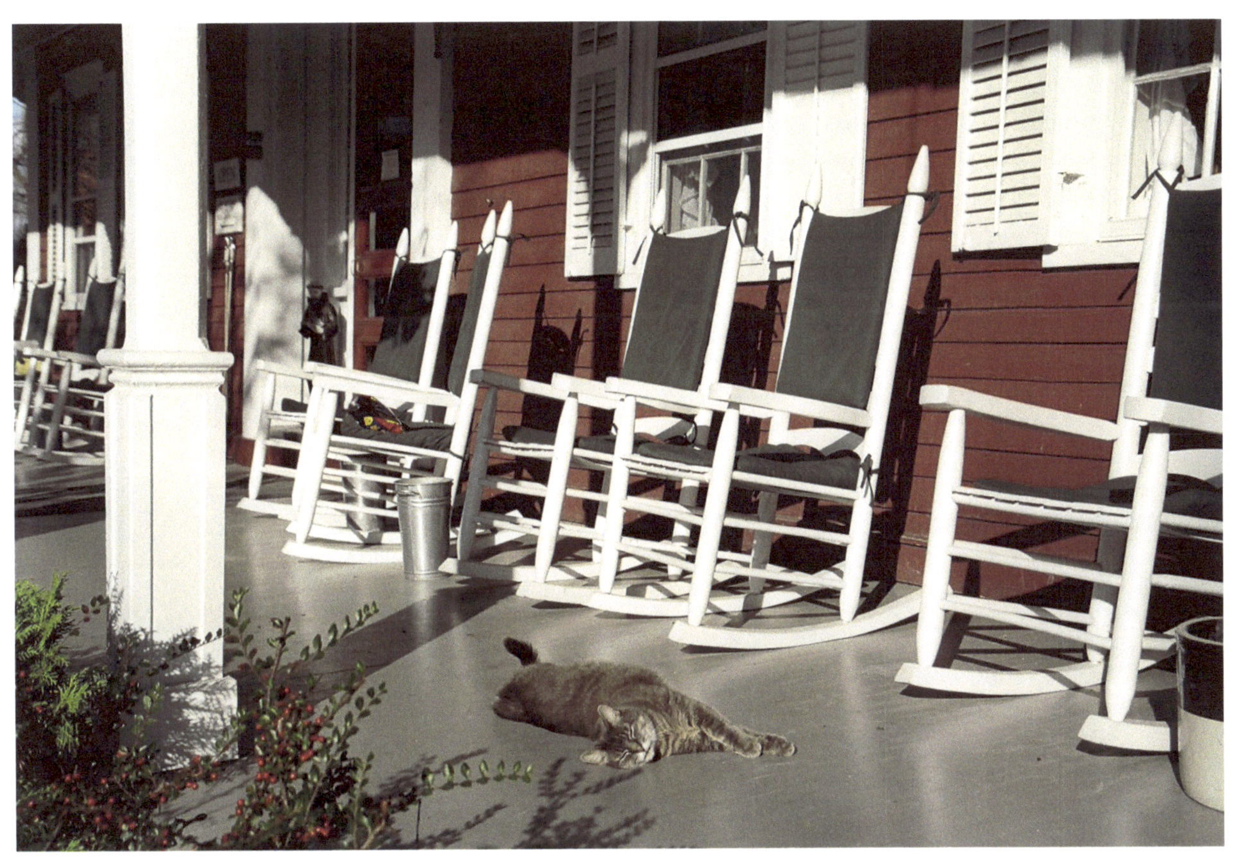

East Dorset, Vermont

Life does not have to be perfect to be wonderful.

--Annette Funicello, 1942 -

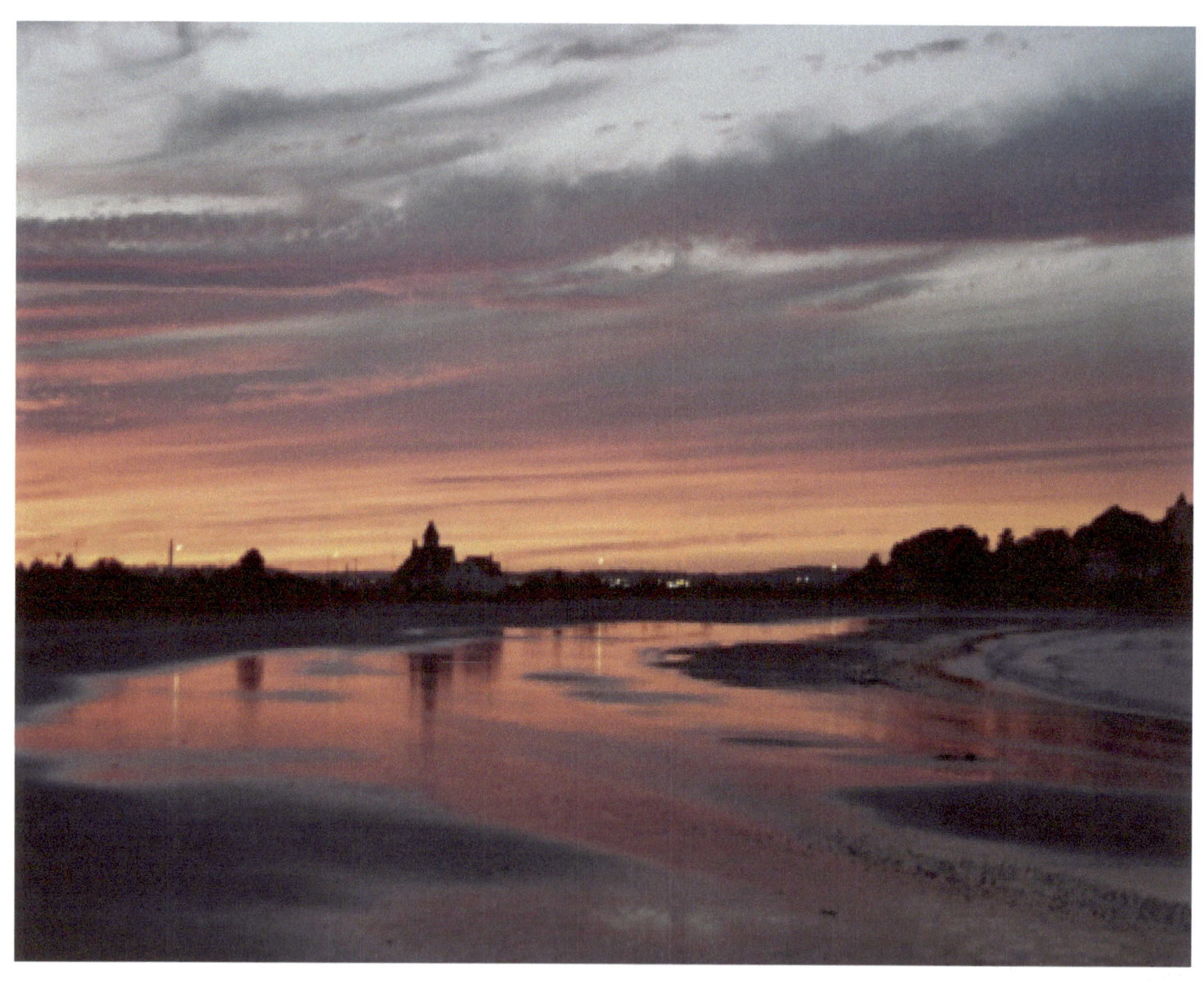

Nahant, Massachusetts

Would you sell the colors of your sunset and the fragrance of your flowers,

and the passionate wonder of your forest for a creed that will not let you dance?

-- Helene Johnson, 1907 - 1995

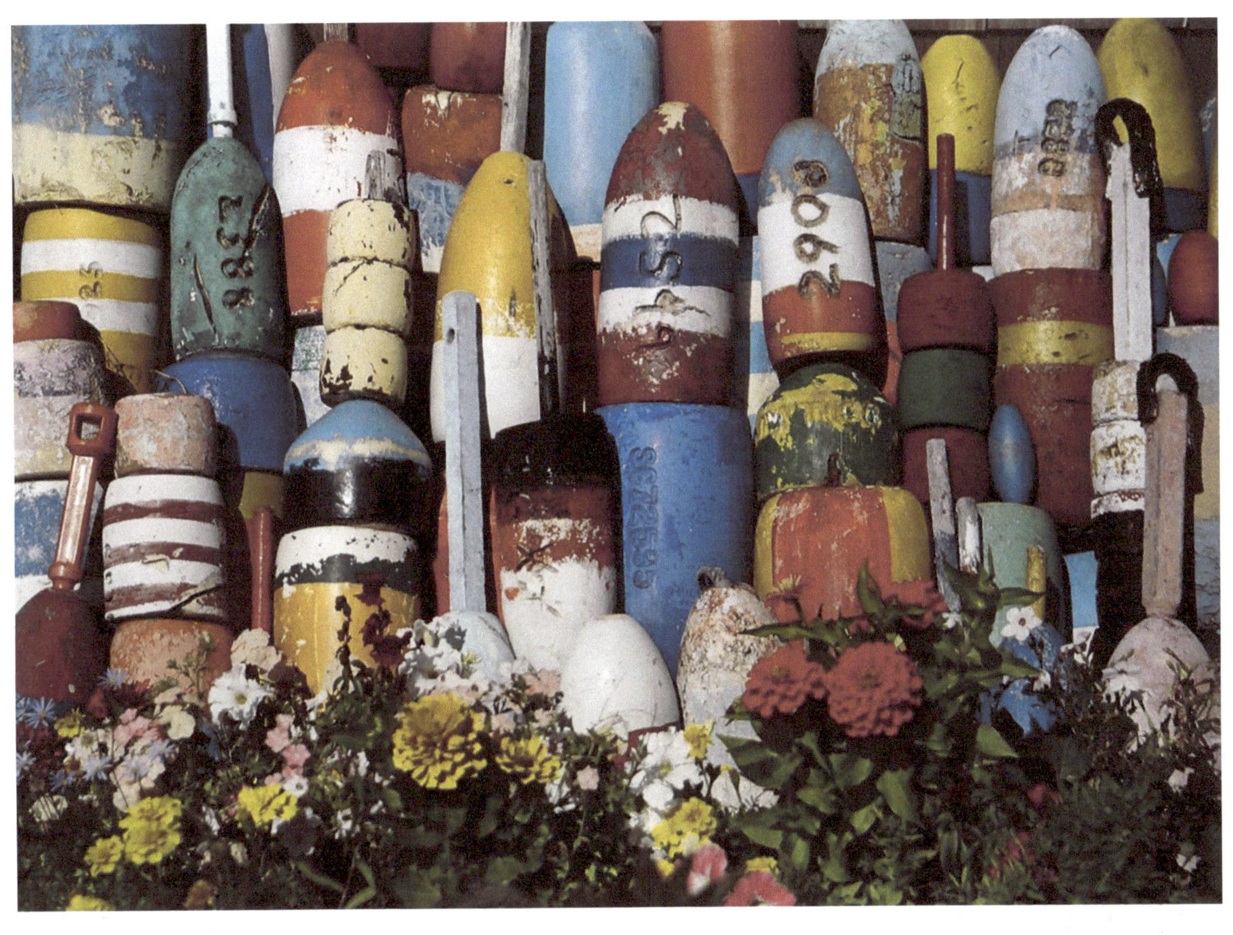

Rockport, Massachusetts

If I try to be like him, who will be like me?
--Yiddish proverb

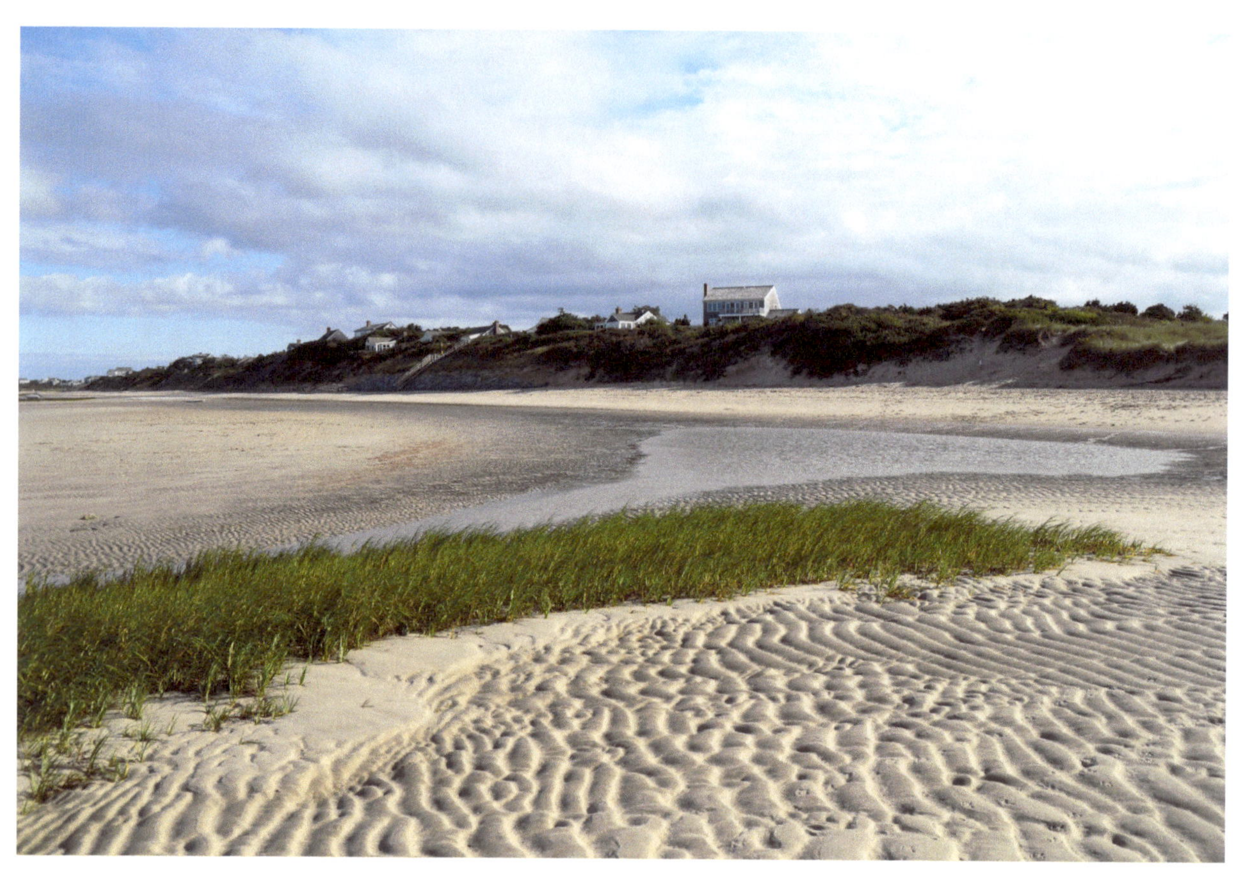

Dennis, Massachusetts

One by one the sands are flowing,
One by one the moments fall;
Some are coming, some are going;
Do not strive to grasp them all.

--Adelaide Proctor, 1825 - 1864

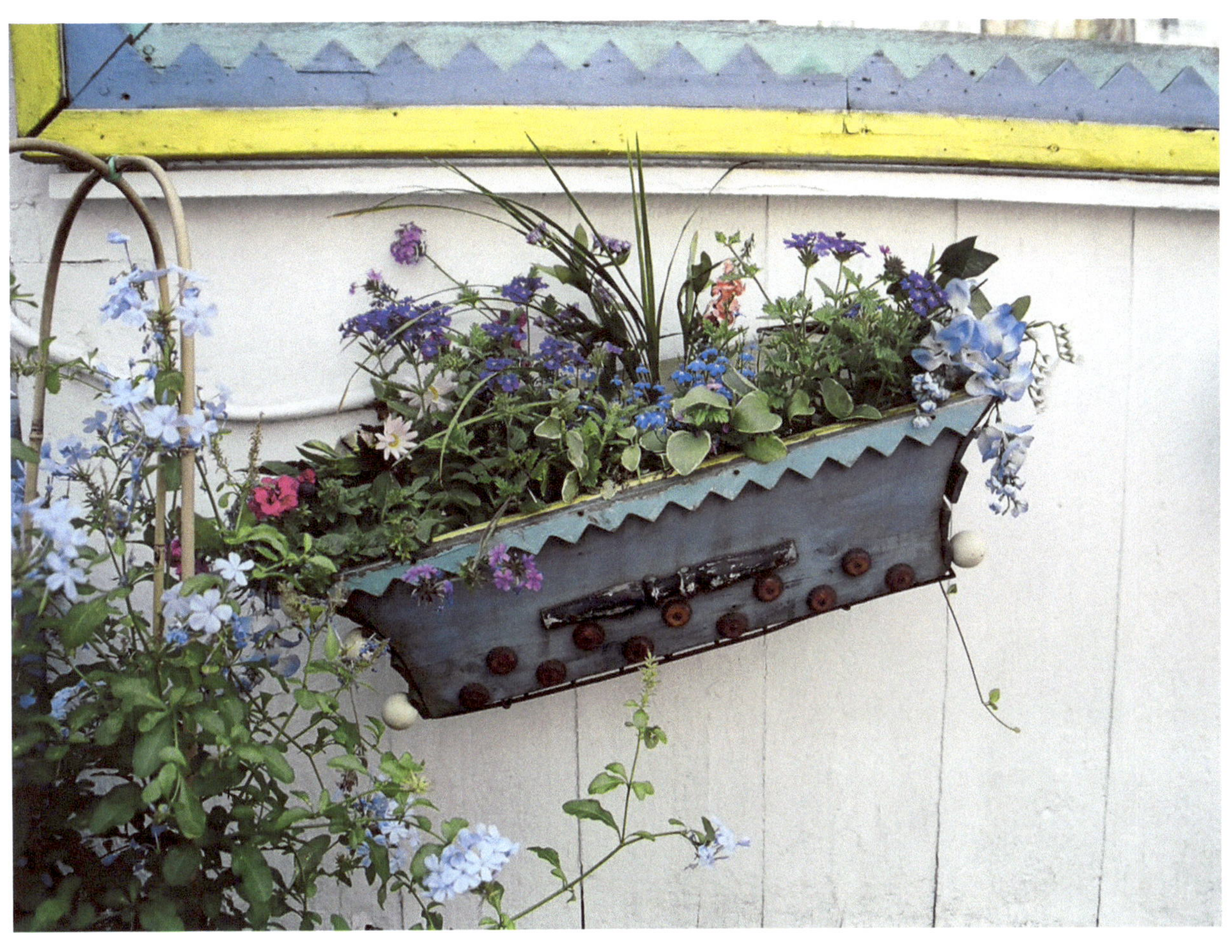

Provincetown, Massachusetts

Joy is but the sign that creative emotion is fulfilling its purpose.

--Charles DuBois, 1661 - 1724

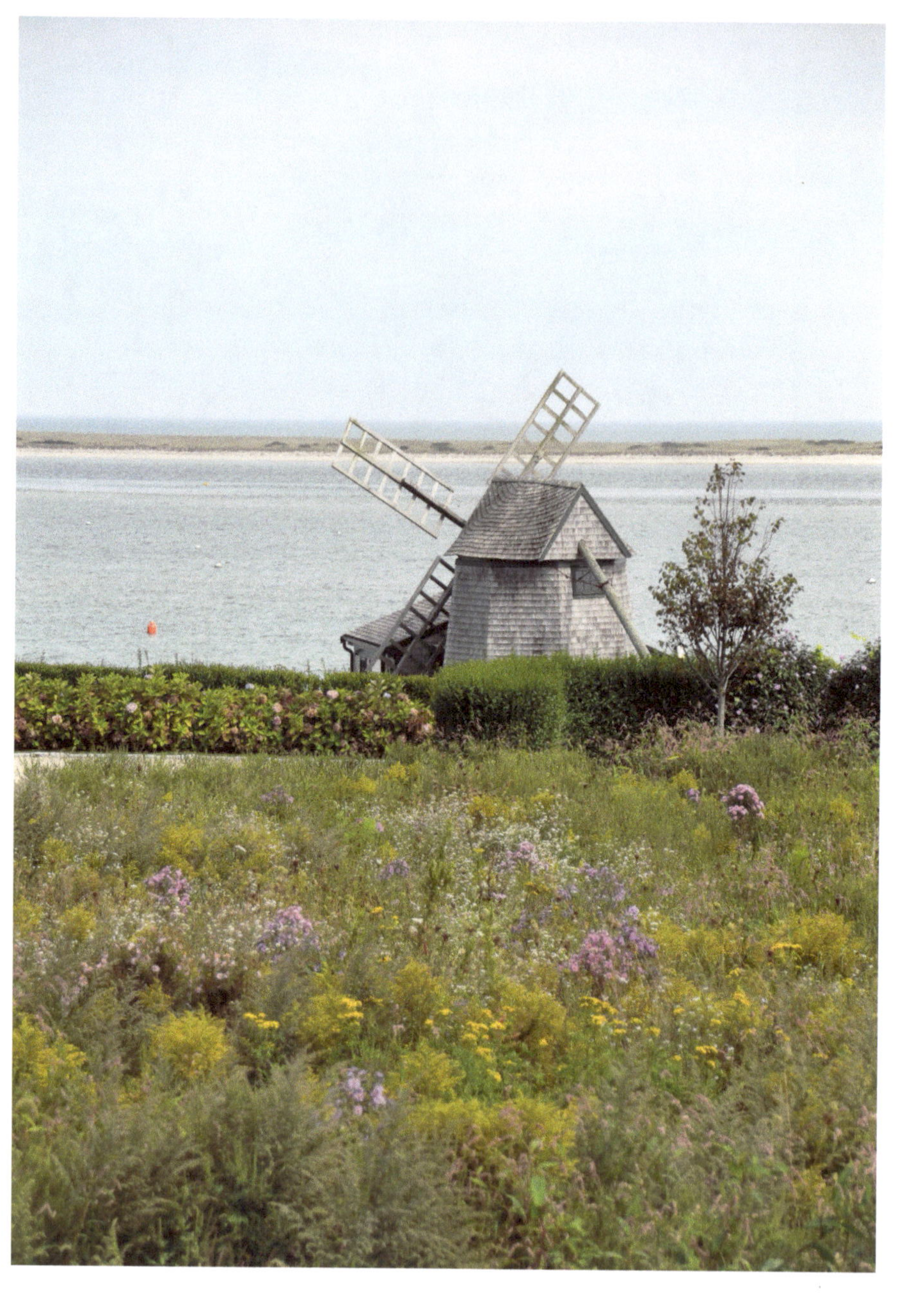

Chatham, Massachusetts

The winds and waves are always on the side of the ablest navigators.

--Edward Gibbon, 1737 - 1794

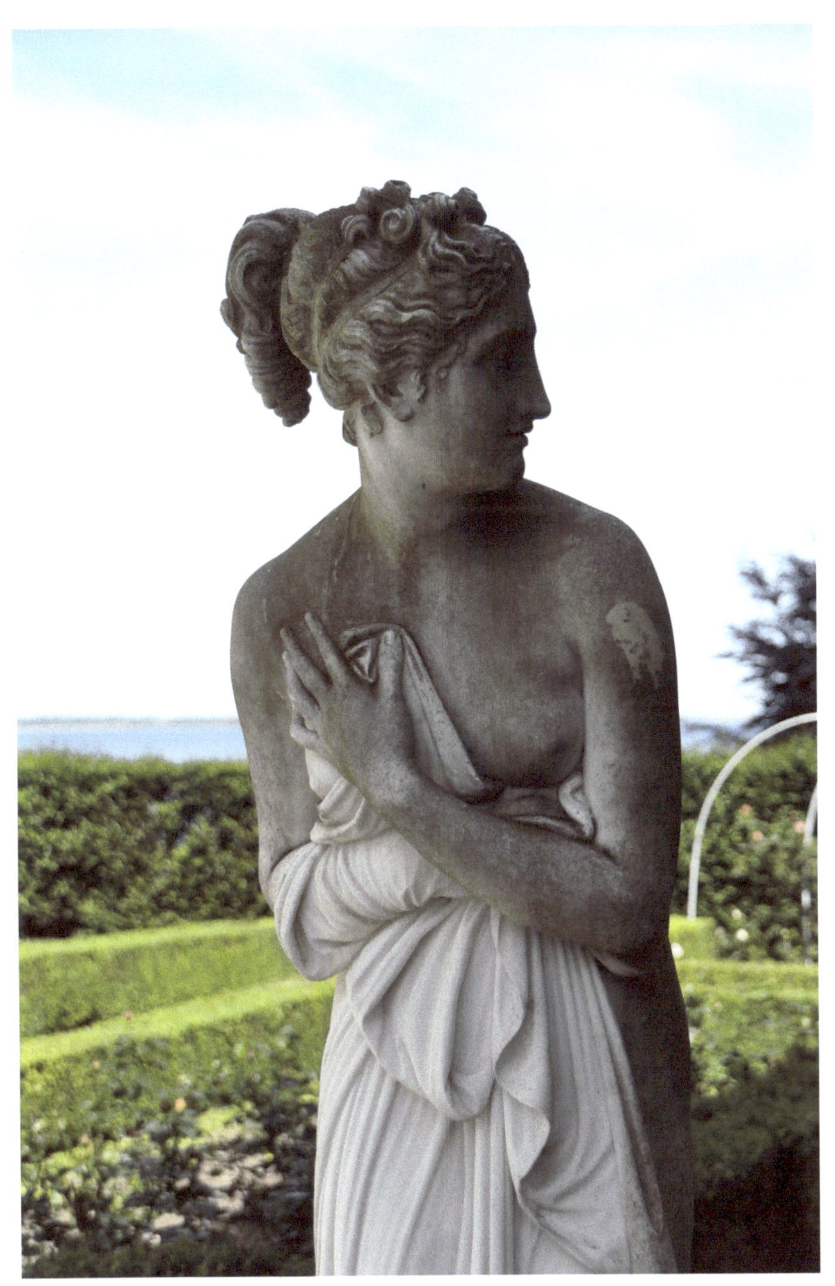

Newport, Rhode Island

When we were children, we used to think that when we were grown-up
we would no longer be vulnerable.
But to grow up is to accept vulnerability...
To be alive is to be vulnerable.
--Madeleine L'Engle, 1918 - 2007

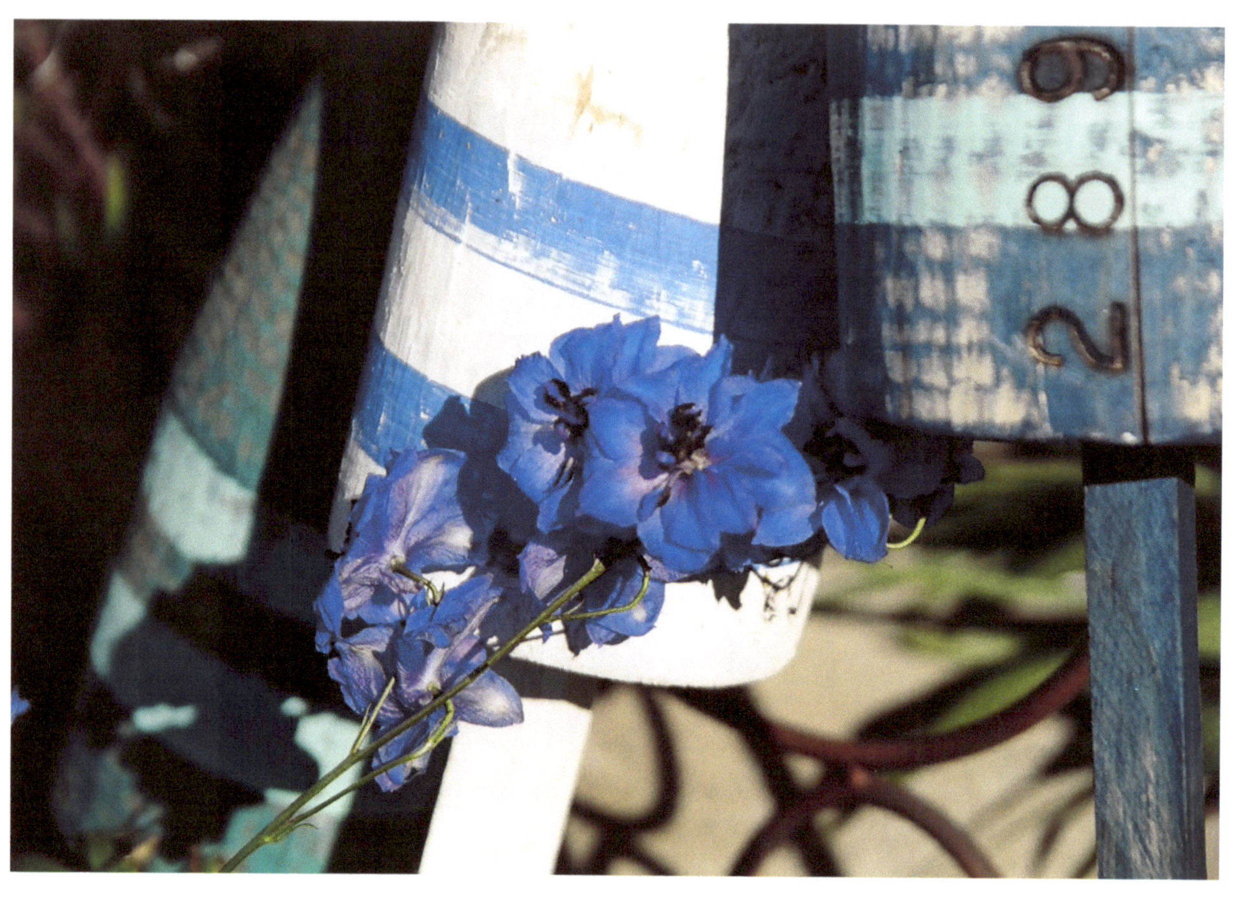

Nahant, Massachusetts

I merely took the energy it takes to pout and wrote some blues.

--Duke Ellington, 1899 - 1974

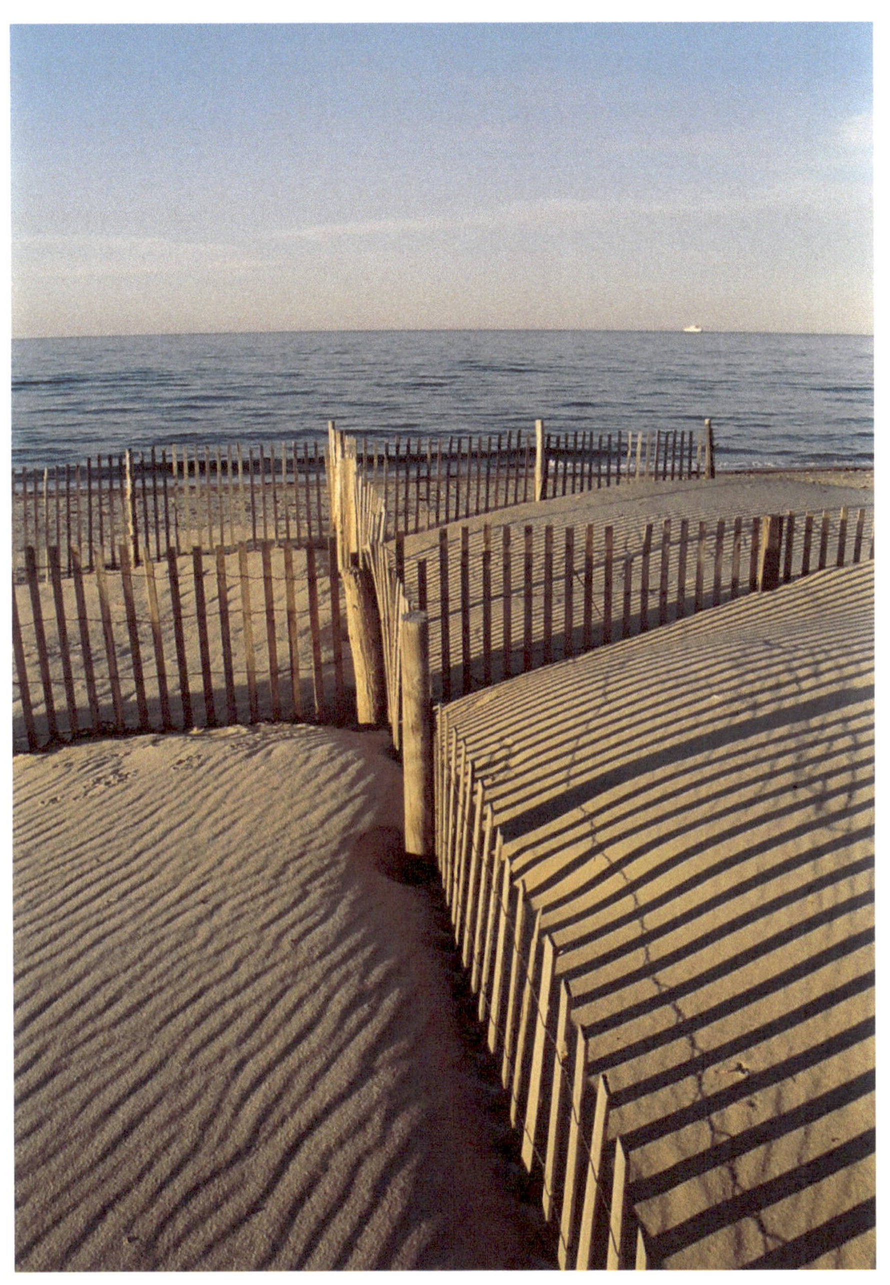

Nantucket, Massachusetts

There can be no friendship where there is no freedom.
Friendship loves a free air, and will not be
fenced up in straight and narrow enclosures.
--William Penn, 1644 - 1718

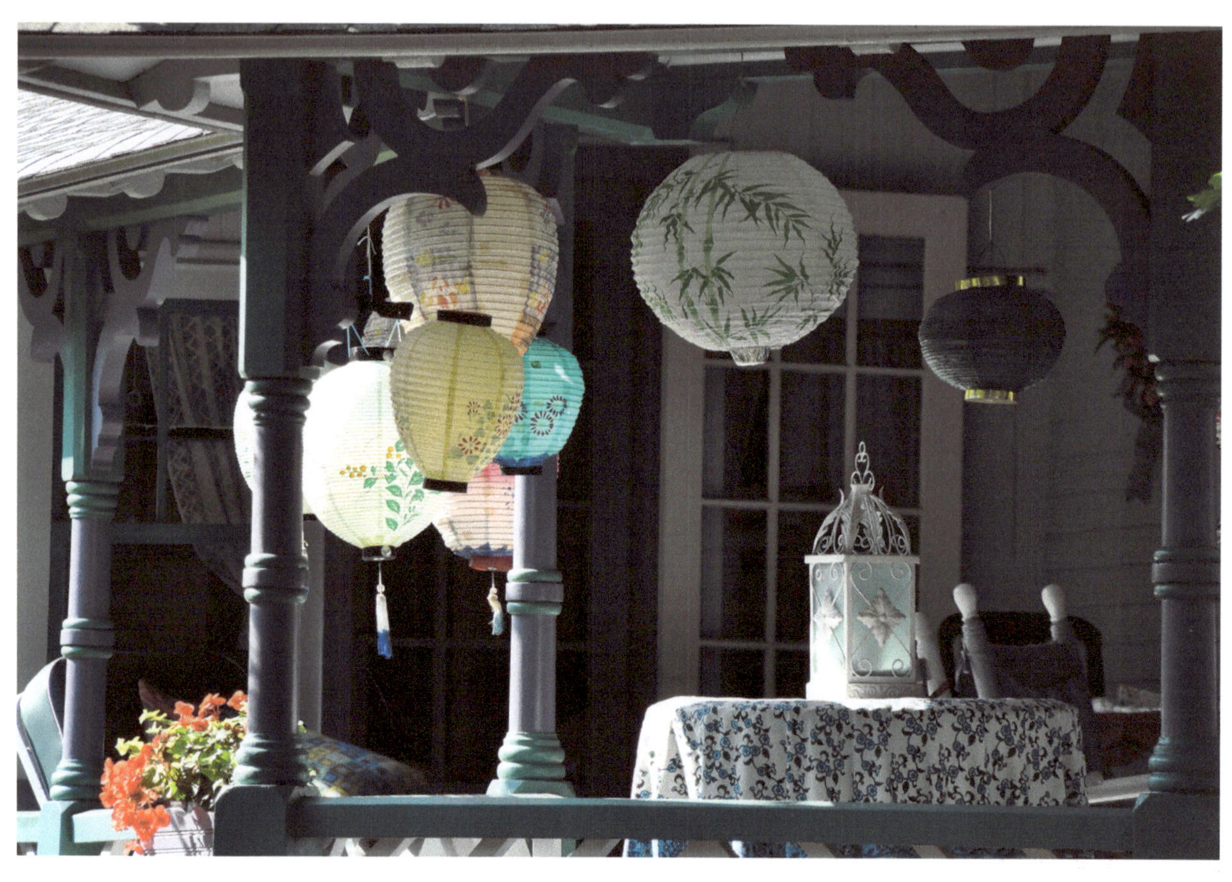

Oak Bluffs, Massachusetts

Every day cannot be a feast of lanterns.

--Chinese Proverb

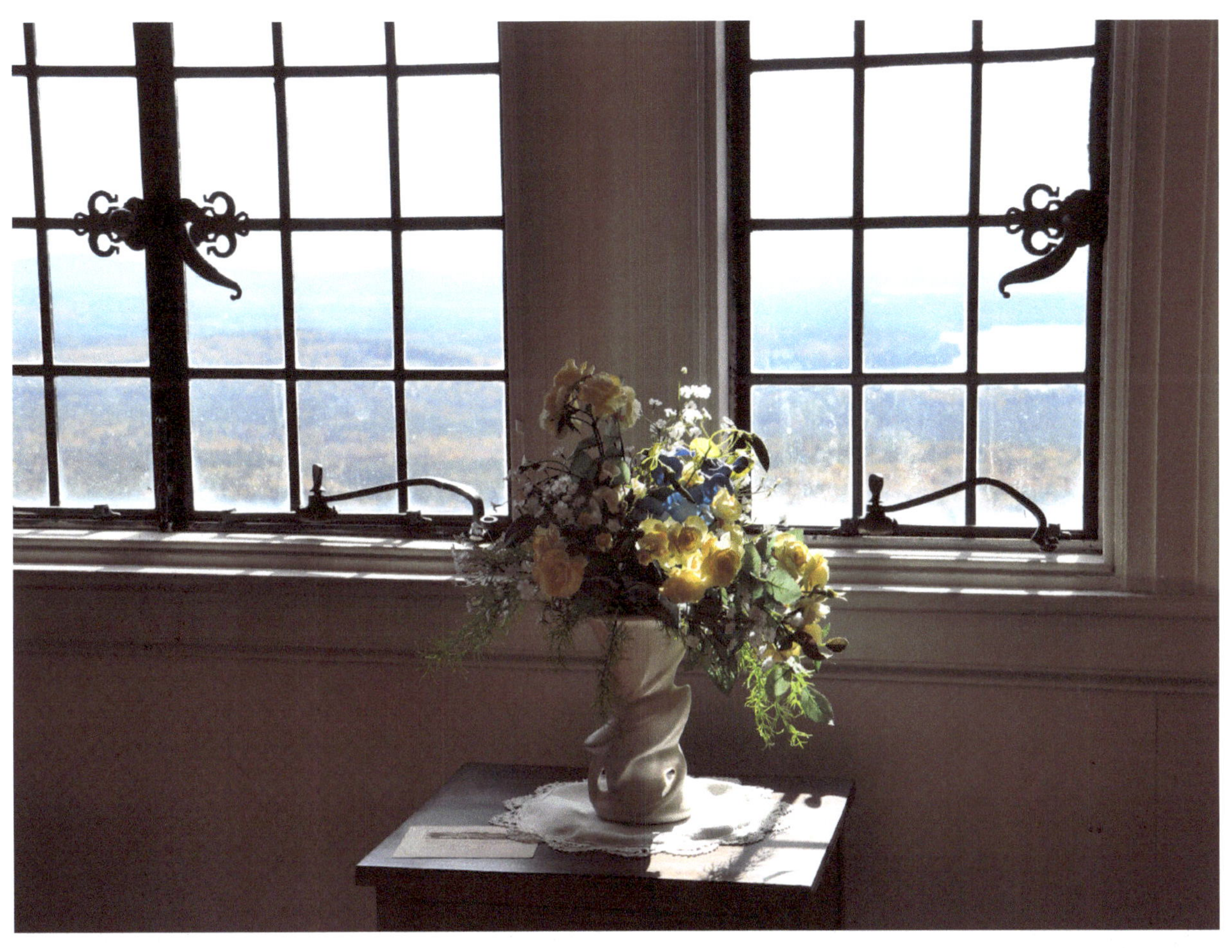

Moultonborough, New Hampshire

Life is a succession of moments. To live each one is to succeed.

--Corita Kent, 1918 - 1986

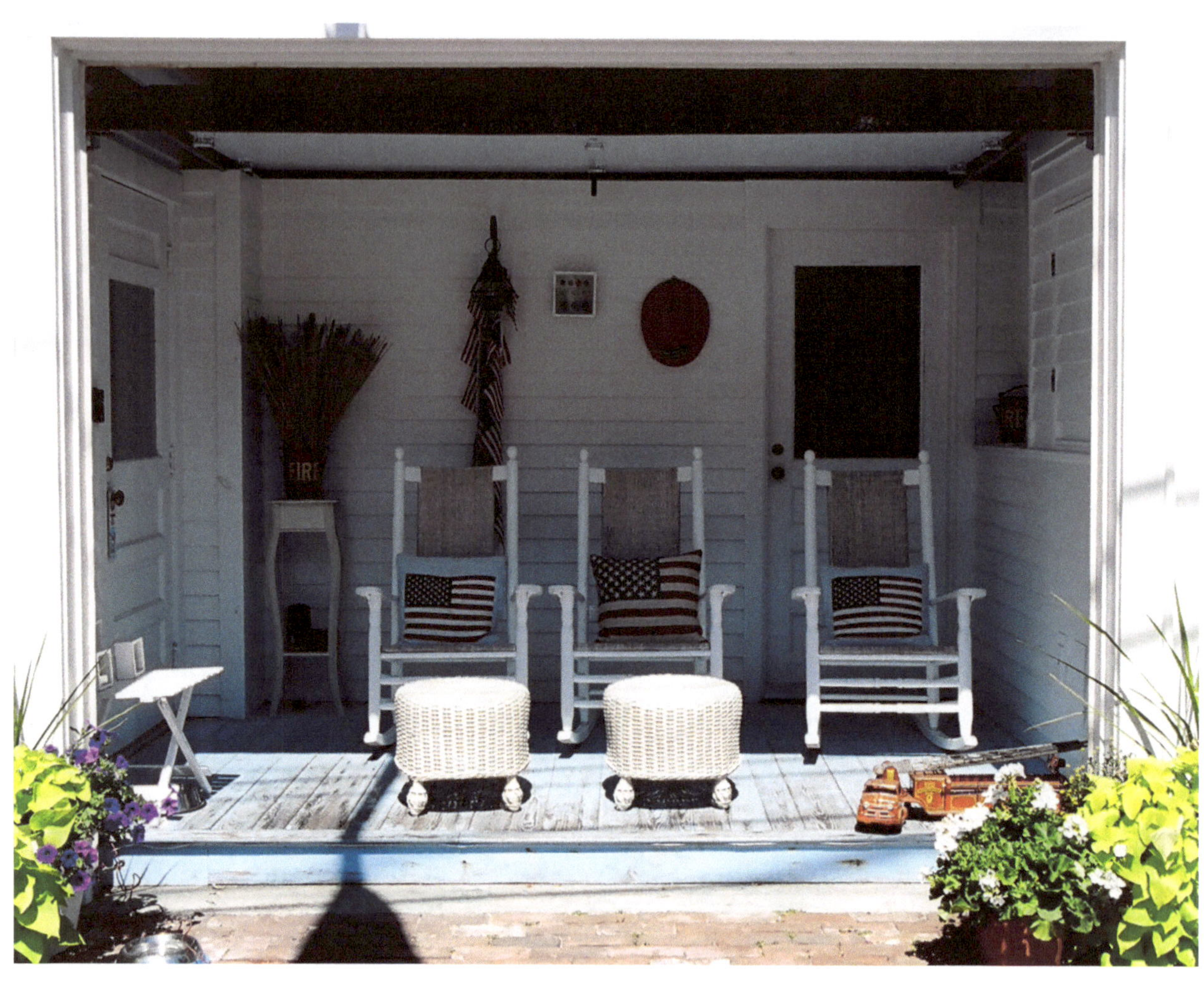

Provincetown, Massachusetts

May you live all days of your life.

-- Jonathan Swift, 1667 - 1745

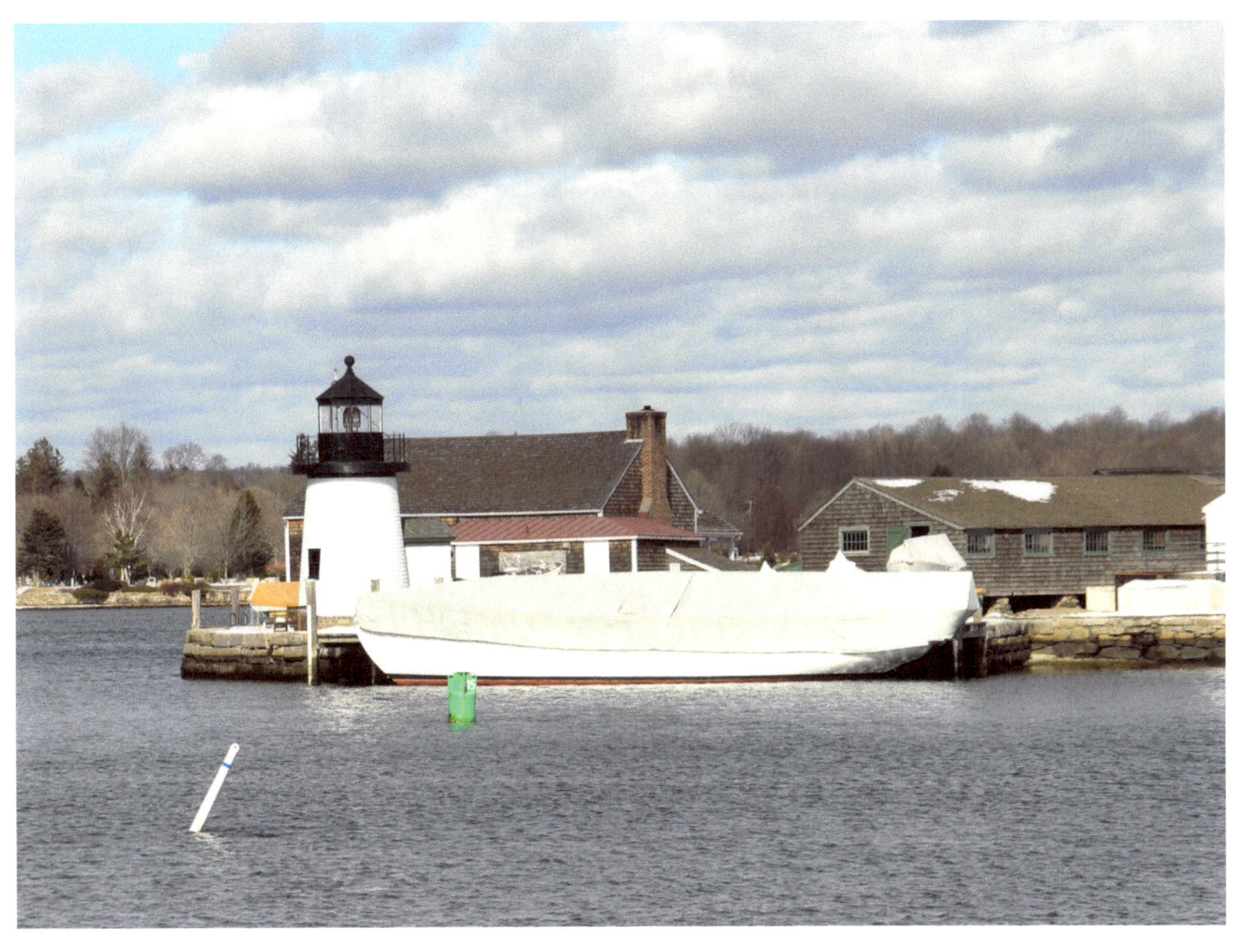

Mystic, Connecticut

The man who goes farthest is generally the one who is willing to do and dare.

The sure-thing boat never gets far from shore.

--Dale Carnegie, 1888 - 1955

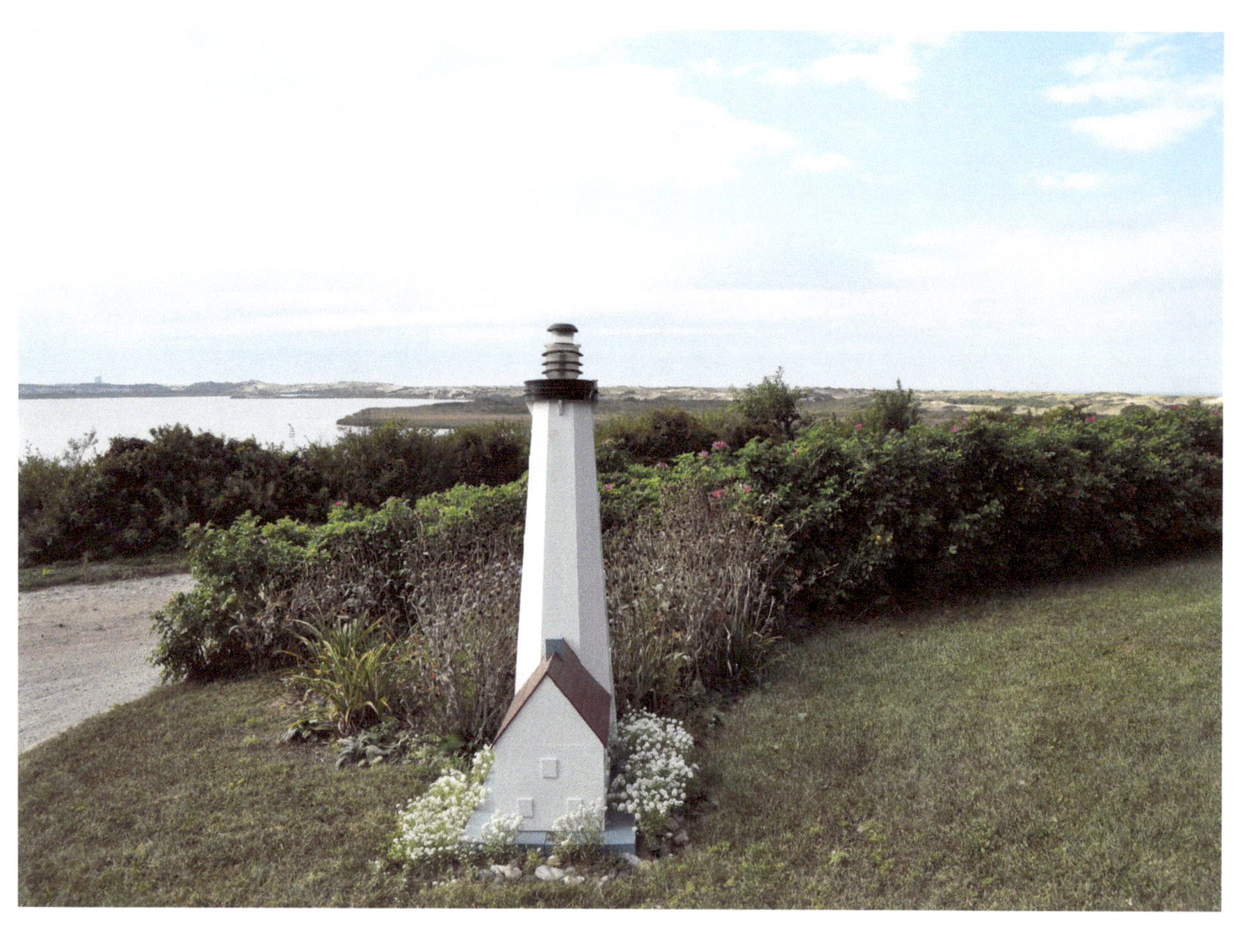

Truro, Massachusetts

The ideals which have lighted my way,

and time after time have given me new courage to face life cheerfully,

have been Kindness, Beauty, and Truth.

--Albert Einstein, 1879 - 1955

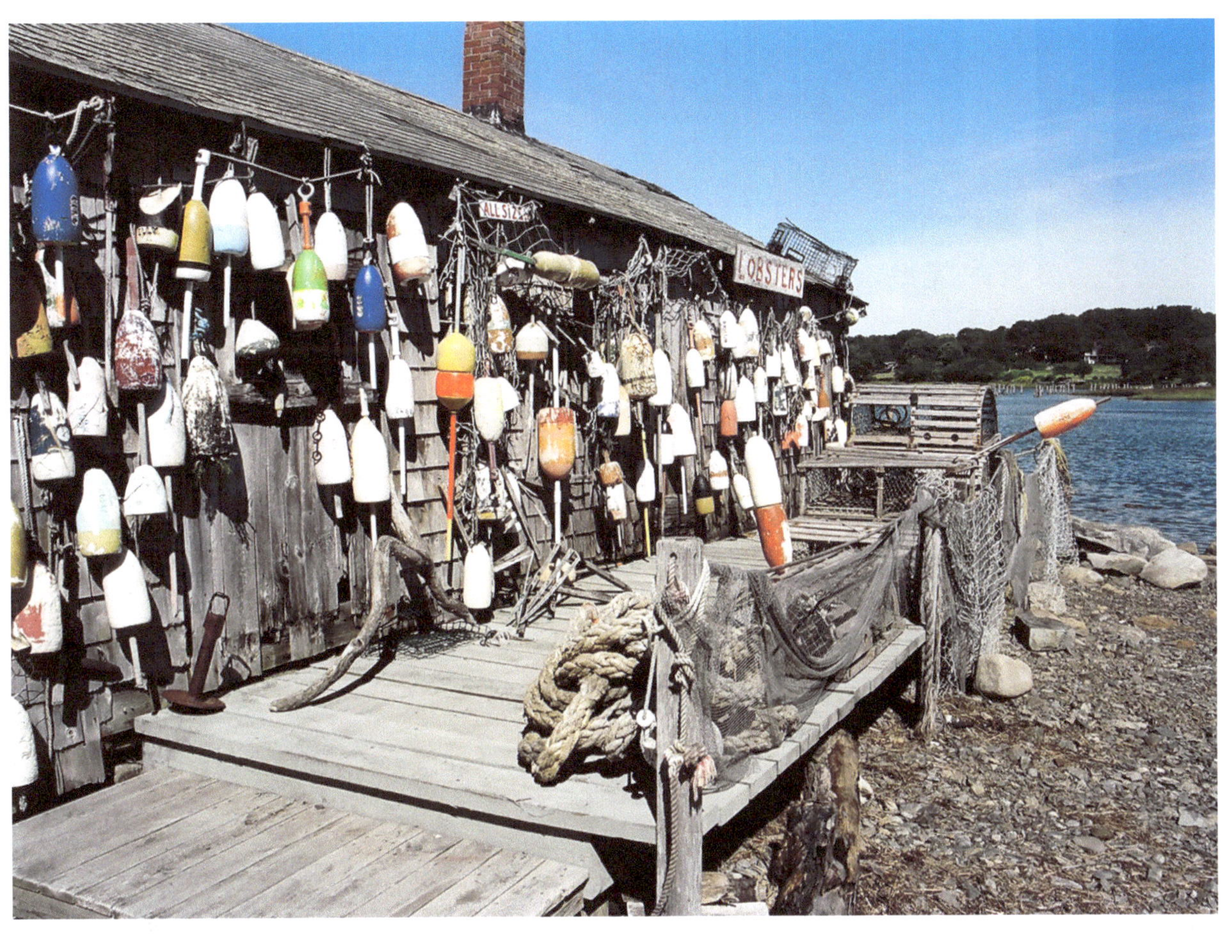

Kennebunk, Maine

May you never suffer the sentiment
of spending a day without purpose.
-- Irish Blessing

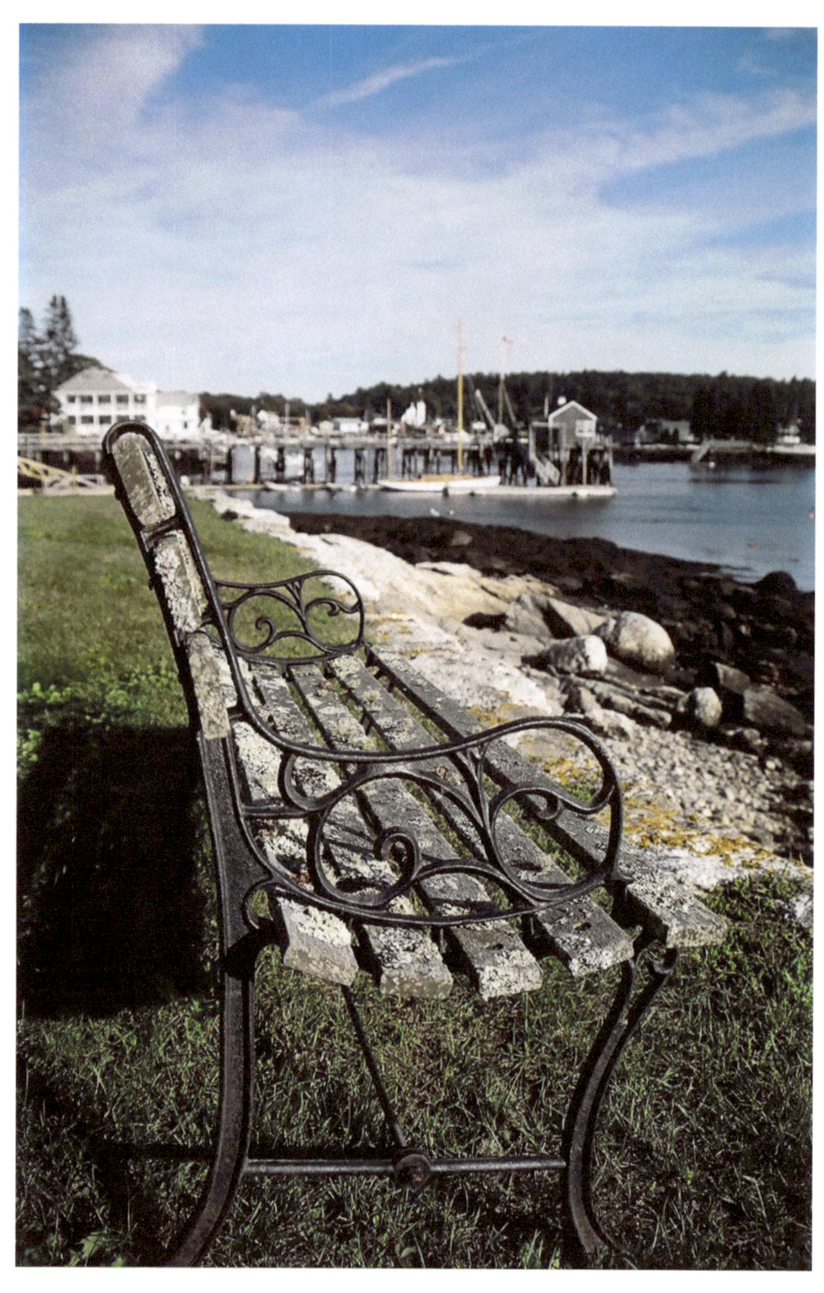

Boothbay Harbor, Maine

There is an art of which every man should be a master, the art of reflection.
If you are not a thinking man, to what purpose are you a man at all?
-- William Hart Coleridge, 1789 - 1842

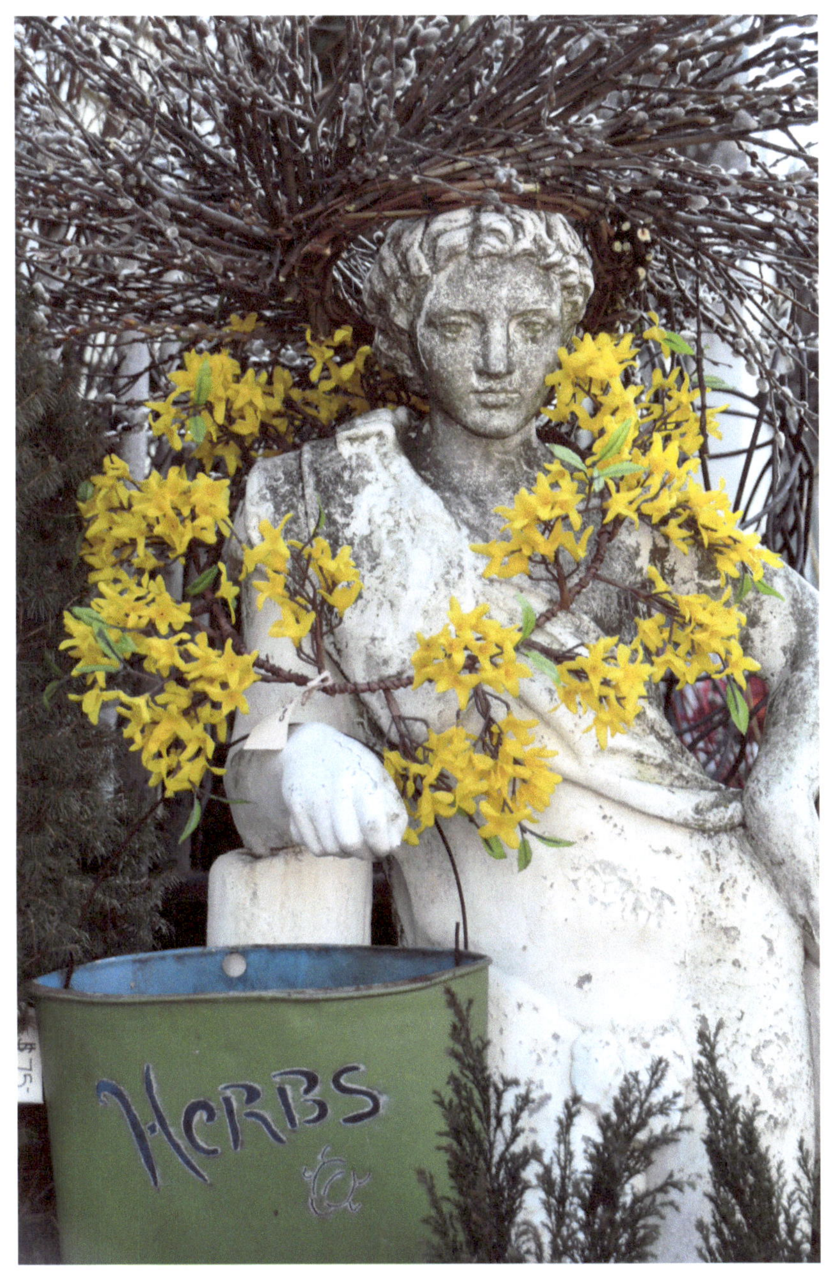

Marblehead, Massachusetts

An optimist is the human personification of spring.

--Susan J. Bissonette

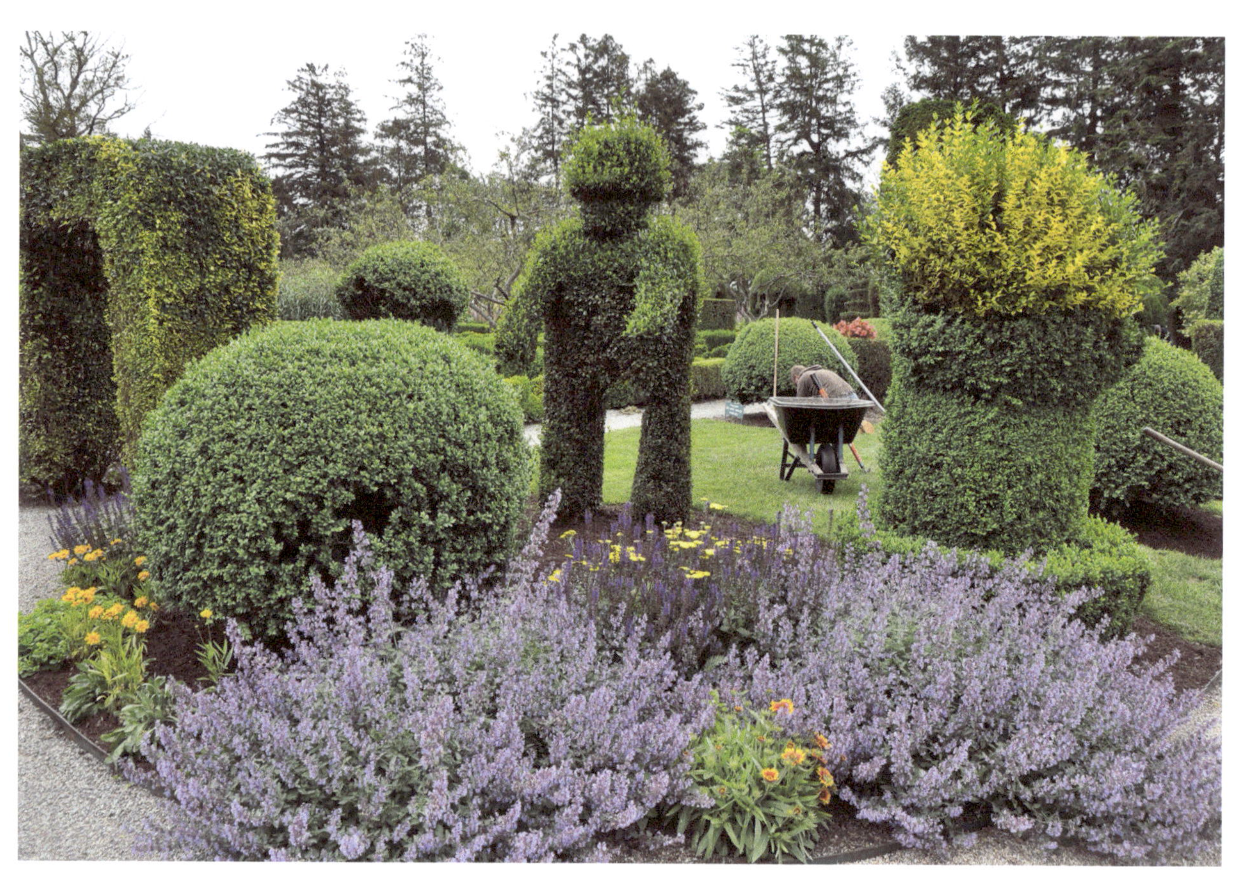

Portsmouth, Rhode Island

If there is no gardener, there is no garden.

--Stephen Covey, 1932 -

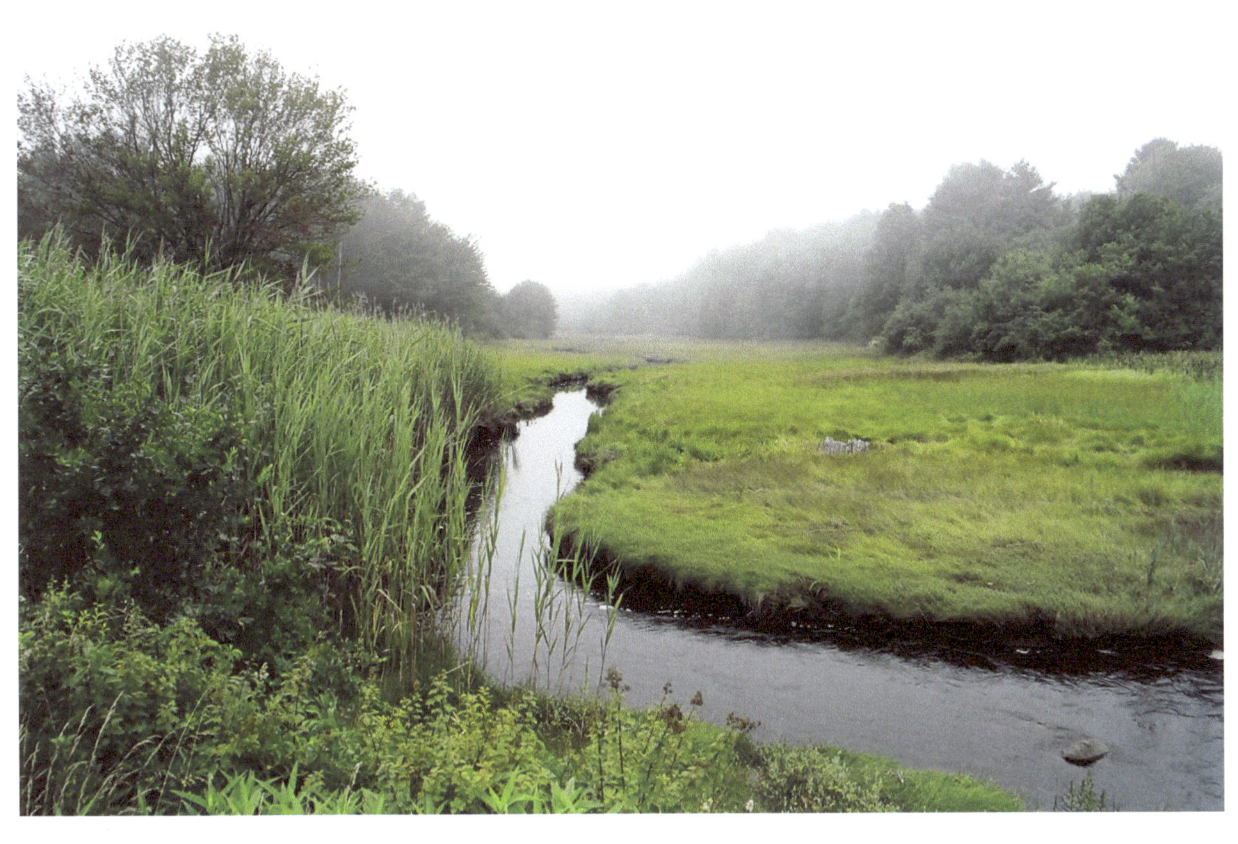

Kennebunk, Maine

A misty morning does not signify a cloudy day.

--Proverb

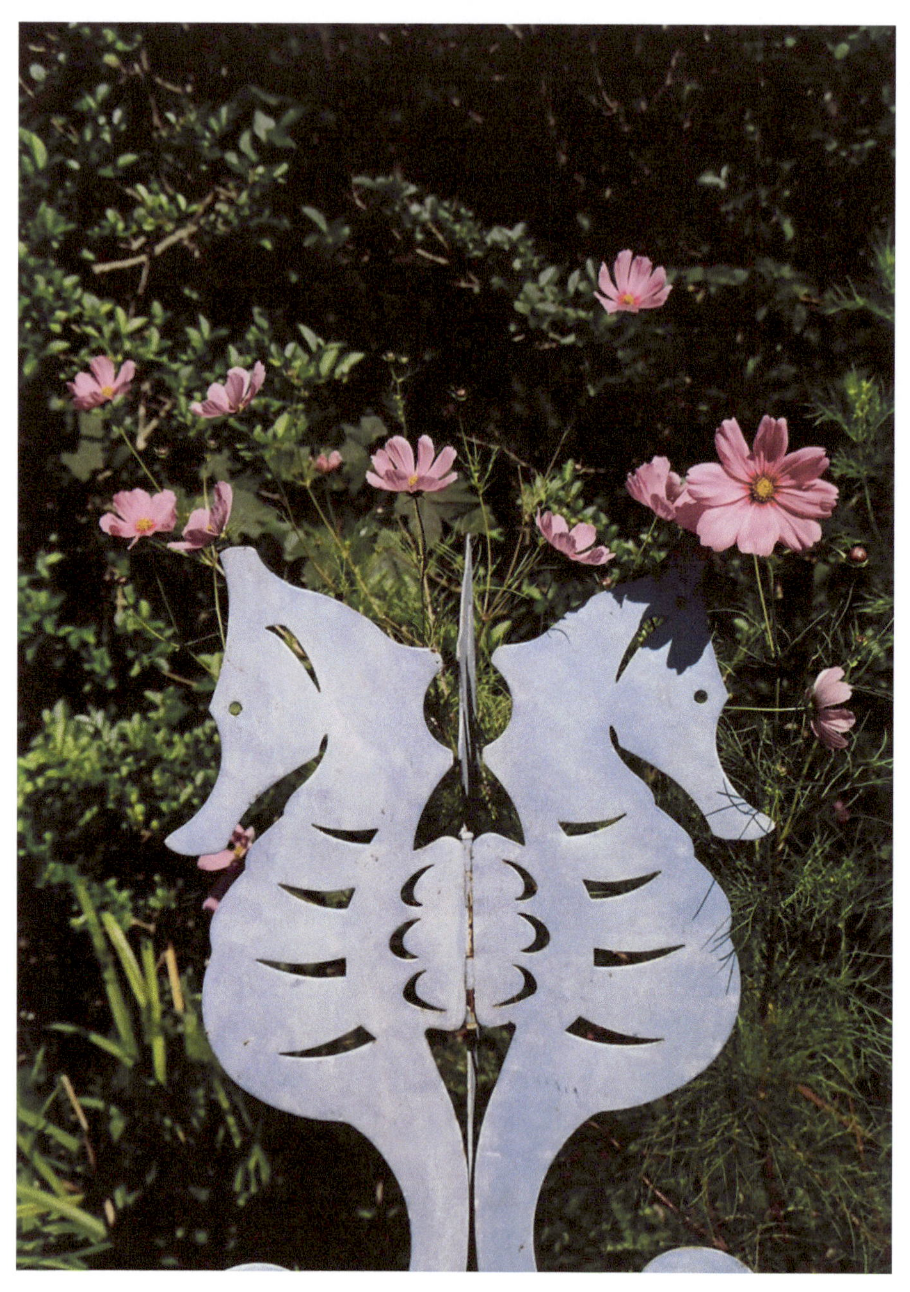

Nahant, Massachusetts

He who lives without folly isn't so wise as he thinks.

--Francois de la Rochefoucauld, 1513 - 1680

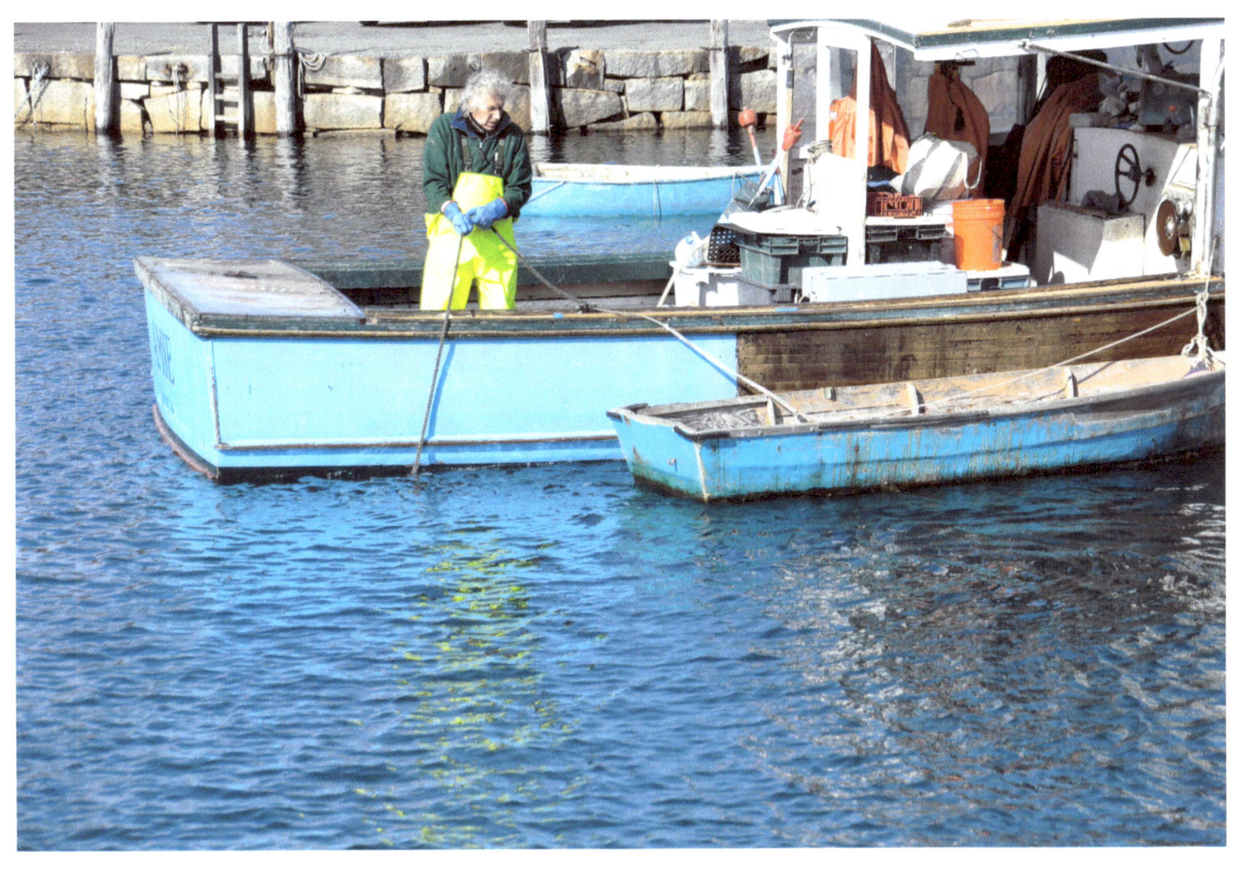

Rockport, Massachusetts

Give a man a fish and you feed him for a day.
Teach a man to fish and you feed him for a lifetime.
--Chinese Proverb

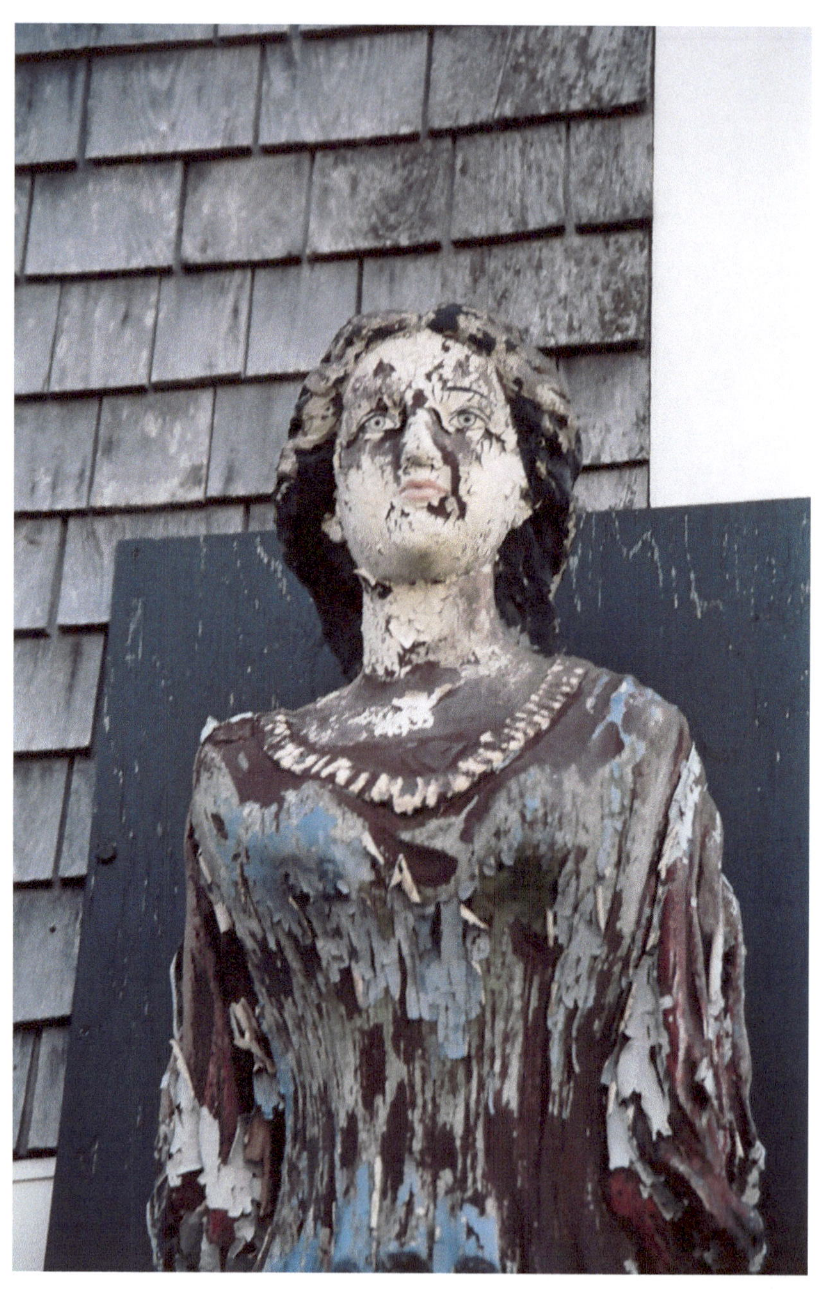

Nantucket, Massachusetts

Is life worth living?
Aye, with the best of us,
Heights of us, depths of us--
Life is the test of us!
--Corinne Roosevelt Robinson, 1861 - 1933

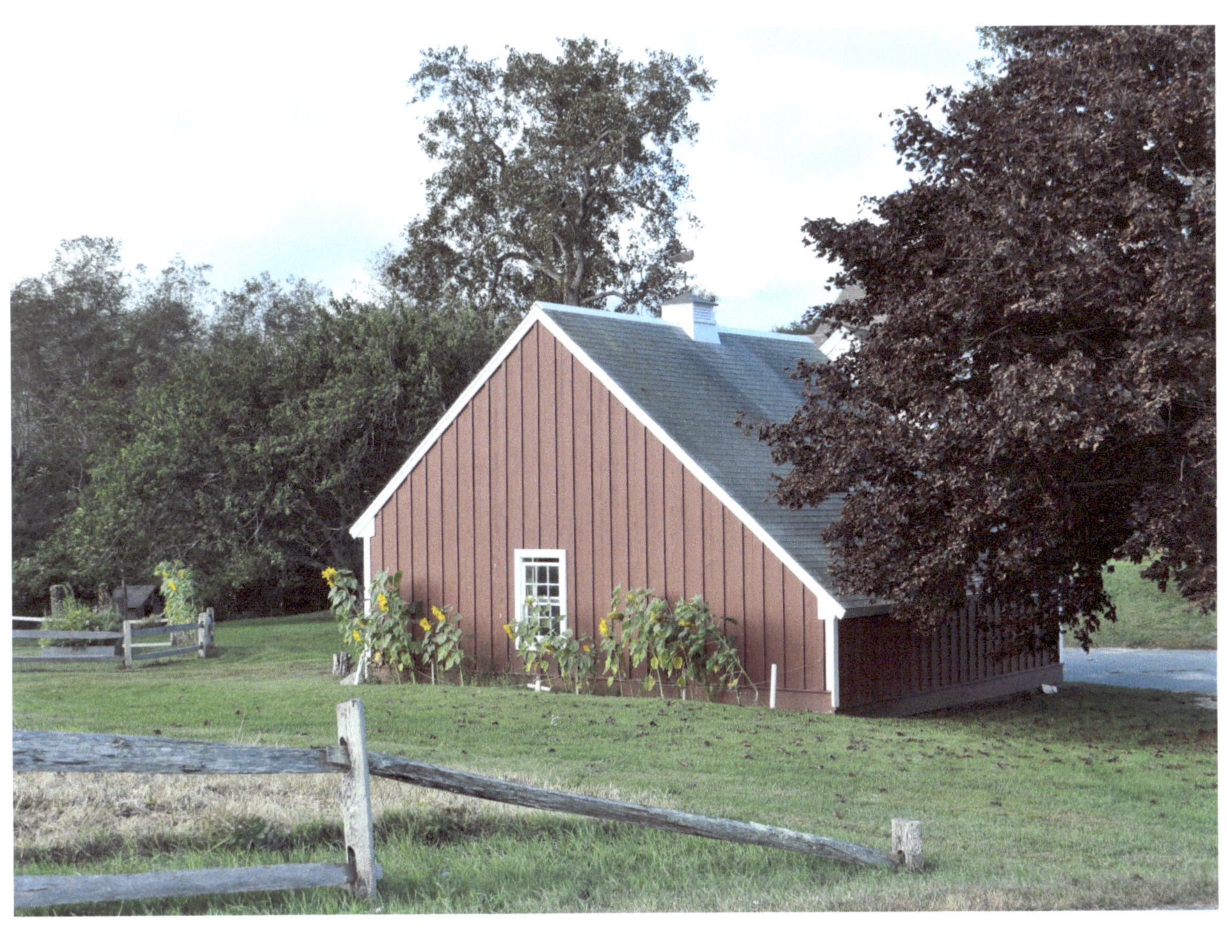

Eastham, Massachusetts

If, every day, I dare to remember that I am here on loan, that this house,
this hillside, these minutes are all leased to me, not given, I will never despair.
--Erica Jong, 1942 -

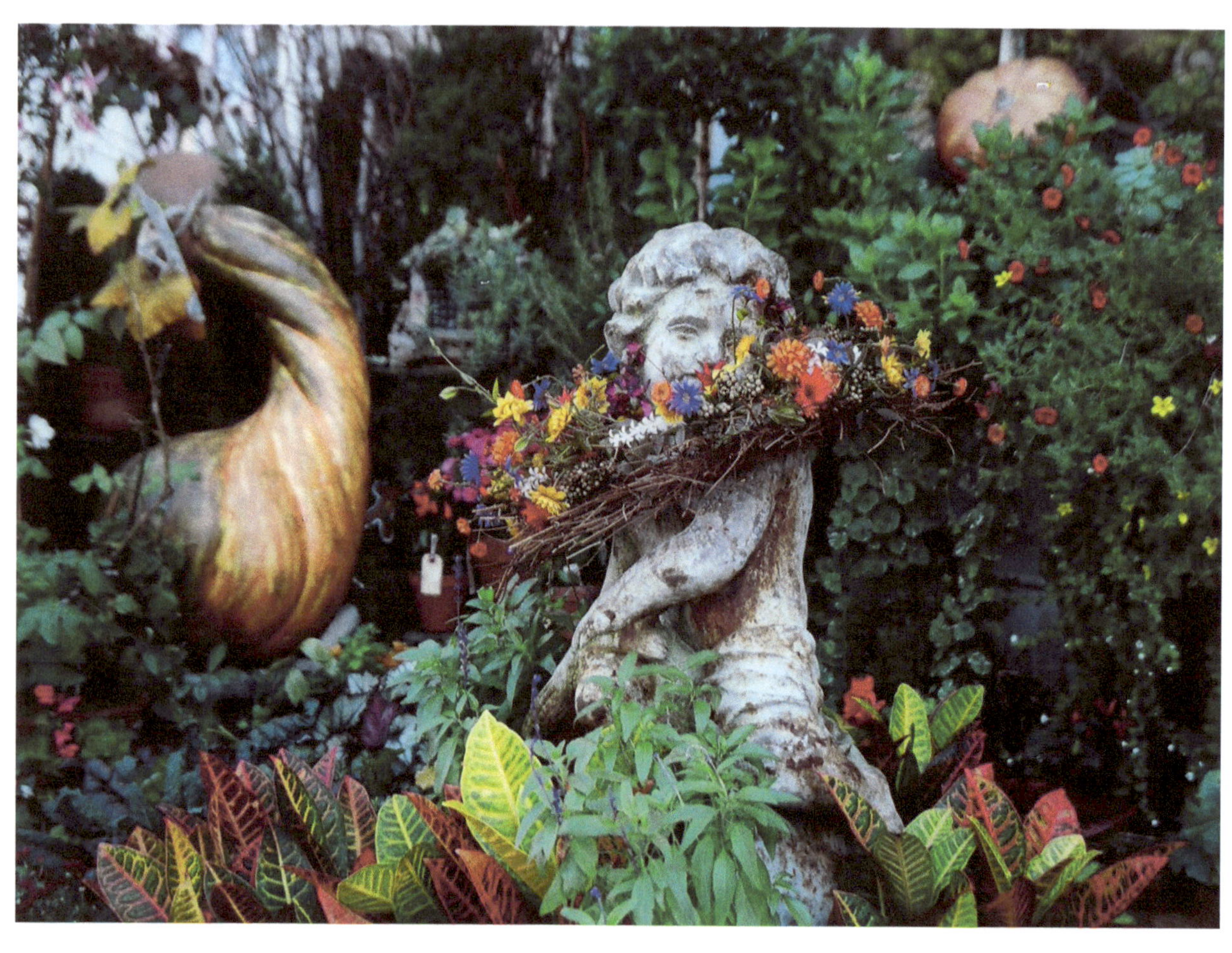

Marblehead, Massachusetts

Autumn is a second spring when every leaf is a flower.
--Albert Camus, 1913 - 1960

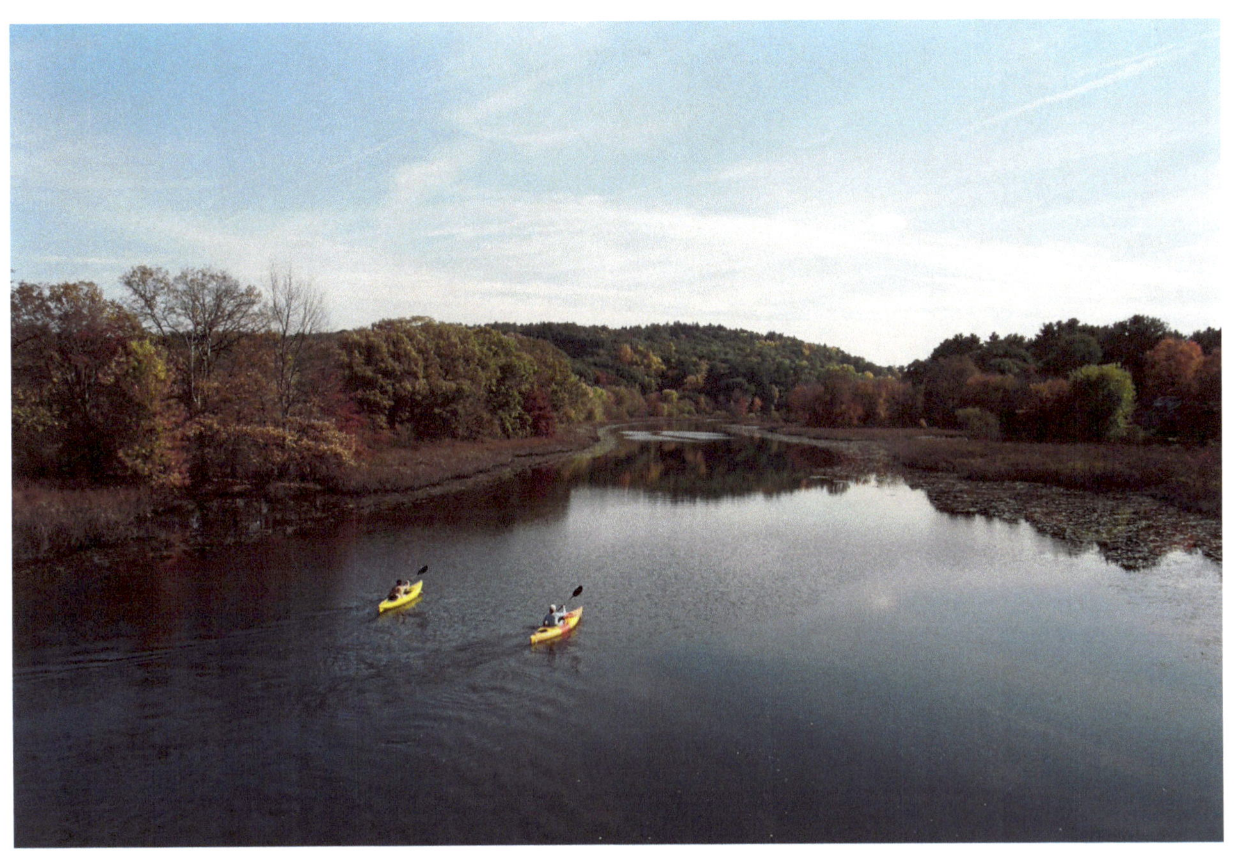

Sudbury, Massachusetts

I am suddenly filled with that sense of peace and meaning which is, I suppose,
what the pious have in mind when they talk about
the practice of the presence of God.
--Valerie Taylor

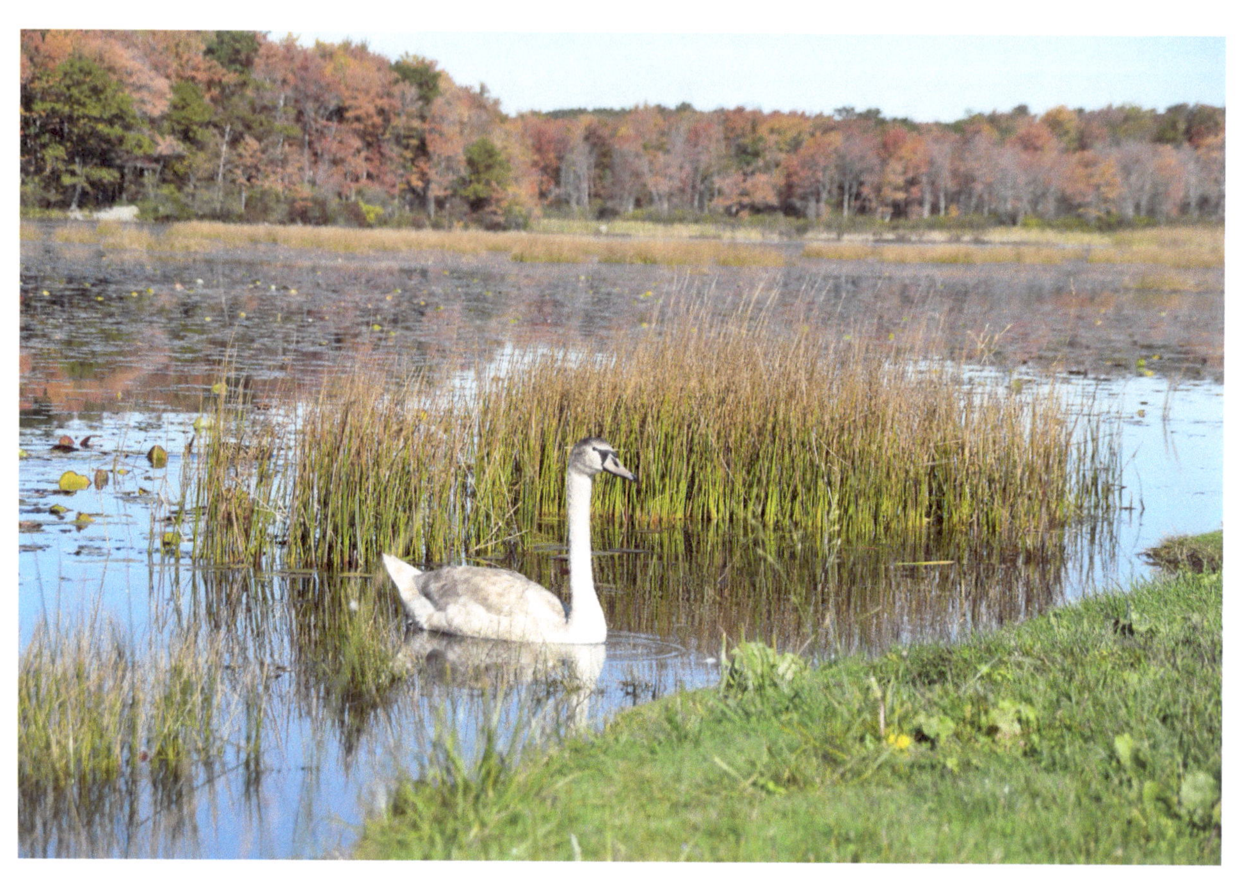

Hampton, New Hampshire

One never knows what each day is going to bring.
The important thing is to be open and ready for it.
--Henry Moore, 1898 - 1986

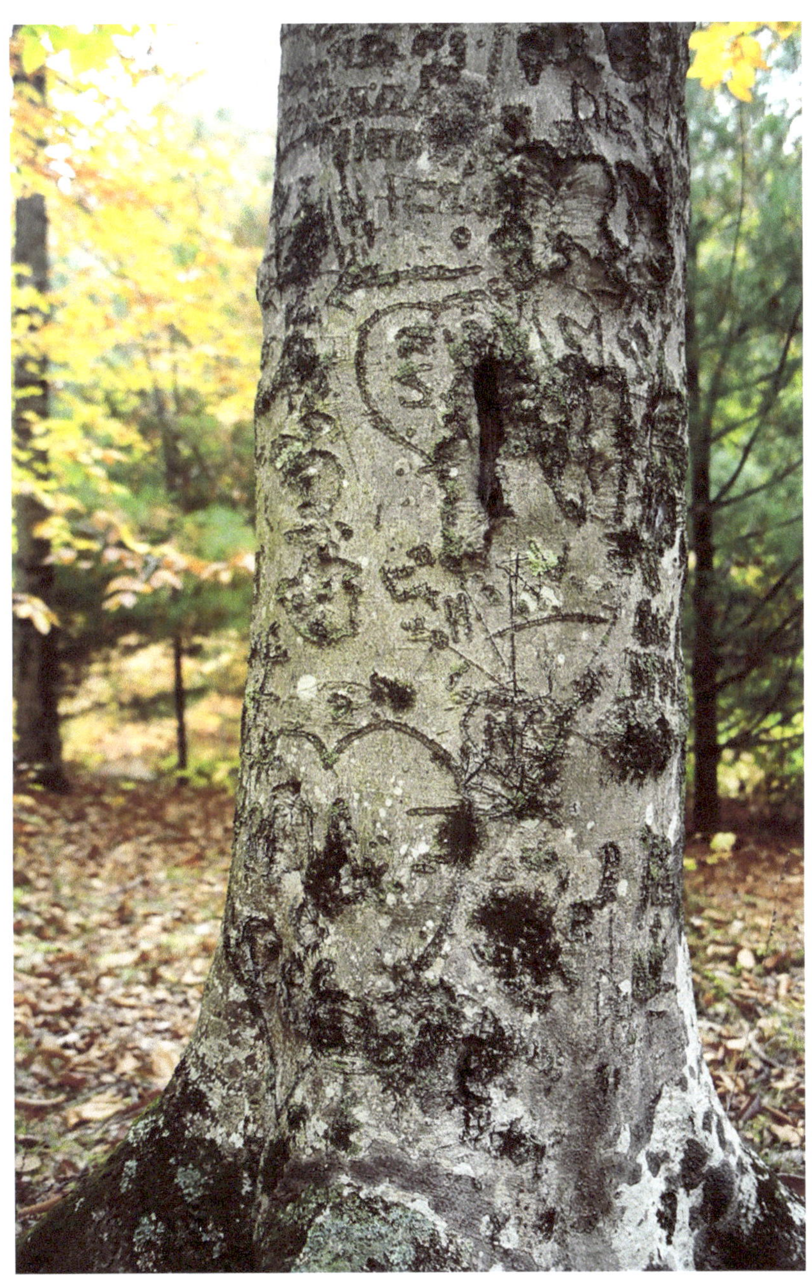

Chatfield Hollow, Connecticut

How we remember, what we remember, and why we remember
form the most personal map of our individuality.
-- Christina Baldwin

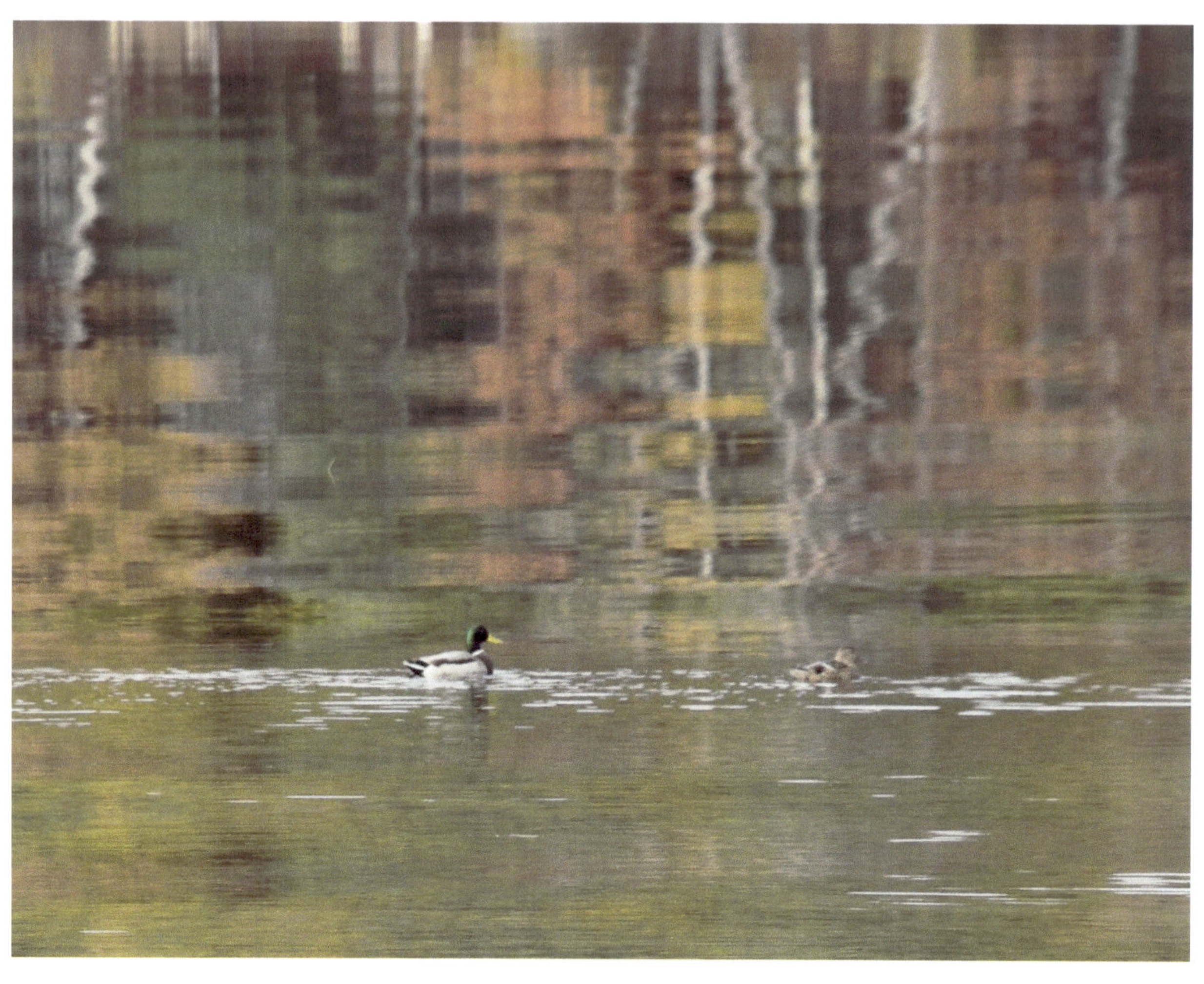

Wolfeboro, New Hampshire

Faith is primarily a process of identification;
the process by which the individual ceases to be himself
and becomes part of something eternal.
---Eric Hoffer, 1902 - 1983

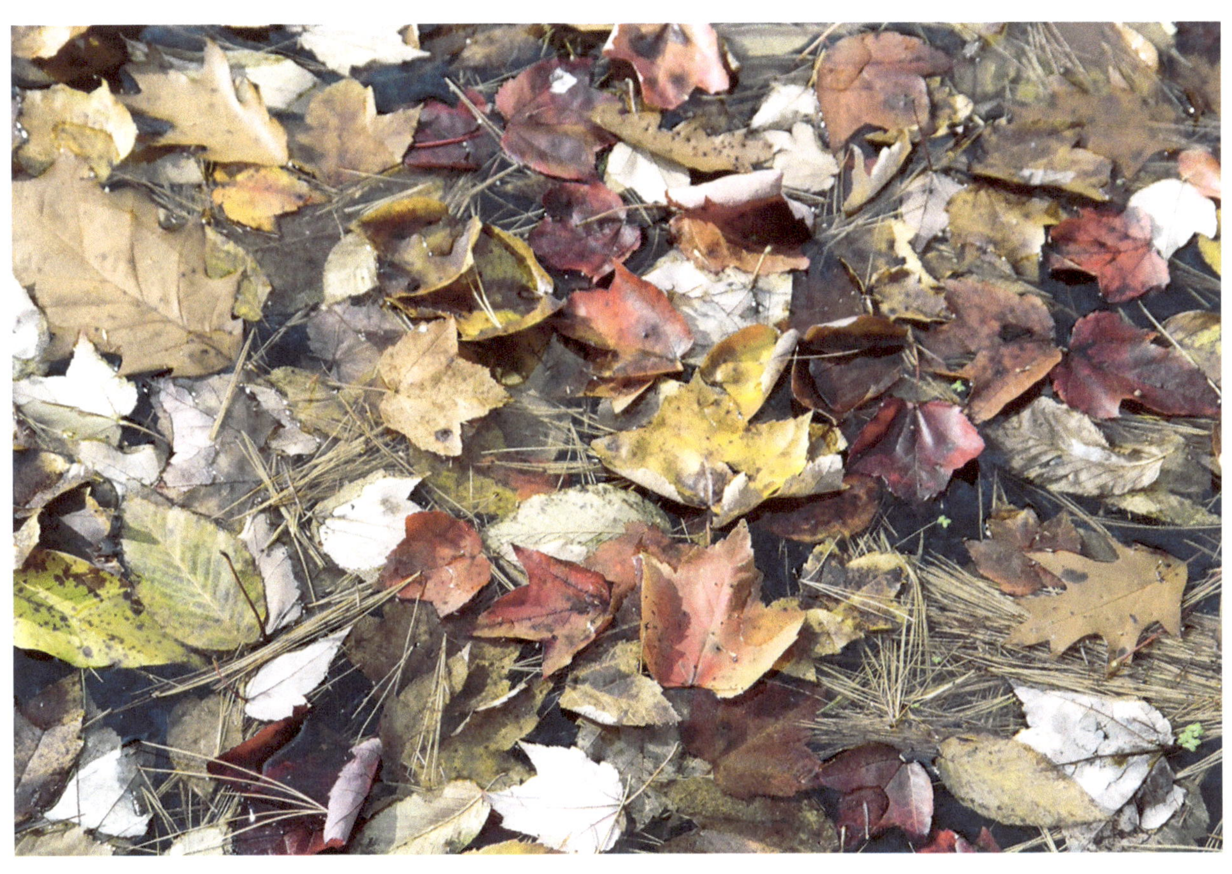

Ogunquit, Maine

We move along... {but} there times when we stop...
we lose ourselves in a pile of leaves or it's memory.
We listen and breezes from a whole other world begin to whisper.
-- James Carroll, 1943 -

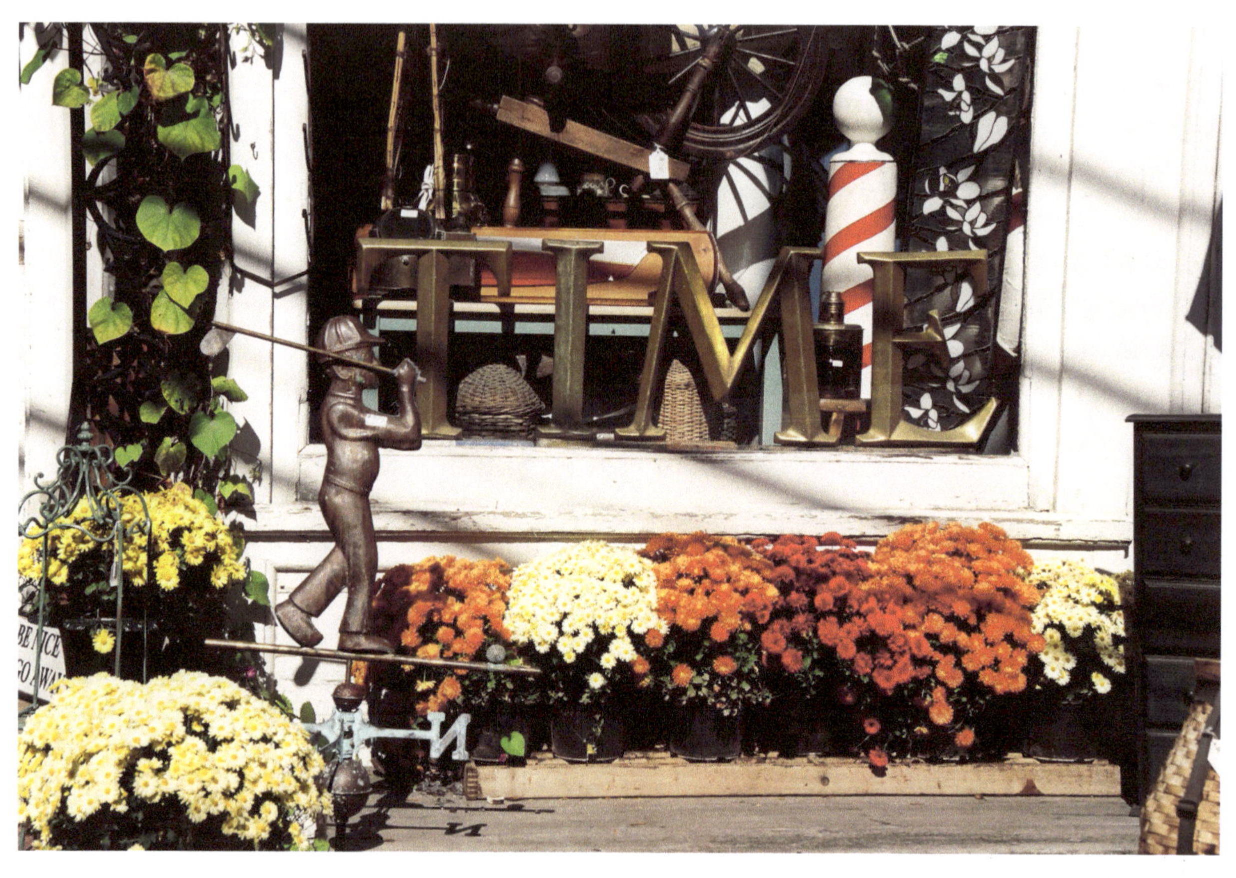

Essex, Massachusetts

We do not remember days, we remember moments.

—Cesare Pavese, 1908 - 1950

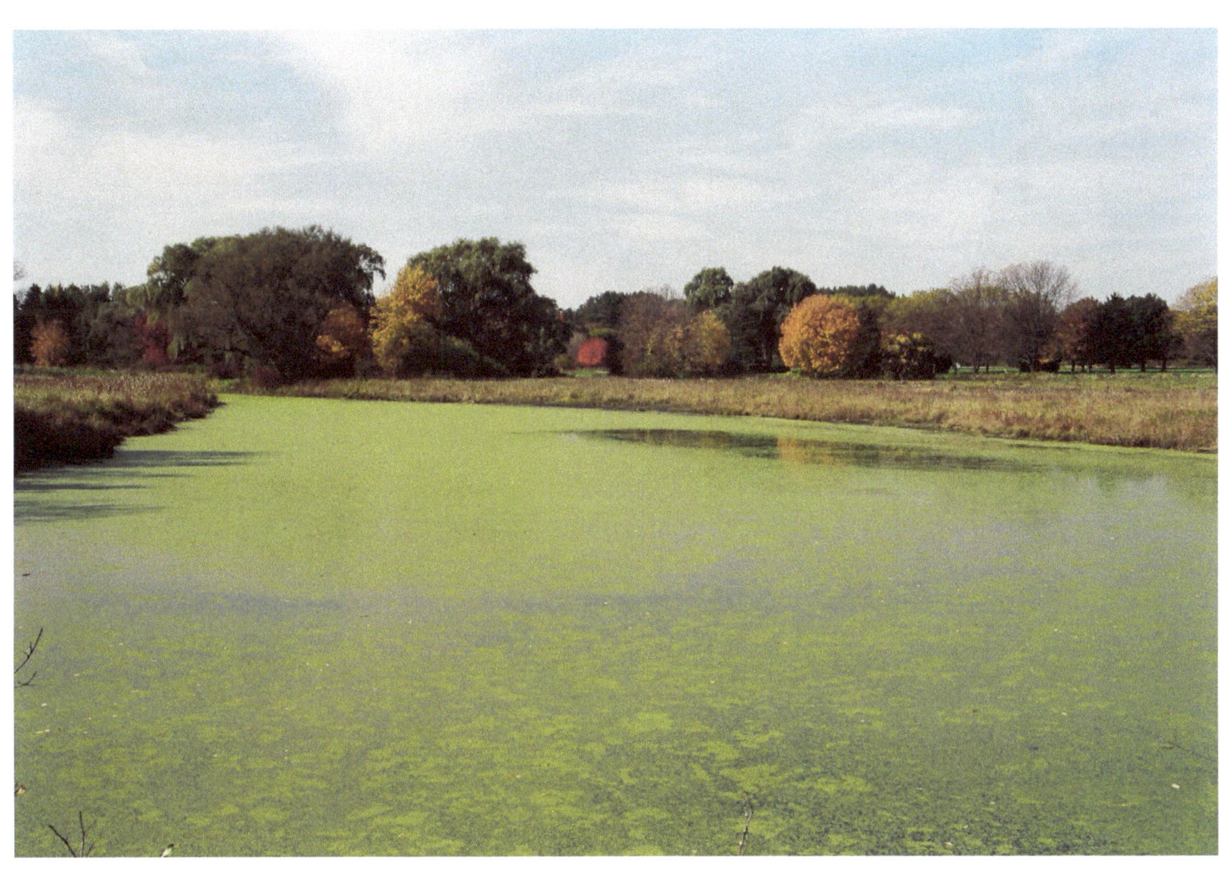

Sudbury, Massachusetts

Love the moment, and the energy of that moment will spread beyond all boundaries.

--Corita Kent, 1918-1986

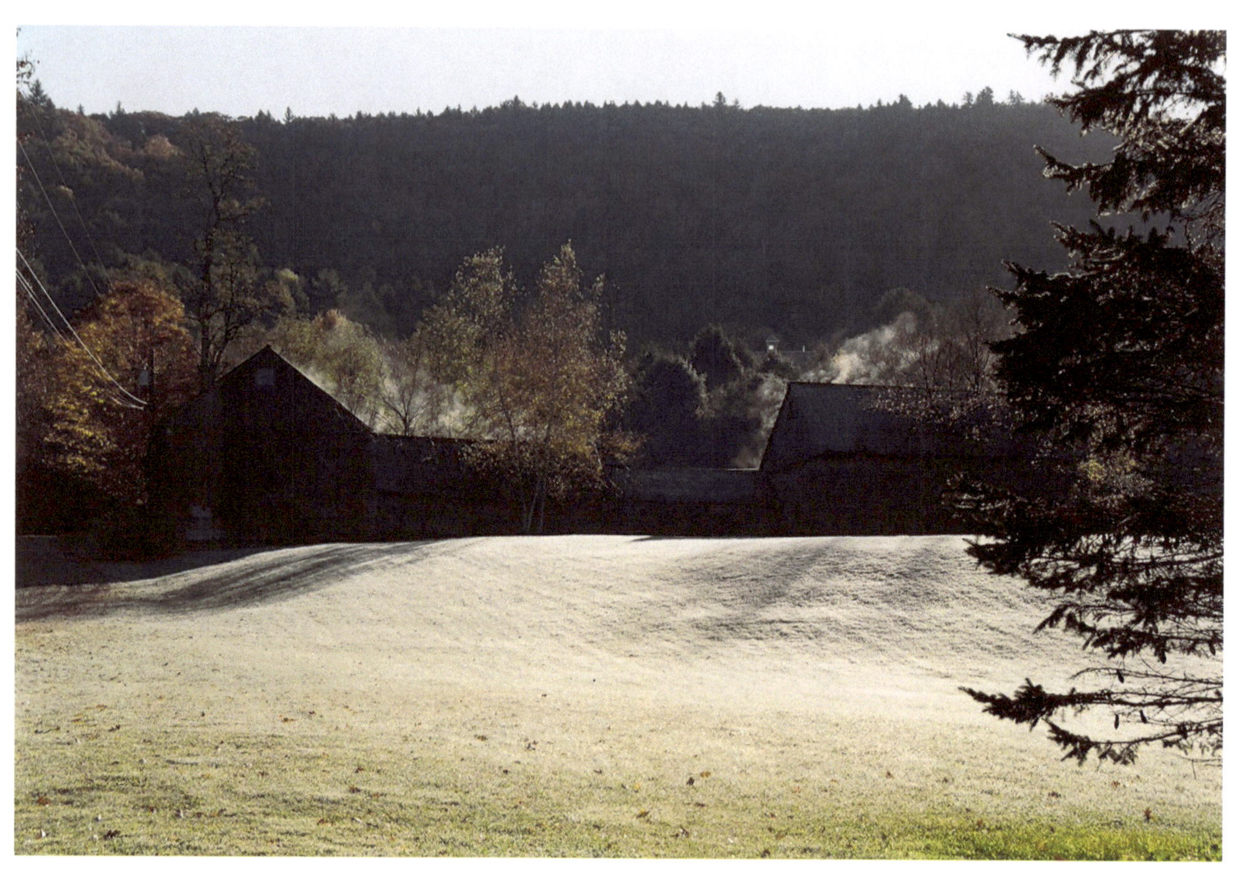

Southern Vermont

On certain mornings, as we turn a corner,
an exquisite dew falls on our heart and then vanishes.
But the freshness lingers, and this, always, is what the heart needs.
The earth must have risen in just such a light the morning the world was born.
--Albert Camus, 1913 - 1960

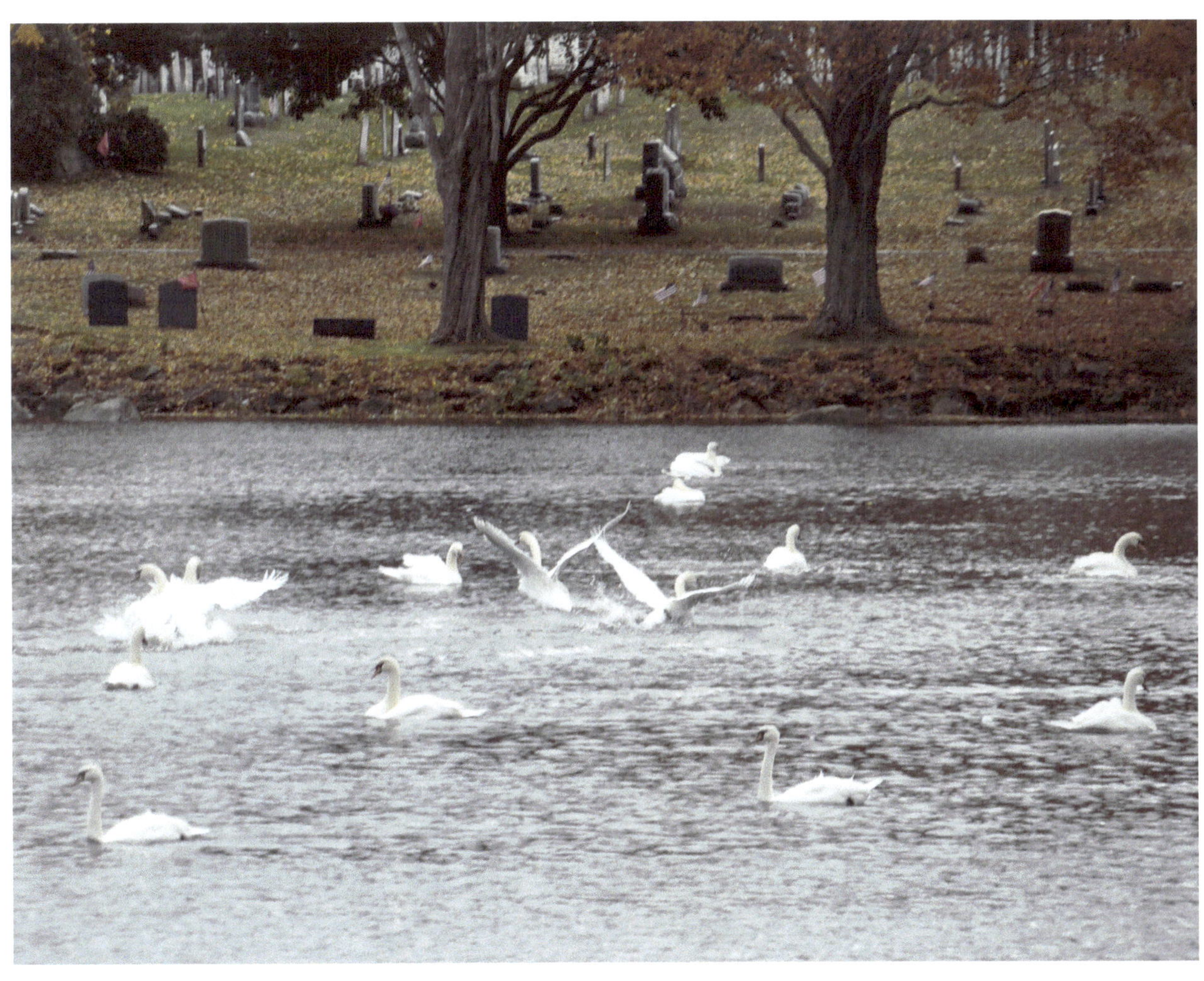

Essex, Connecticut

Faith is an act of a finite being who is grasped by, and turned to, the infinite.

--Paul Tillich, 1886 - 1965

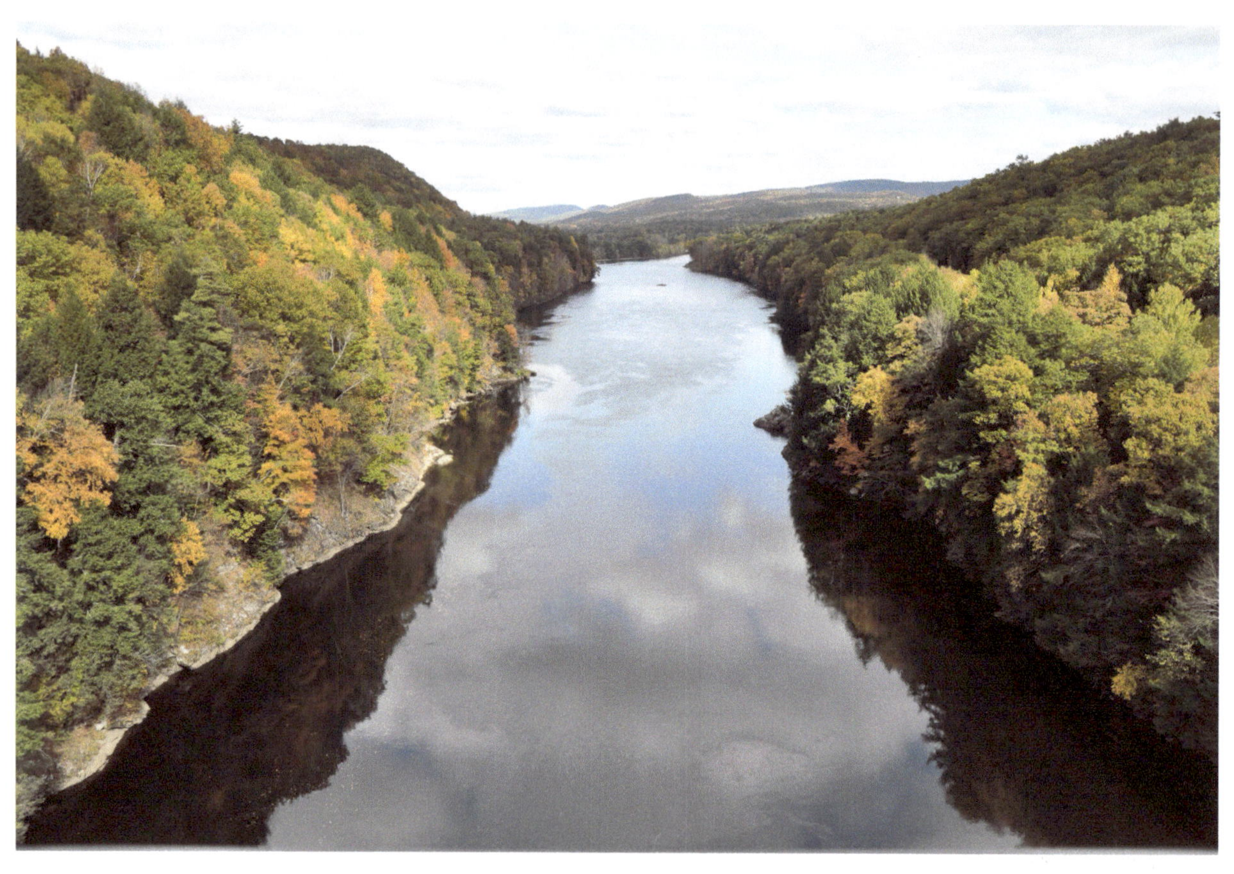

Turners Falls, Massachusetts

I thank You God for this most amazing day;
for the leaping greenly spirits of trees and a true blue dream of sky;
and for everything which is natural which is infinite which is yes.

—e.e. cumings, 1894 - 1962

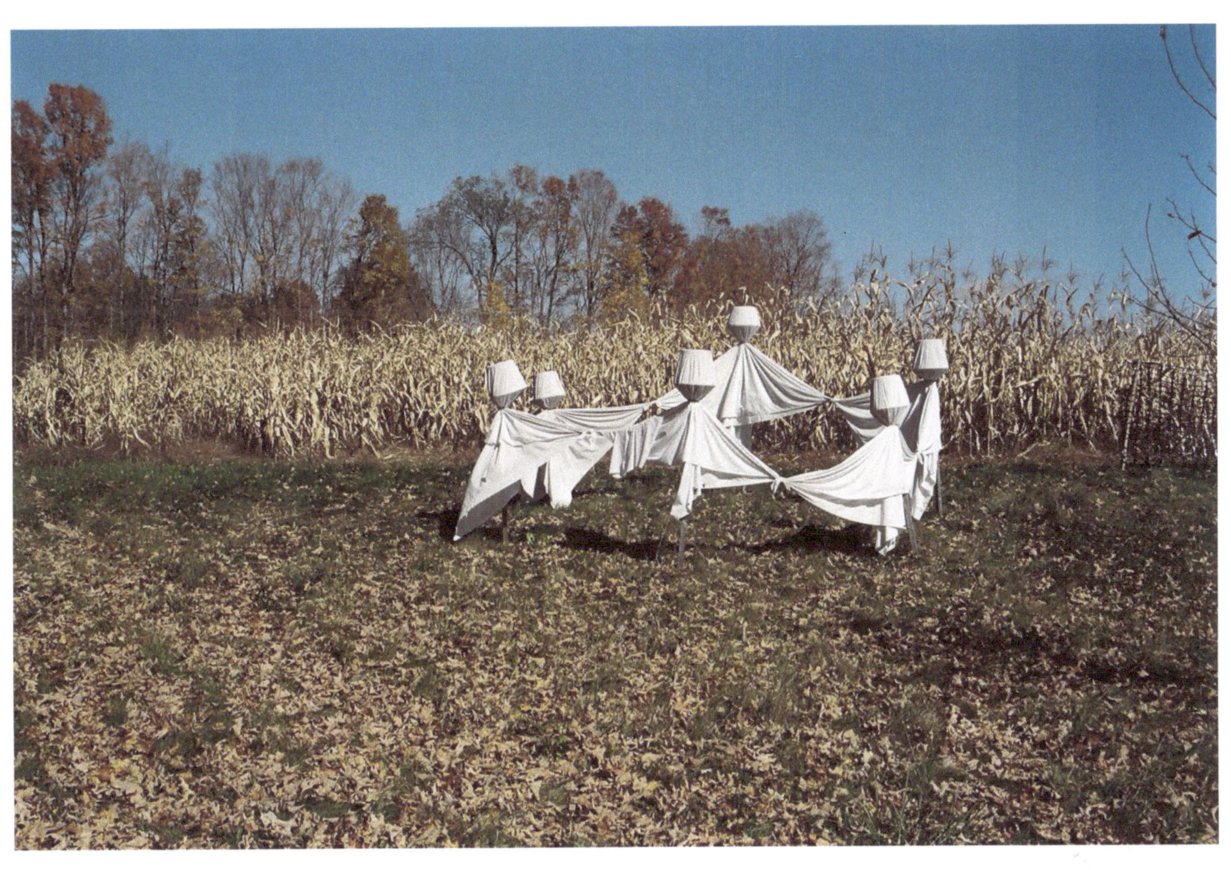

Southern Vermont

Be aware of wonder. Live a balanced life -- learn some and think some and draw and paint and sing and dance and play and work every day some.

--Robert Fulghum, 1937 -

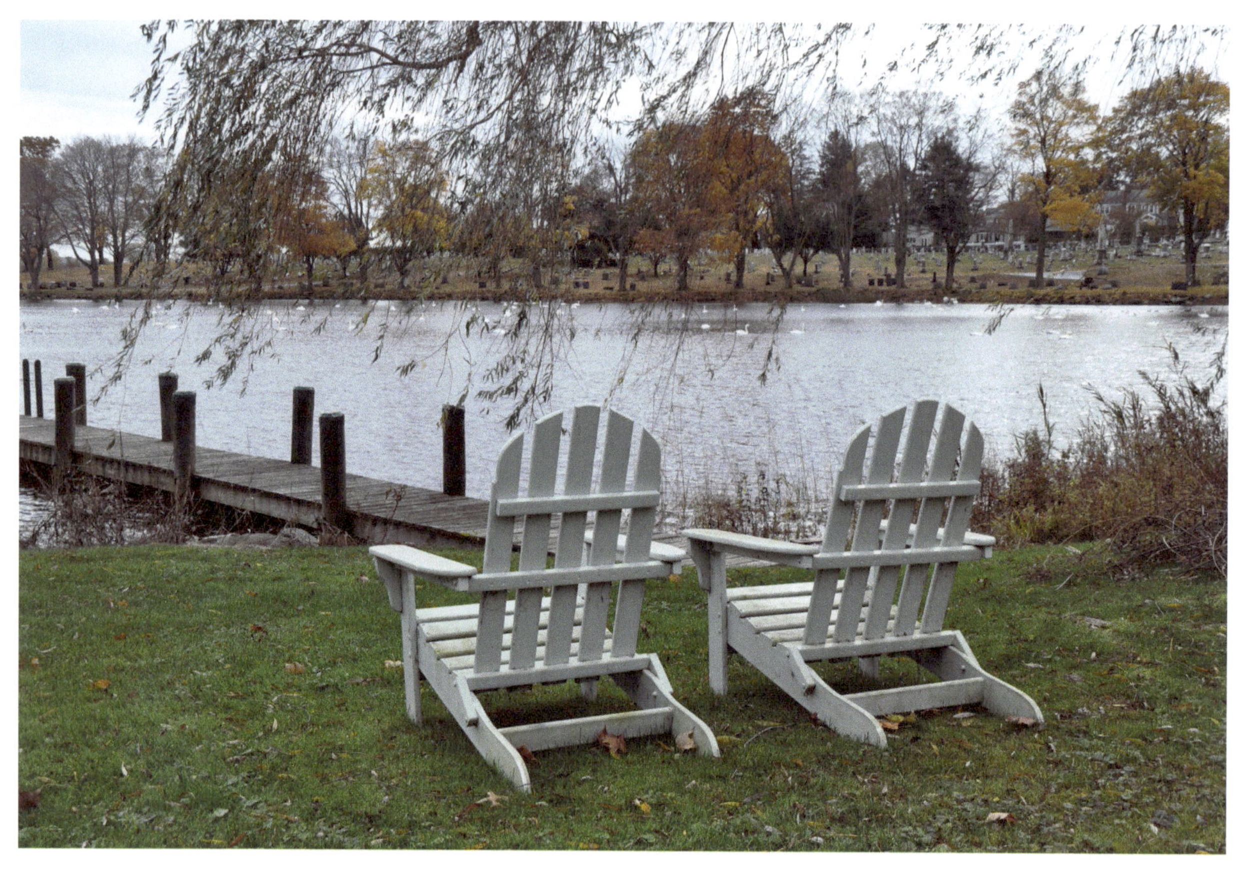

Essex, Connecticut

Grow old along with me! The best is yet to be.

--Robert Browning, 1812 - 1889

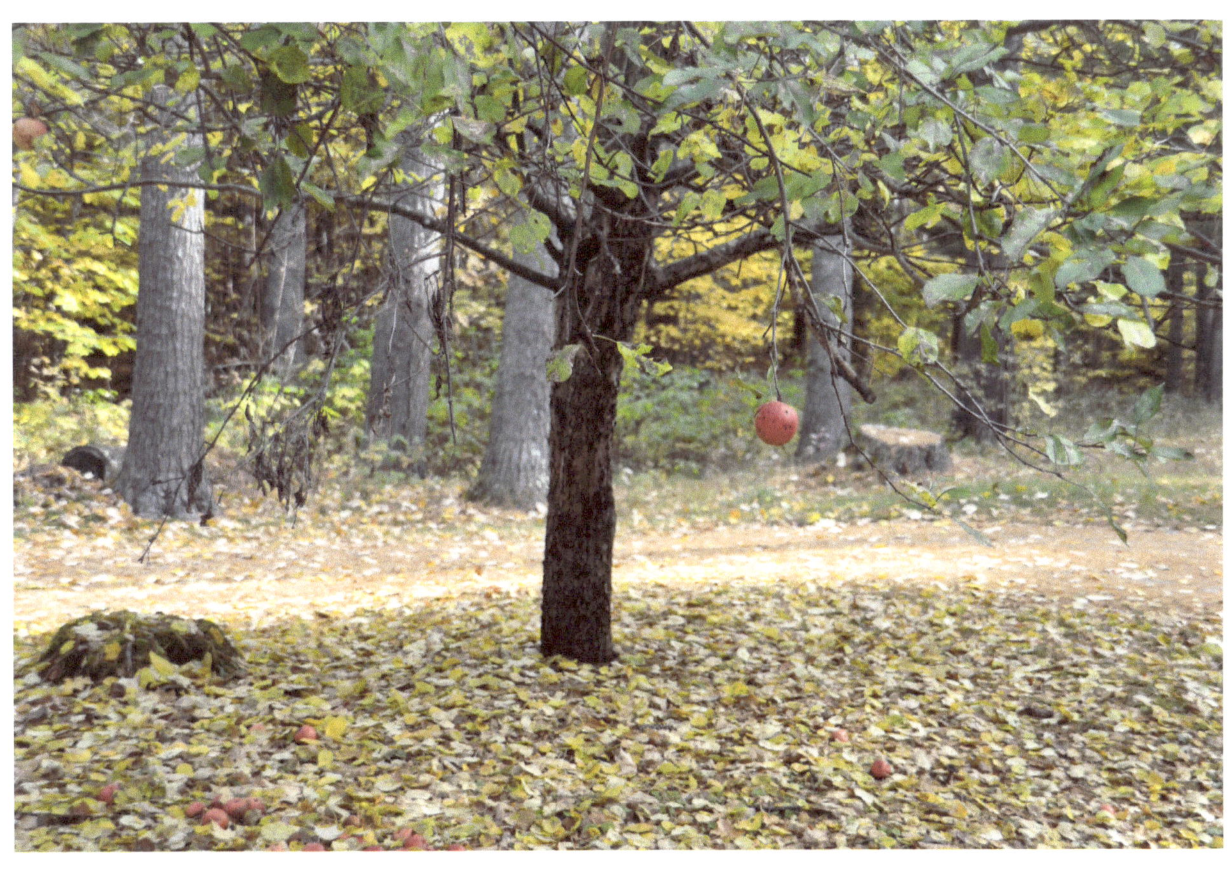

Moultonborough, New Hampshire

Success seems to be largely a matter of hanging on after others have let go.

--William Feather, 1908 - 1976

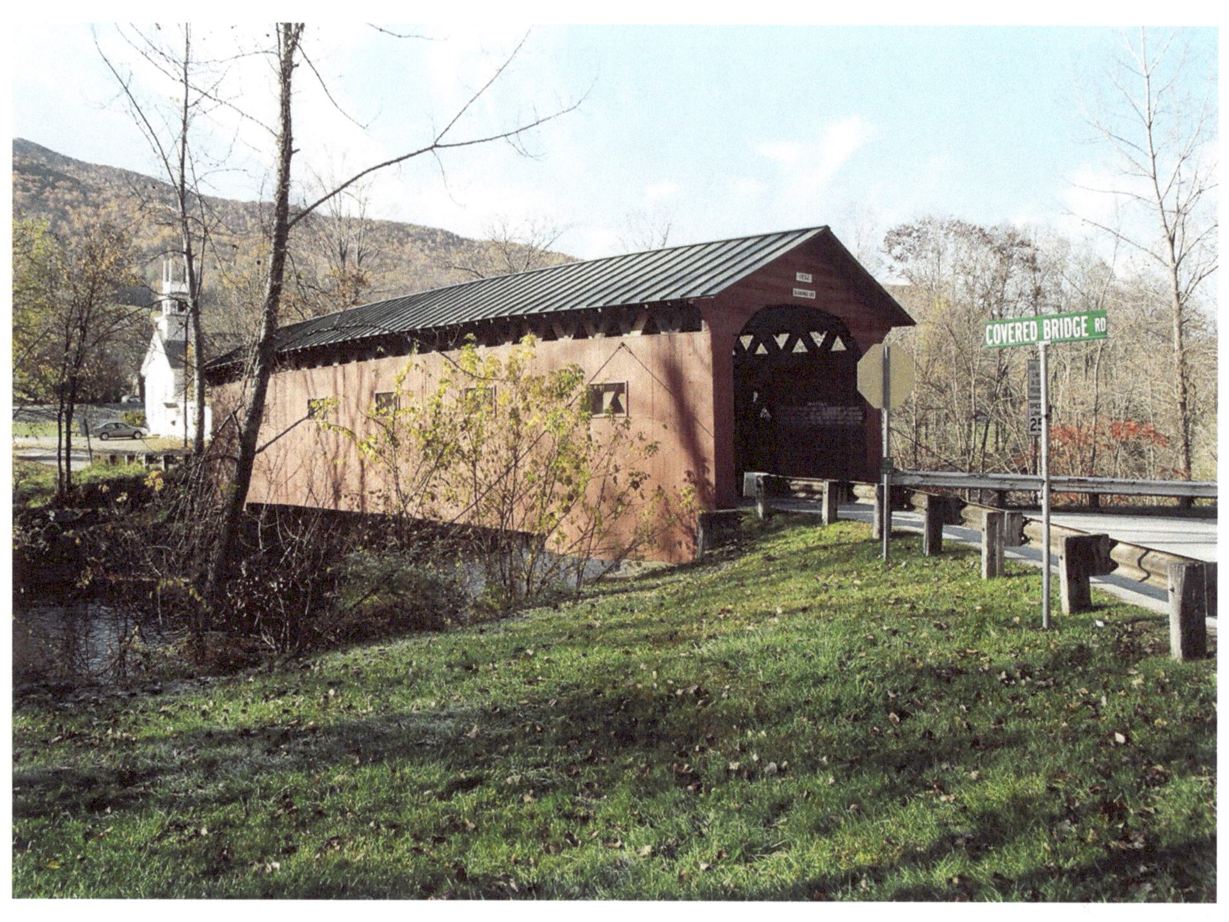

Southern Vermont

Probably no one alive hasn't at one time or another brooded over the possibility of going back to an earlier, ideal age in his existence and living a different kind of life.

--Hal Boyle, 1911 - 1974

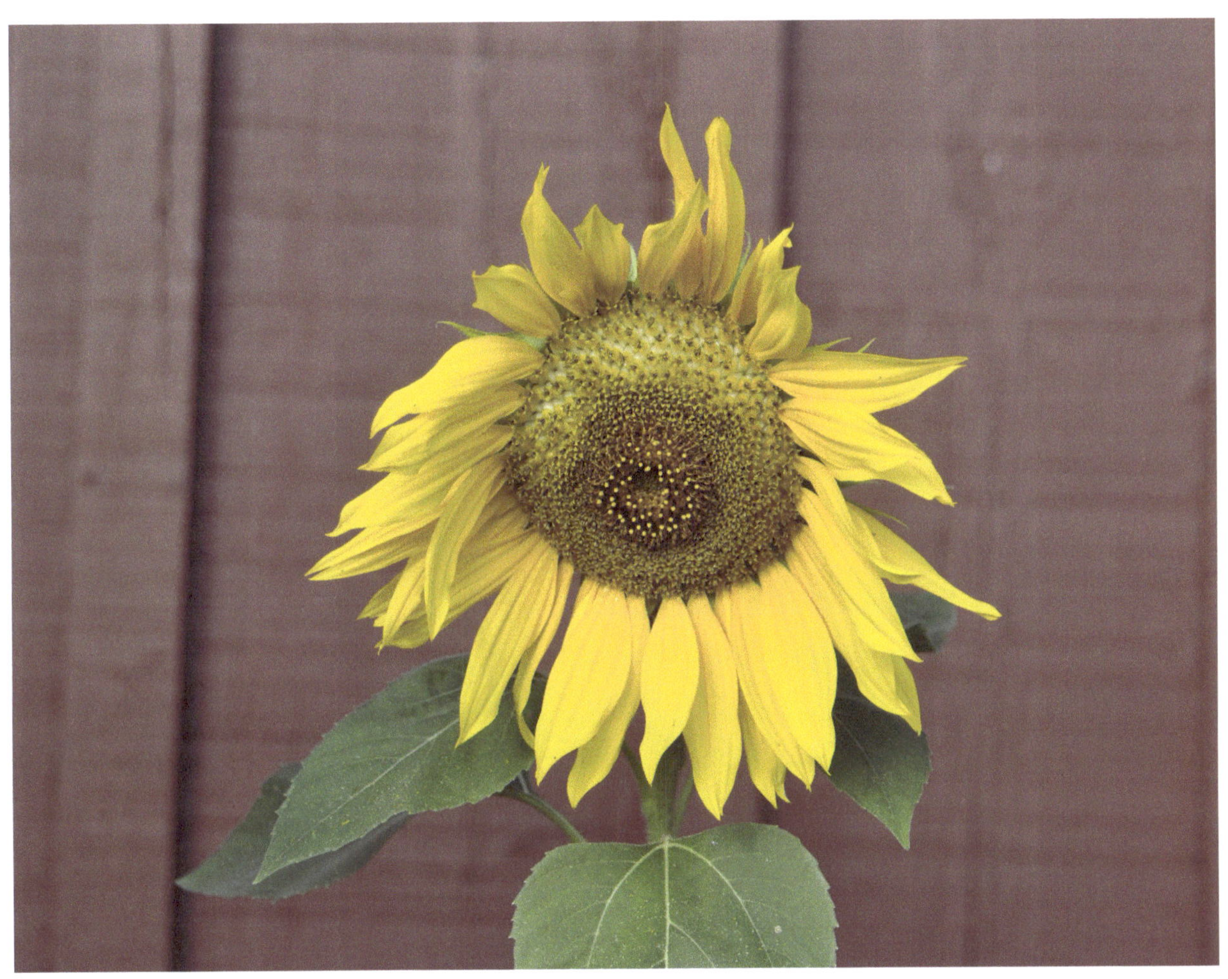

Eastham, Massachusetts

Nor is it an objection to say that we must understand a prayer if it is to have its true effect.
That simply is not the case. Who understands the wisdom of a flower?
Yet we can take pleasure in it.
--Rudolph Steiner, 1861 - 1925

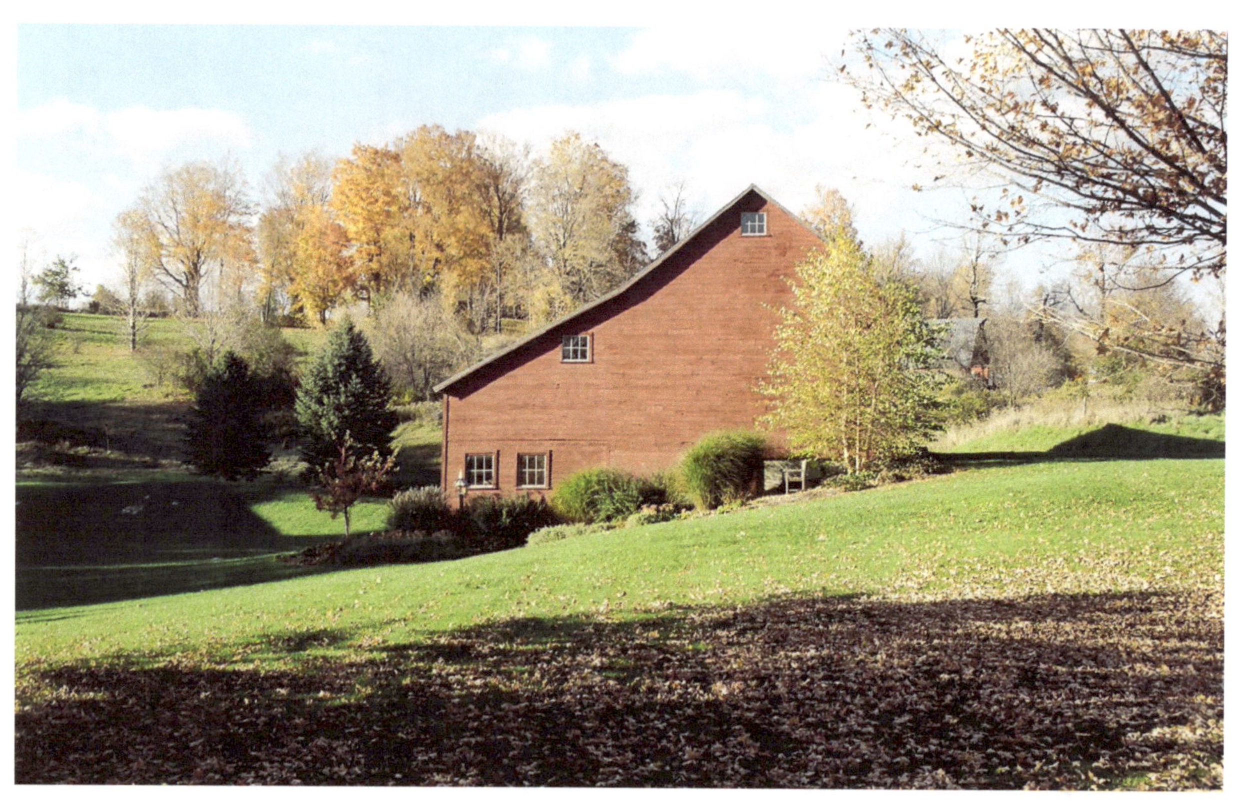

Southern Vermont

Gratitude unlocks the fullness of life. It turns what we have into enough, and more.
It turns denial into acceptance, chaos to order, confusion to clarity.
It can turn a meal into a feast, a house into a home, a stranger into a friend.
Gratitude makes sense of our past, brings peace for today, and creates a vision for tomorrow.

--Melody Beattie, 1948 -

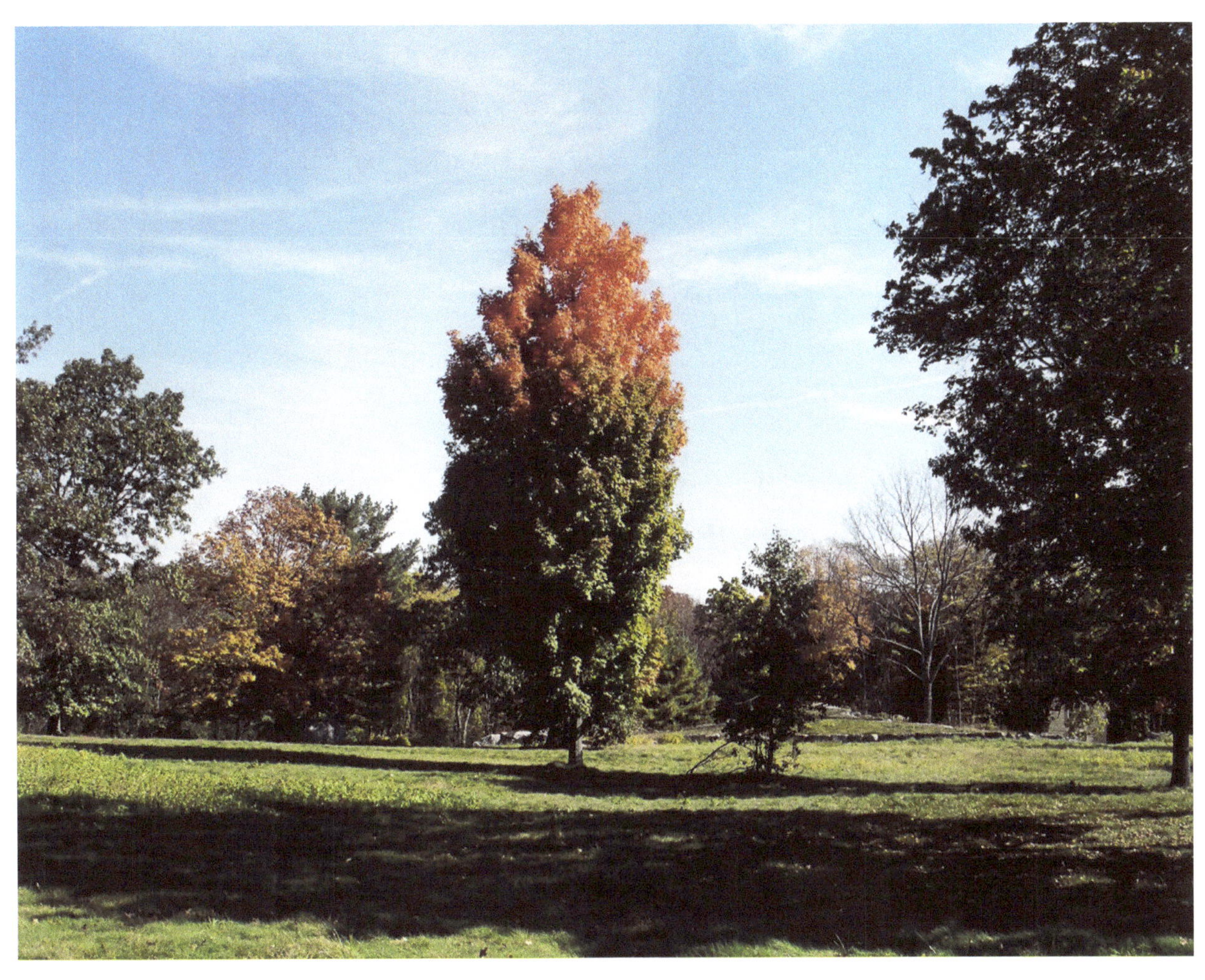

Concord, Massachusetts

When we are no longer able to change a situation...
we are challenged to change ourselves.
--Viktor Frankl, 1905 - 1997

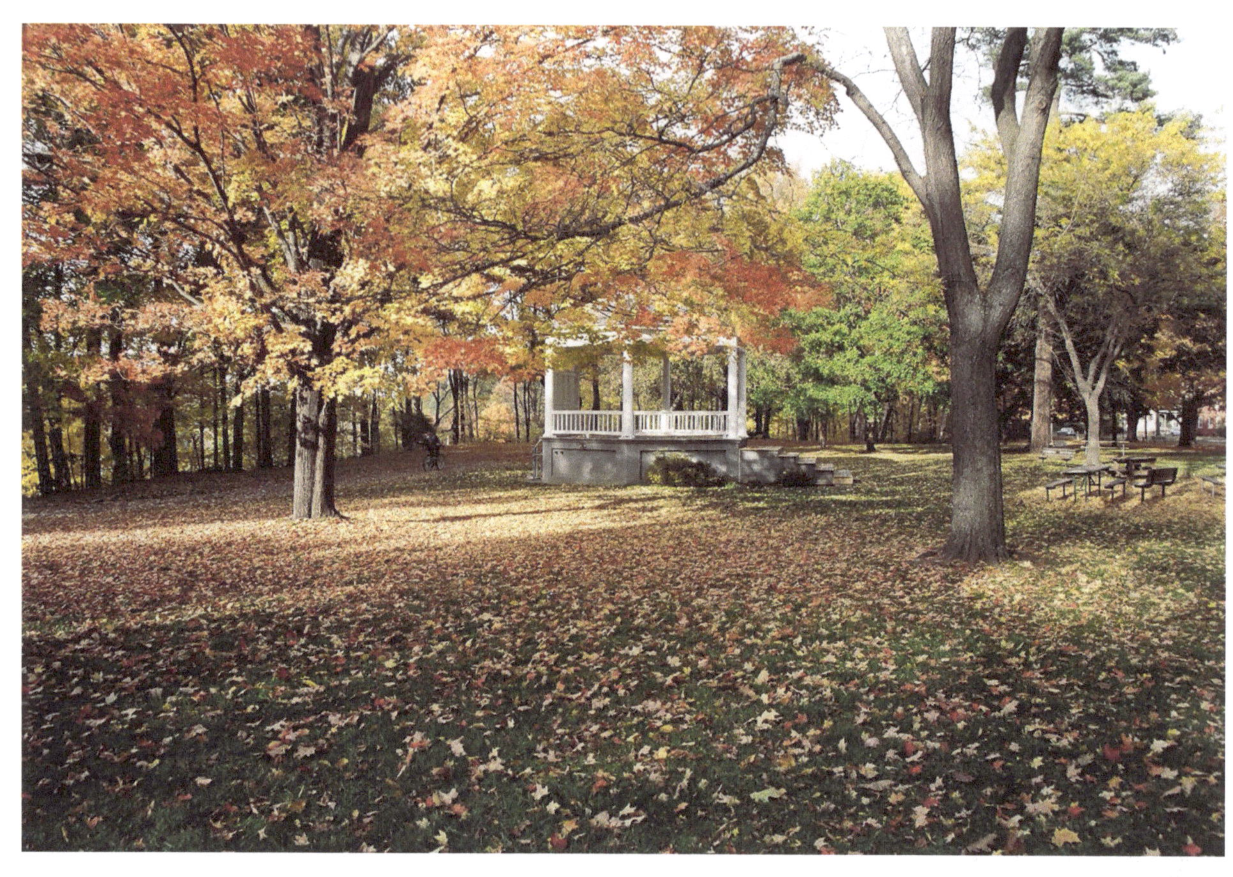

Brattleboro, Vermont

What is life, but the gentle effacement of a tree shedding its leaves?

--Harrison Christian

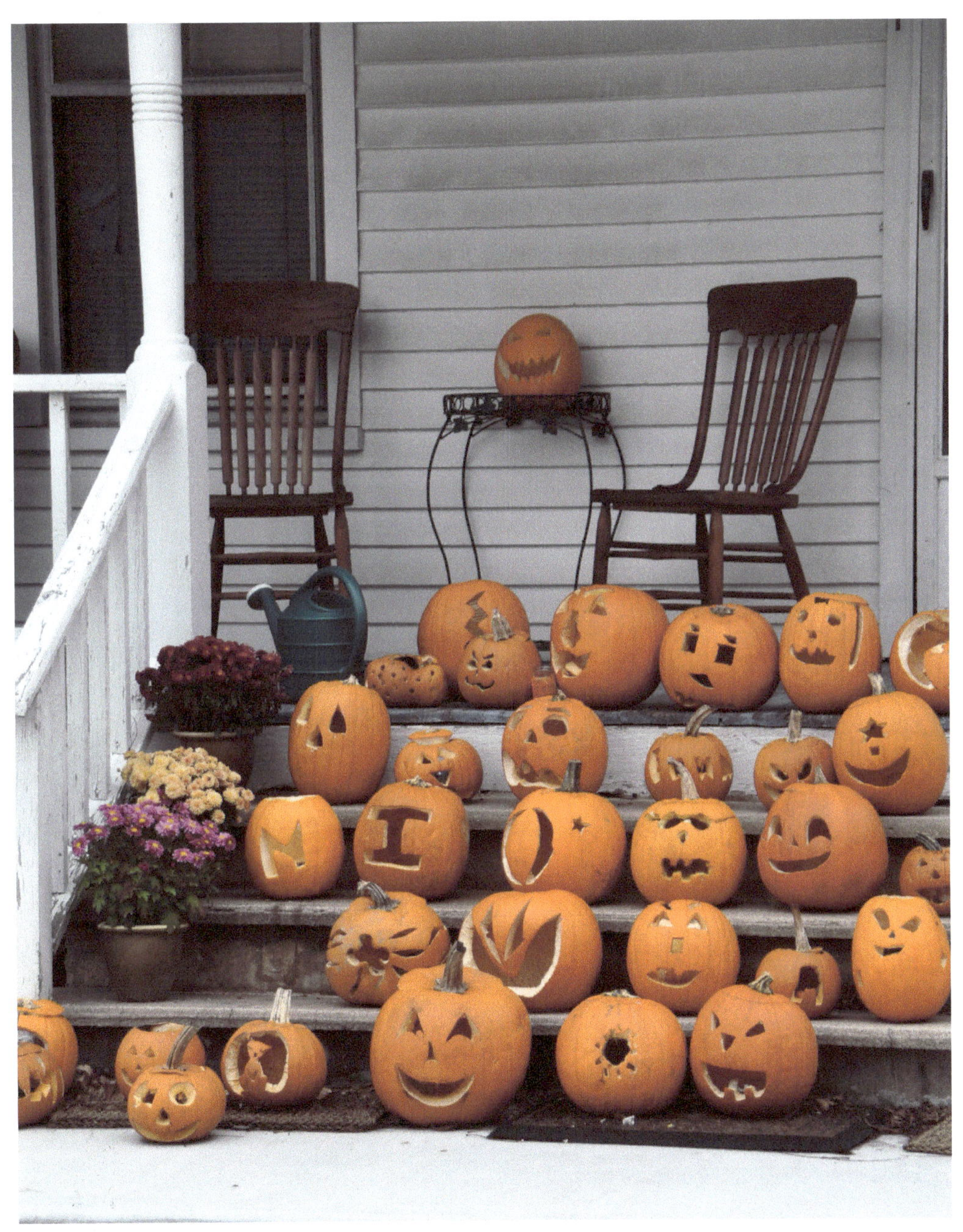

Ivoryton, Connecticut

Each day, and the living of it, has to be a conscious creation in which discipline and order are relieved with some play and pure foolishness.

--May Sarton, 1912 - 1995

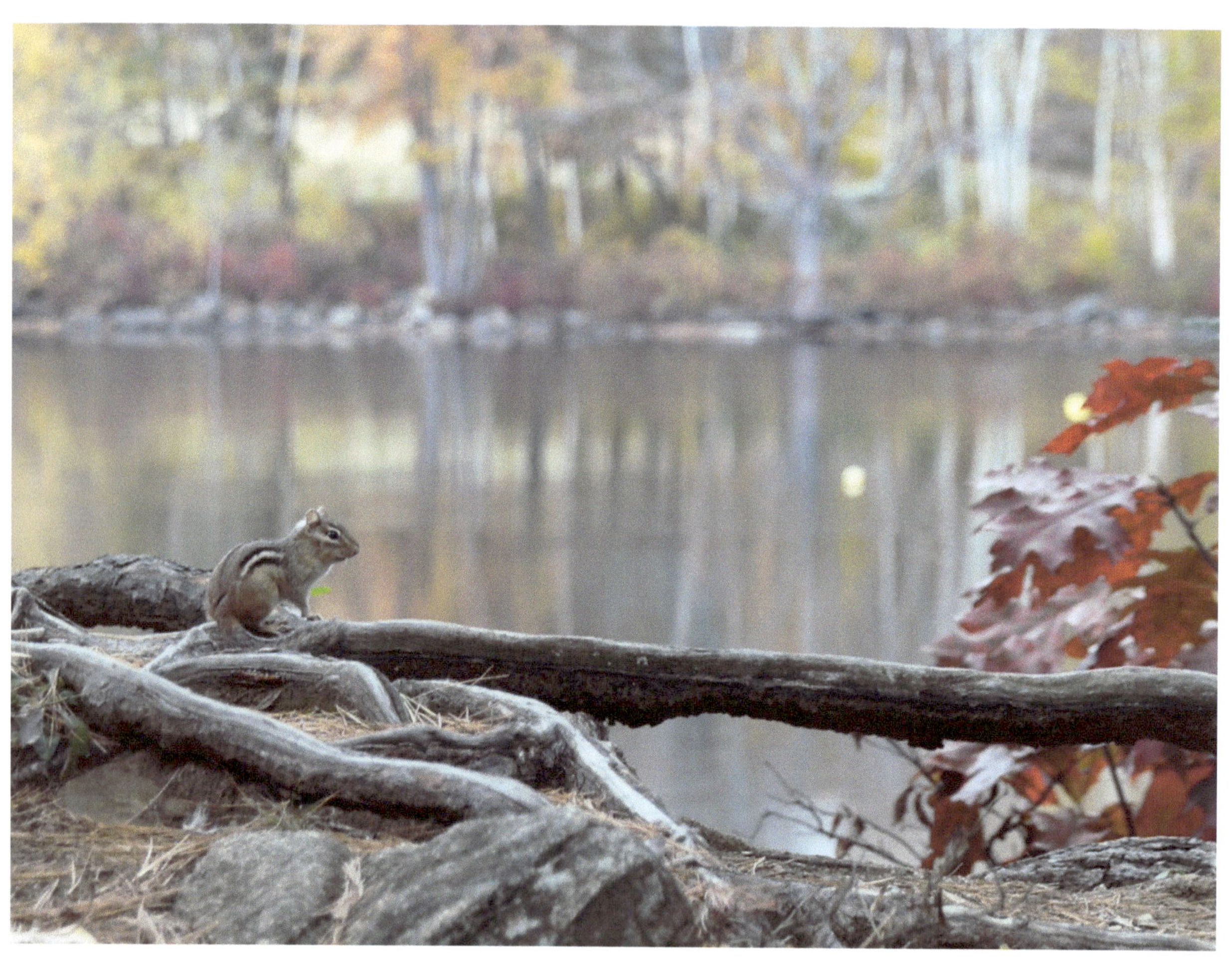

Wolfeboro, New Hampshire

There is one thing we can do, and the happiest people are those
who do it to the limit of their ability. We can be completely present. We can be all here.
We can... give all our attention to the opportunity before us.
--Mark Van Doren, 1894 - 1972

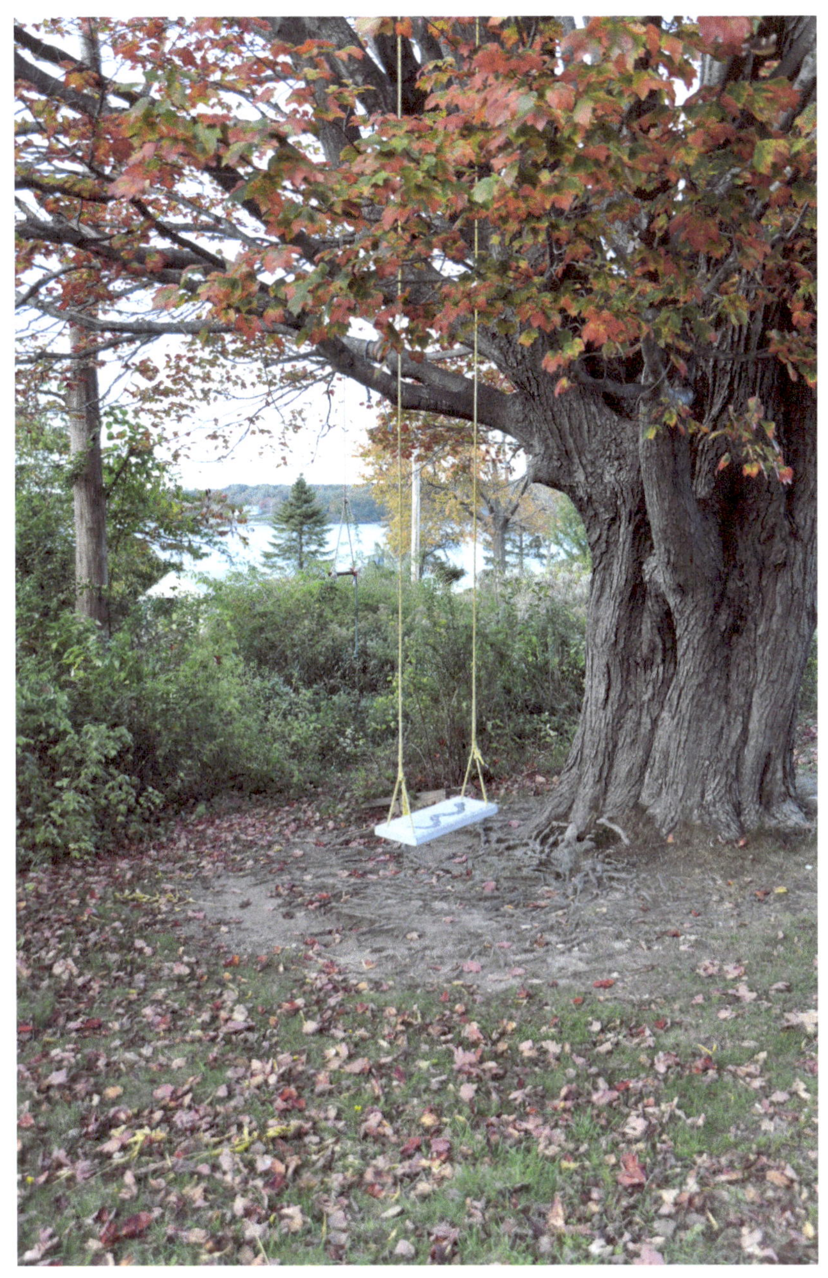

Peaks Island, Maine

The events in our lives happen in a sequence in time,
but in their significance to ourselves, they find their own order...
the continuous thread of revelation.
--Eudora Welty 1909 - 2001

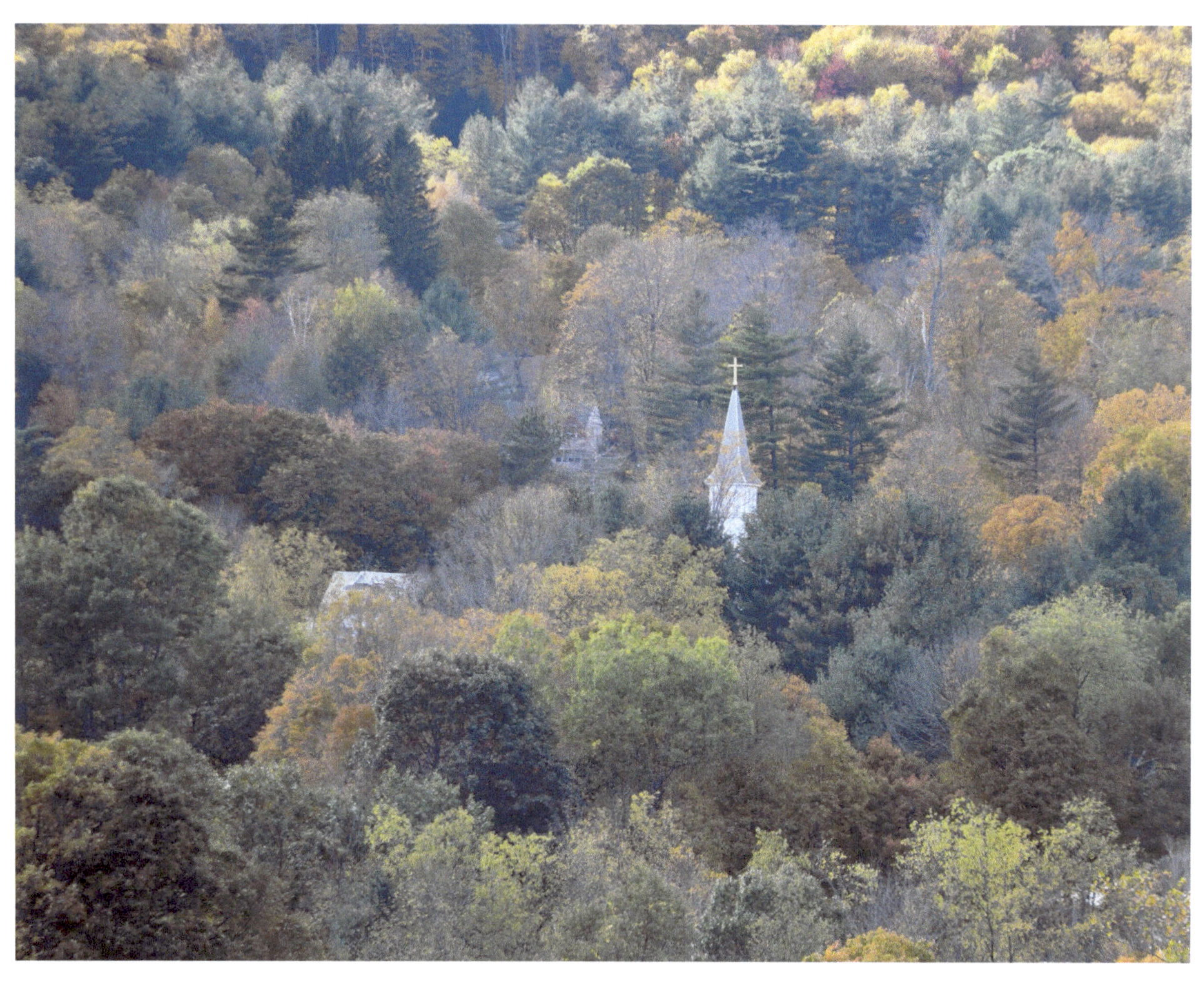

Shelburne Falls, Massachusetts

Life is a wilderness of twists and turns, where faith is your only compass.

---Paul Santaguida

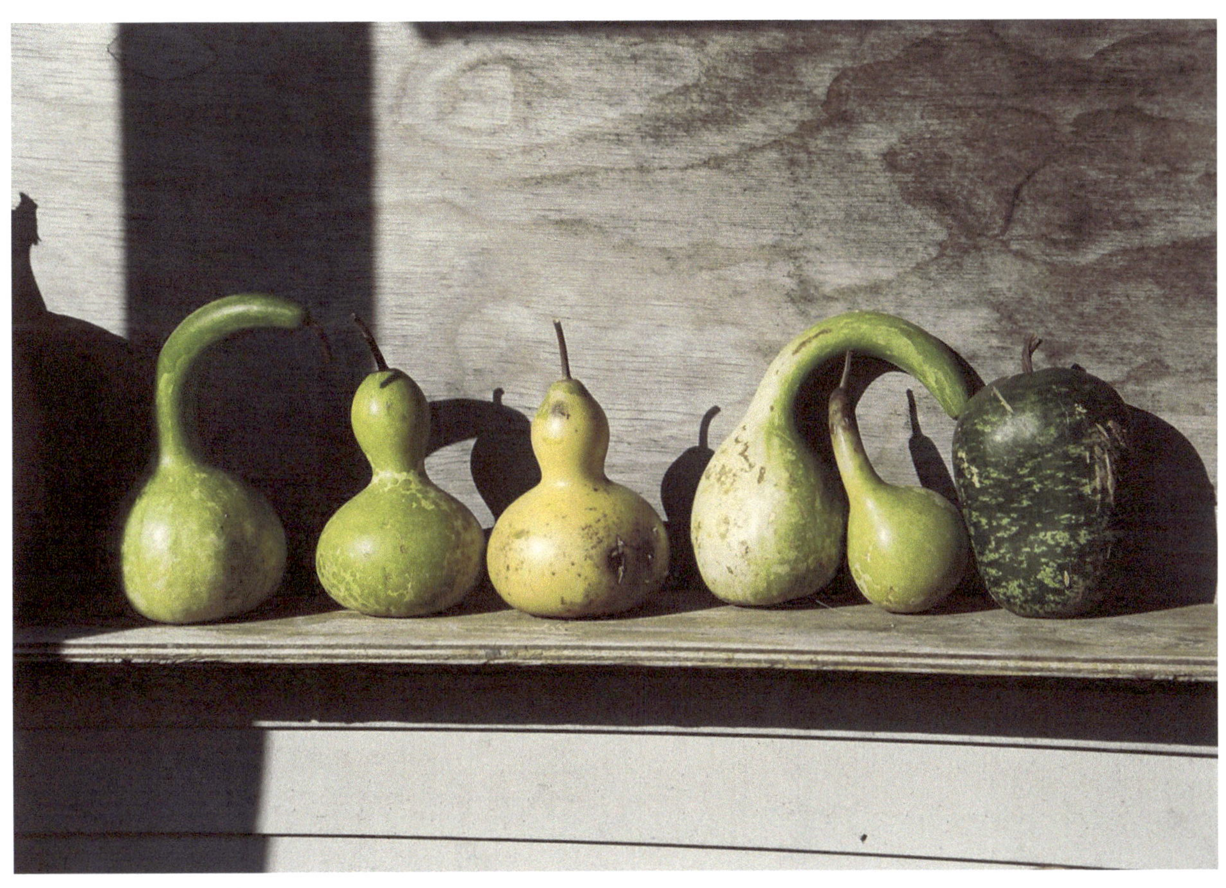

Southern Vermont

Be a first rate version of yourself,
not a second rate version of someone else.
--Judy Garland, 1922-1969

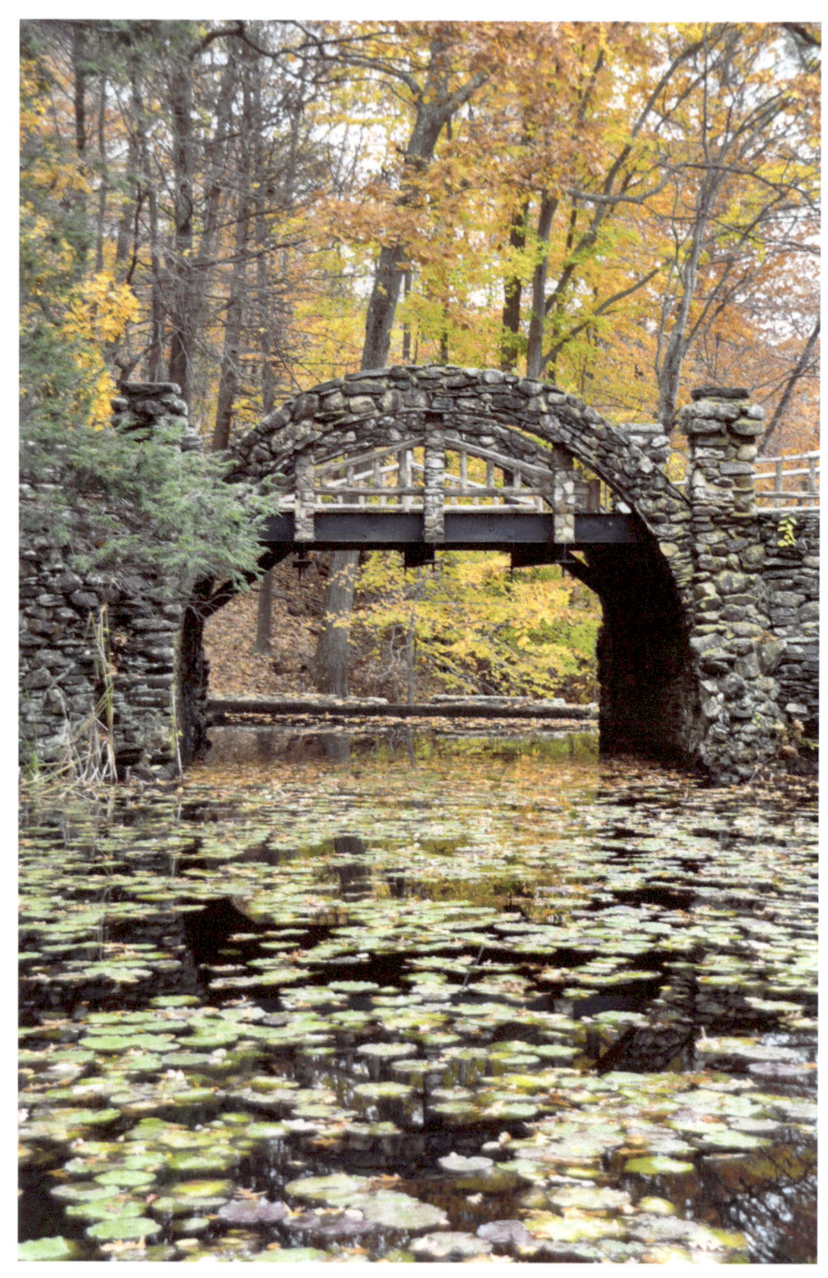

East Haddam, Connecticut

Don't be afraid to take a big step if one is indicated.
You can't cross a chasm in two small jumps.
--David Lloyd George, 1863 - 1945

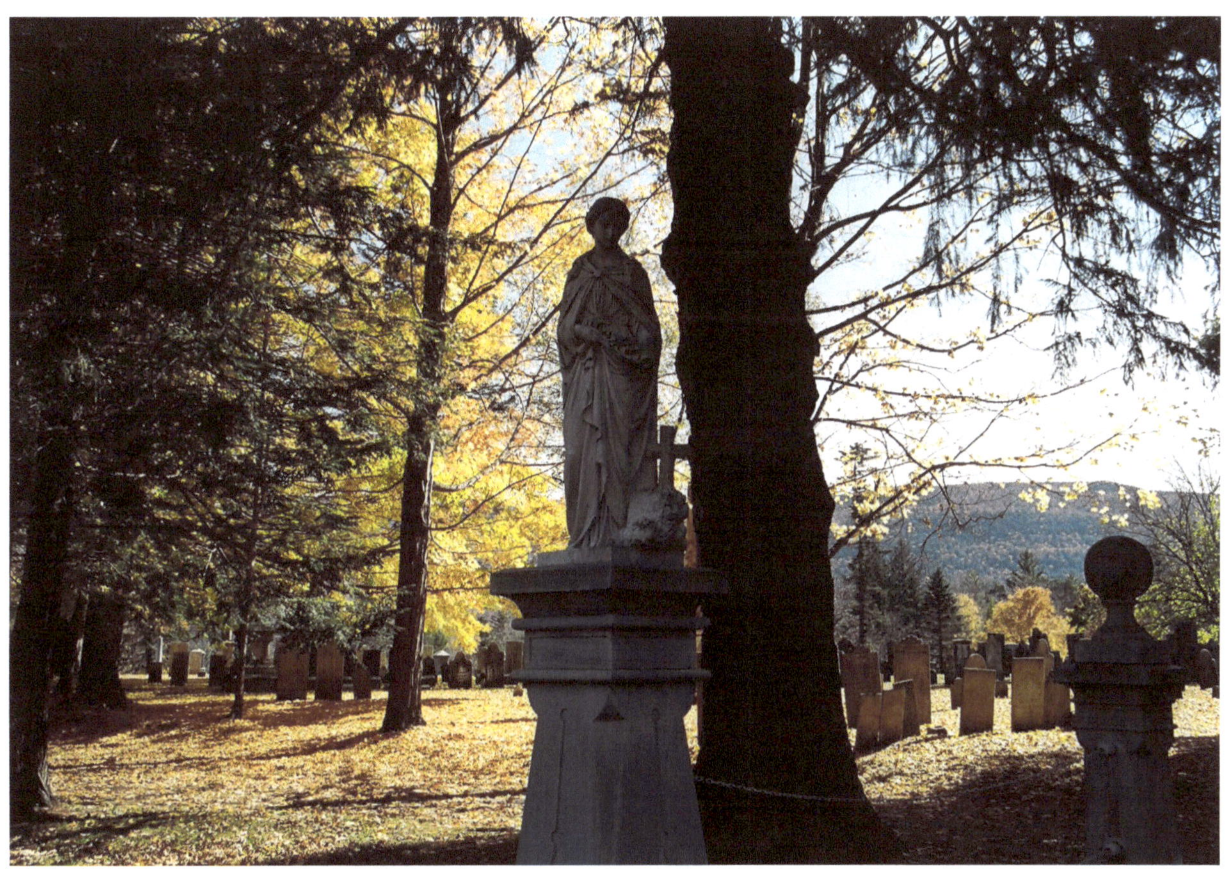

Southern Vermont

Peace is when time doesn't matter as it passes by.

--Maria Schell

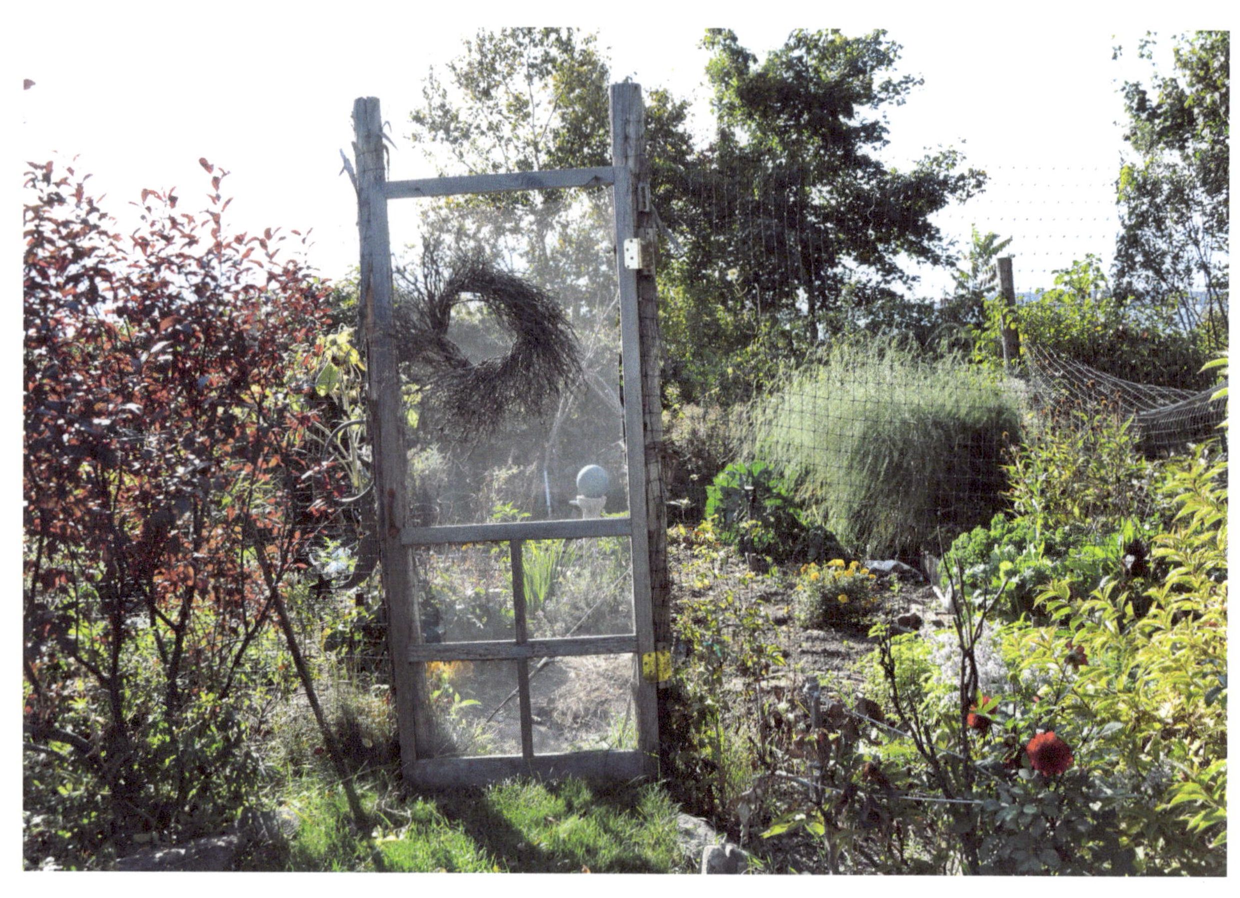

Peaks Island, Maine

Within your heart, keep one still, secret spot where dreams may go.

--Louise Driscoll, 1875 - 1957

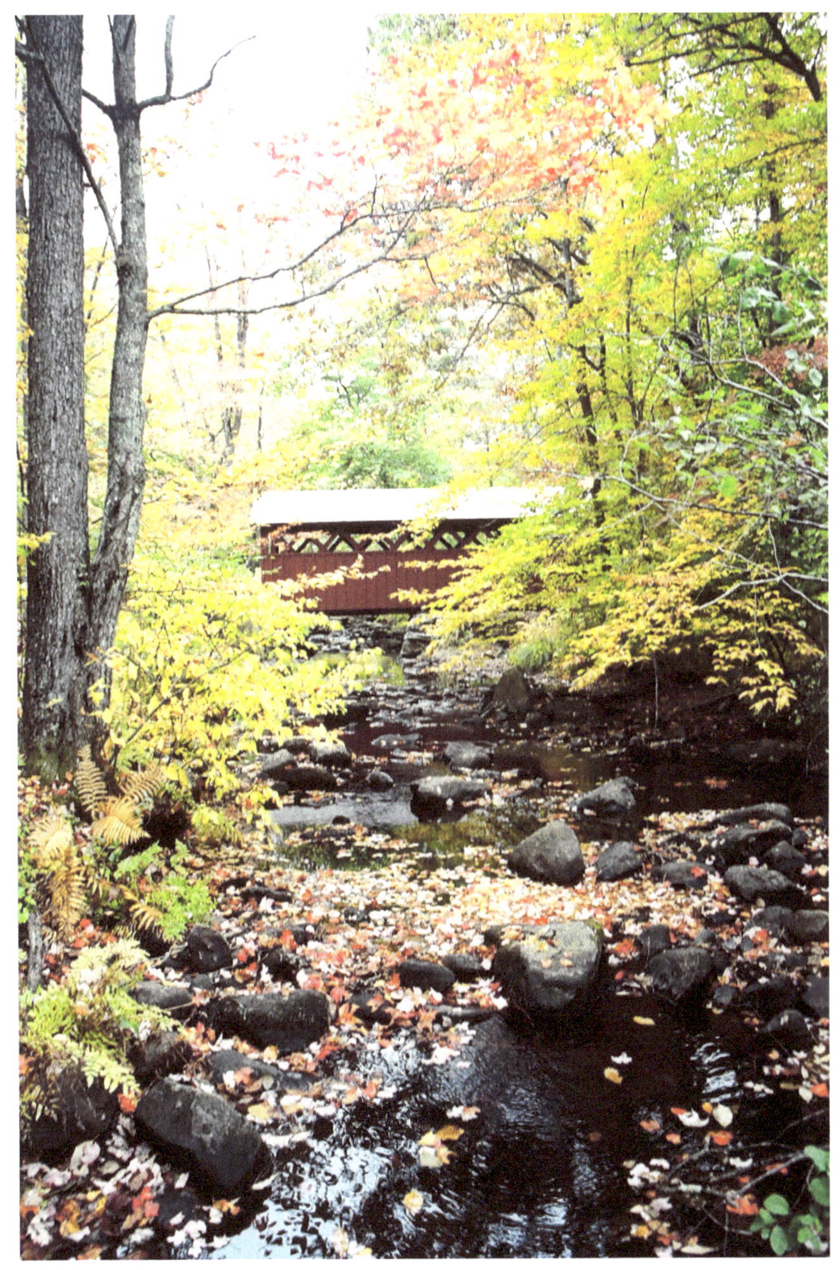

Chatfield Hollow, Connecticut

He that cannot forgive others breaks the bridge over which he himself must pass if he would ever reach heaven; for everyone has need to be forgiven.

--Edward, Lord Herbert, 1582 - 1648

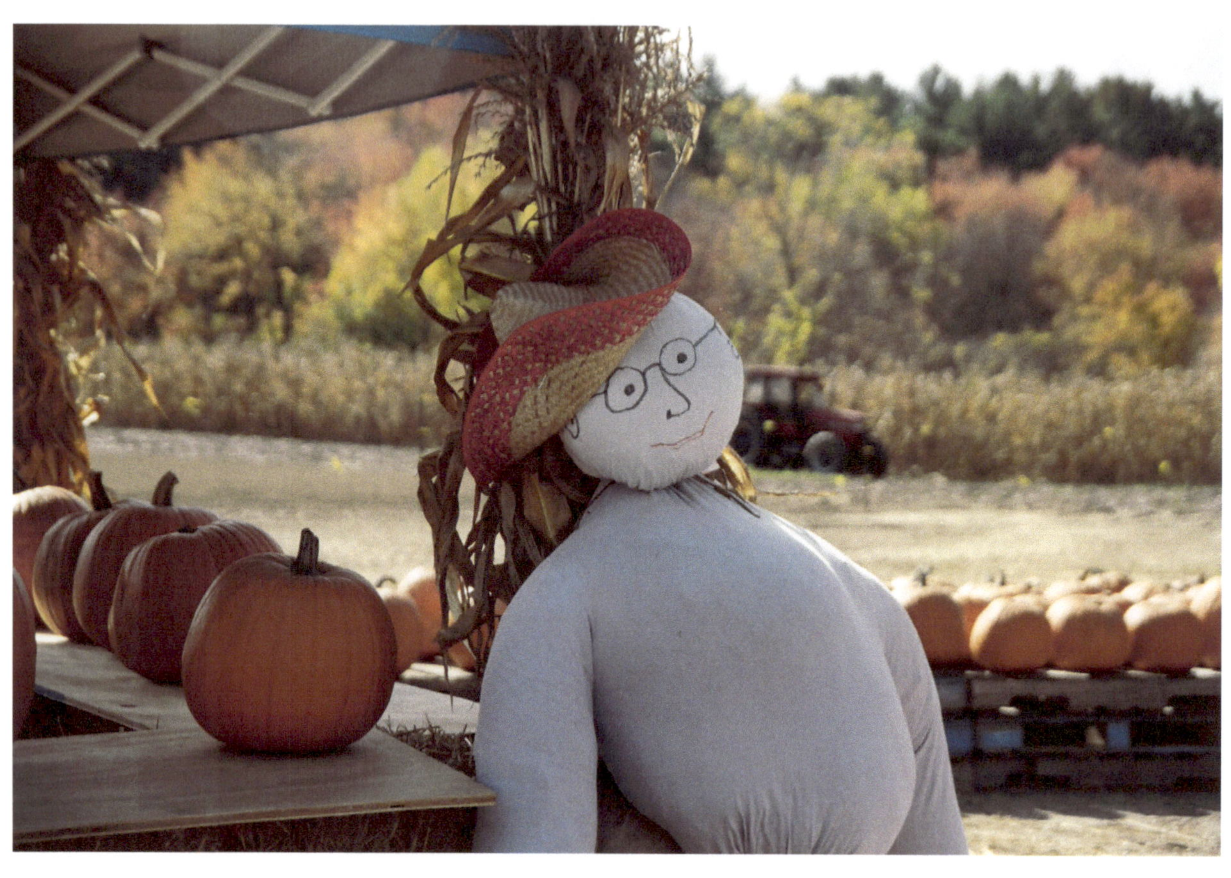

Sudbury, Massachusetts

Of all the things you wear, your expression is the most important.

--Janet Lane, 1978 -

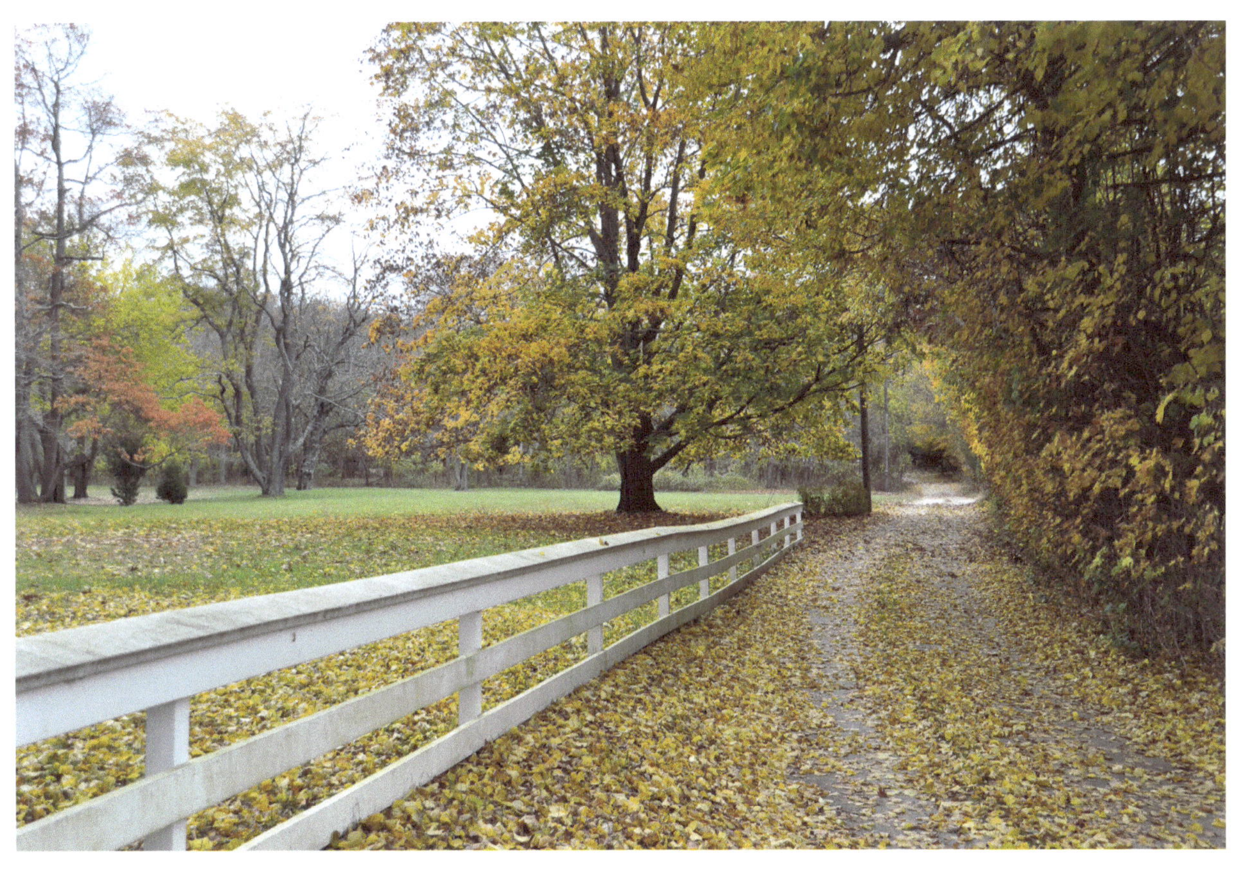

Essex, Connecticut

In the life of the spirit, there is no ending that is not a beginning.

--Henrietta Zolde

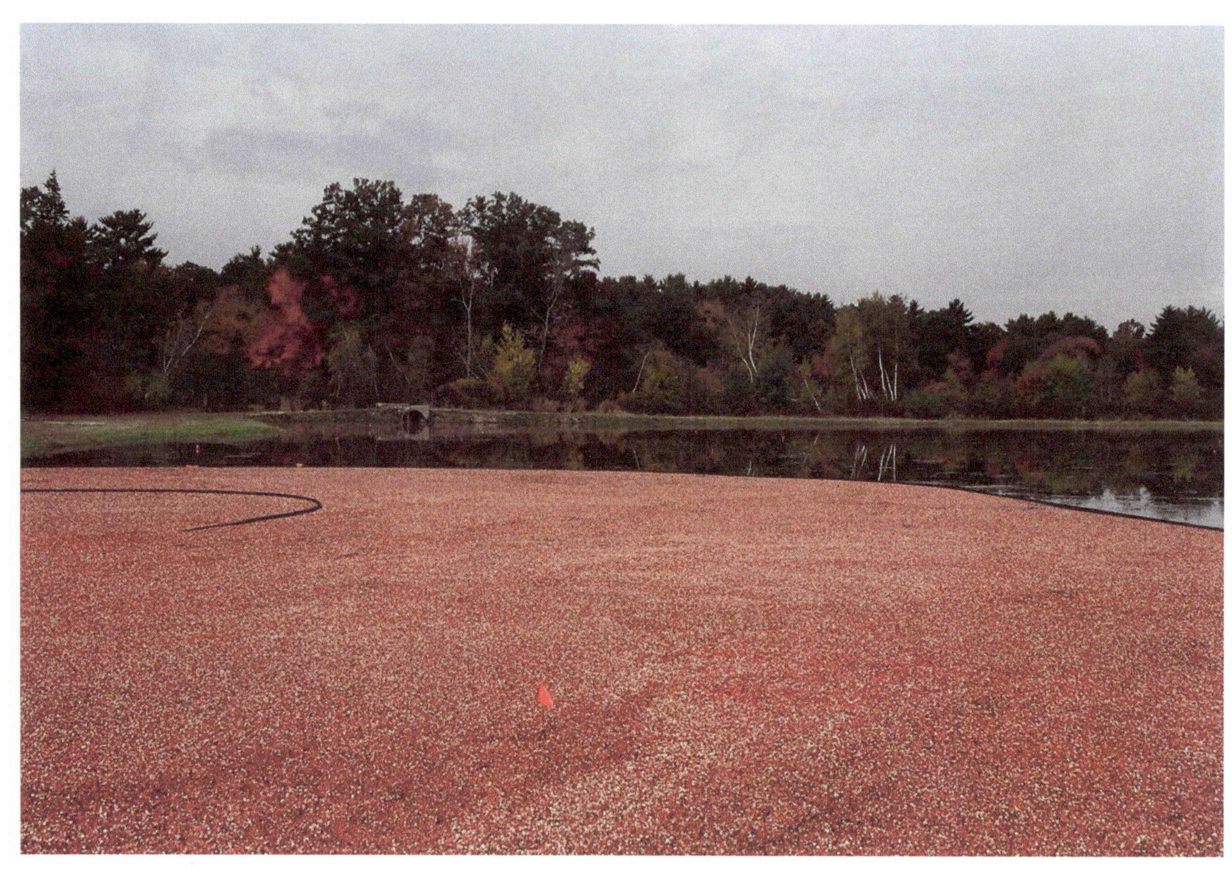

Hanson, Massachusetts

Stuff your eyes with wonder . . . live as if you'd drop dead in ten seconds.
See the world. It's more fantastic than any dream made or paid for in factories.
--Ray Bradbury, 1920 -

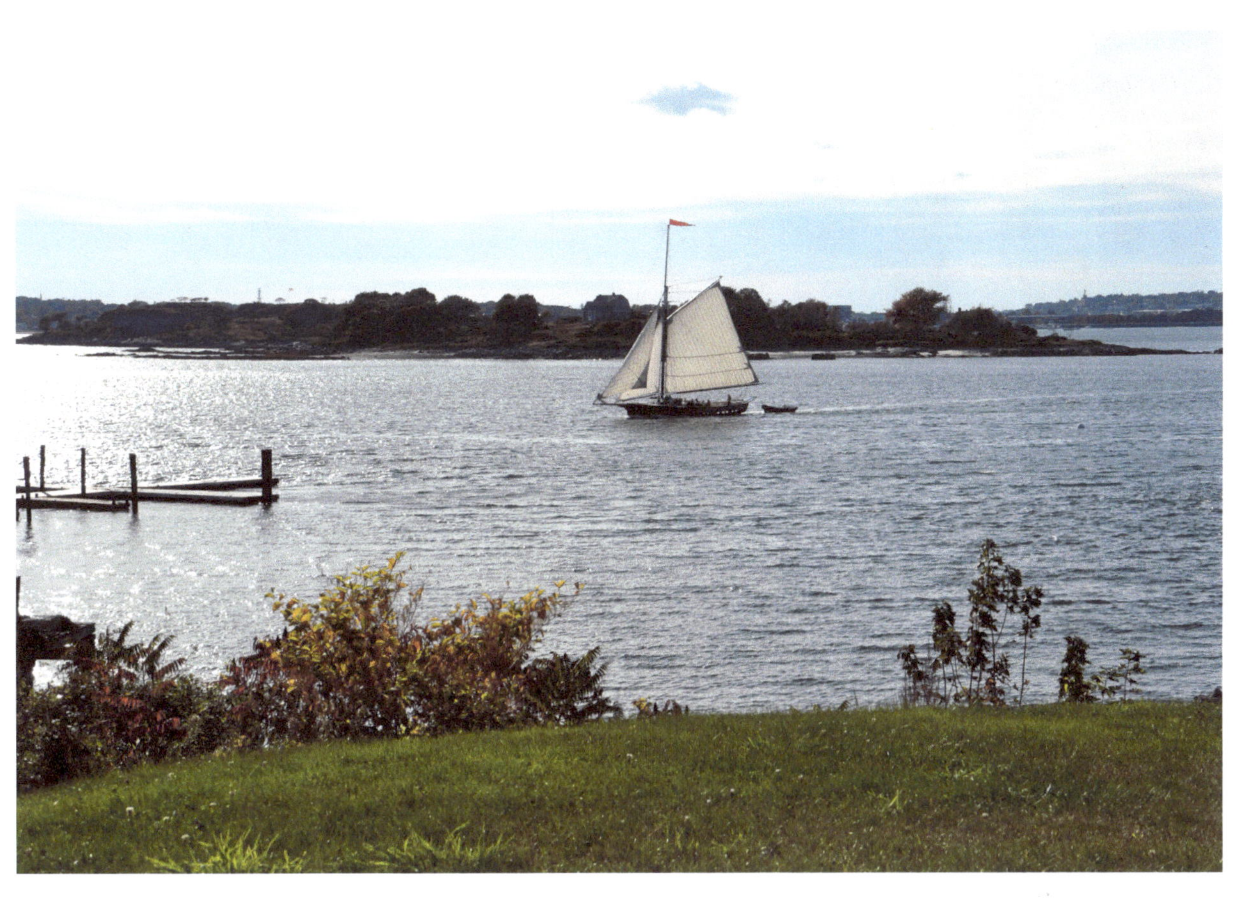

Peaks Island, Maine

We cannot direct the wind, but we can adjust the sails.

--Bertha Calloway, 1925 -

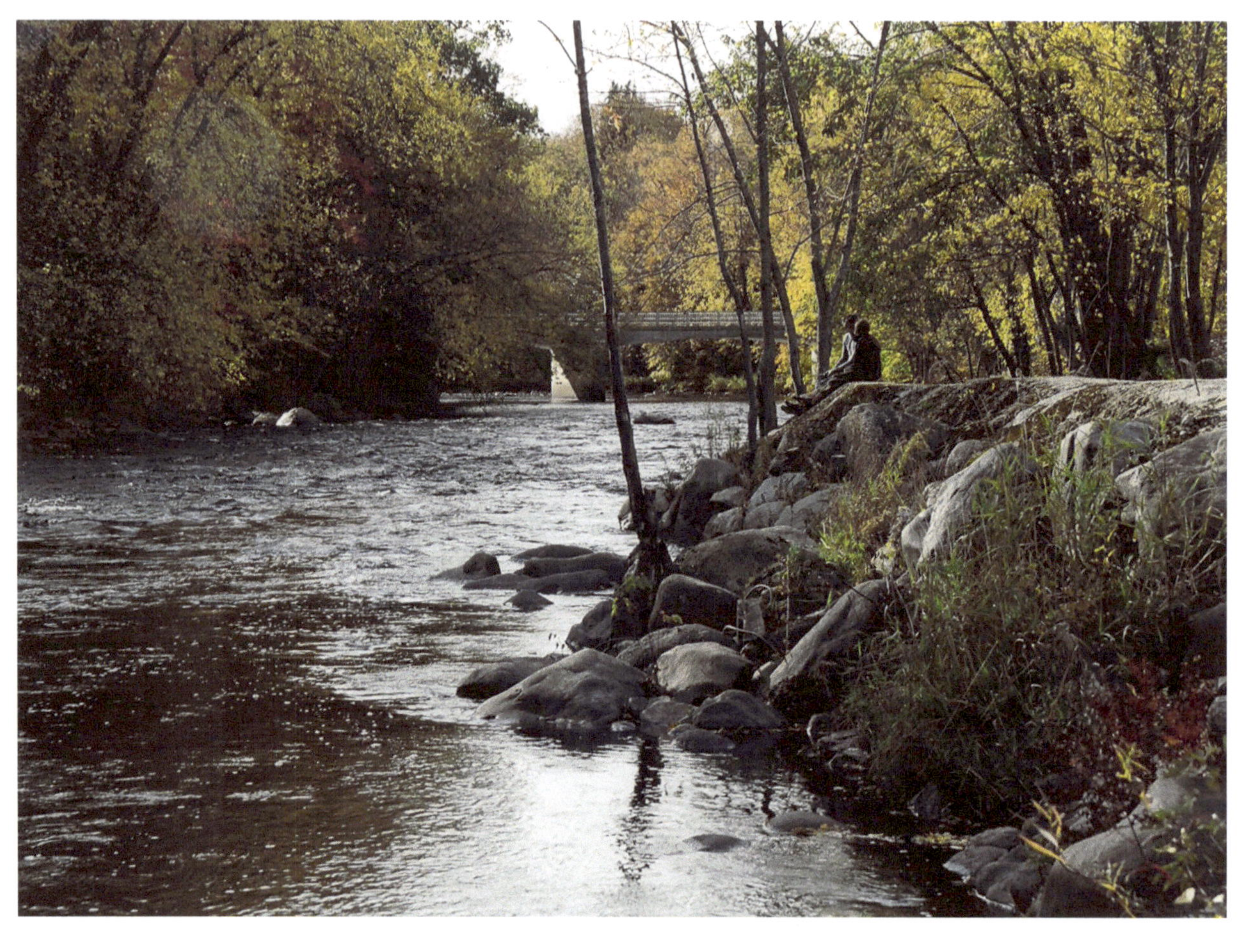

Southern Vermont

Time is but the stream I go a-fishing in.
--Henry David Thoreau, 1817 - 1862

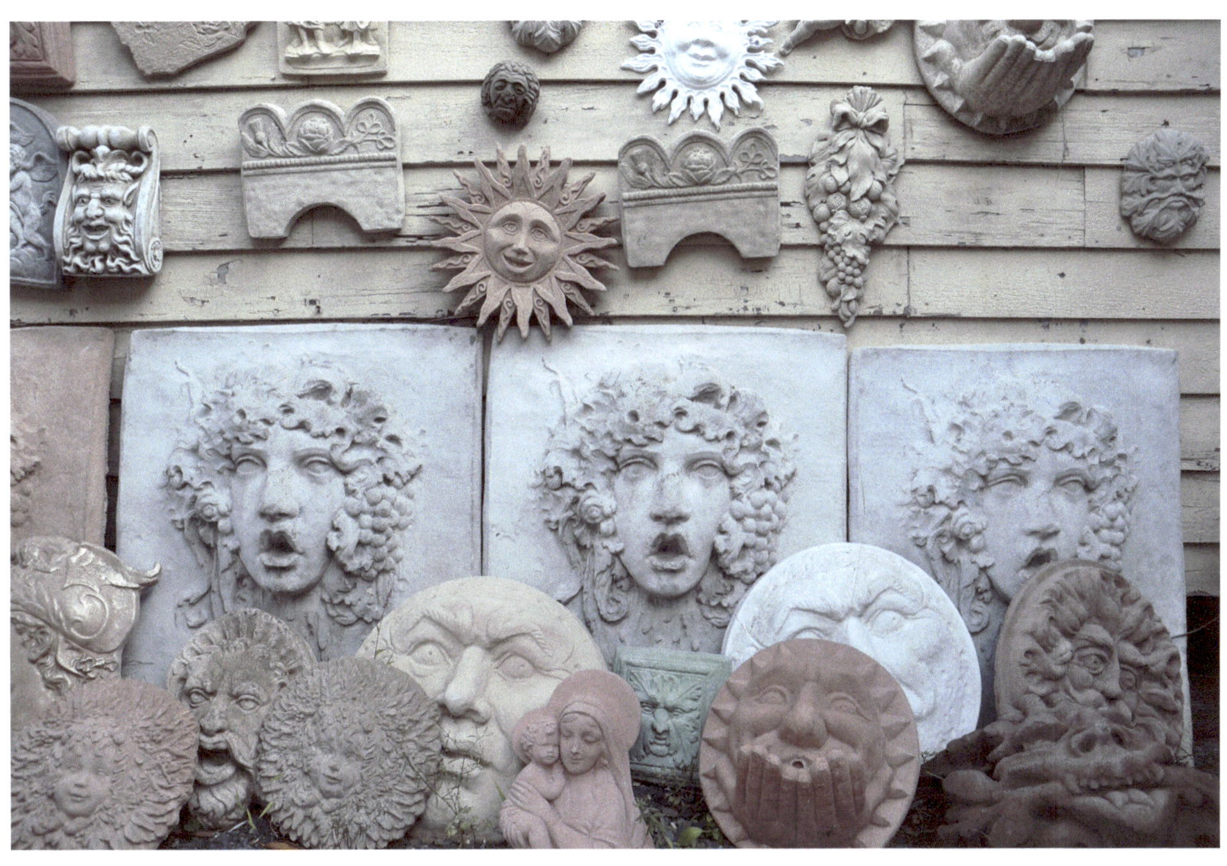

Turners Falls, Massachusetts

Whether we name divine presence synchronicity, serendipity, or graced moments matters little.
What matters is the reality that our hearts have been understood.
Nothing is as real as a healthy dose of magic which restores our spirits.
--Nancy Long

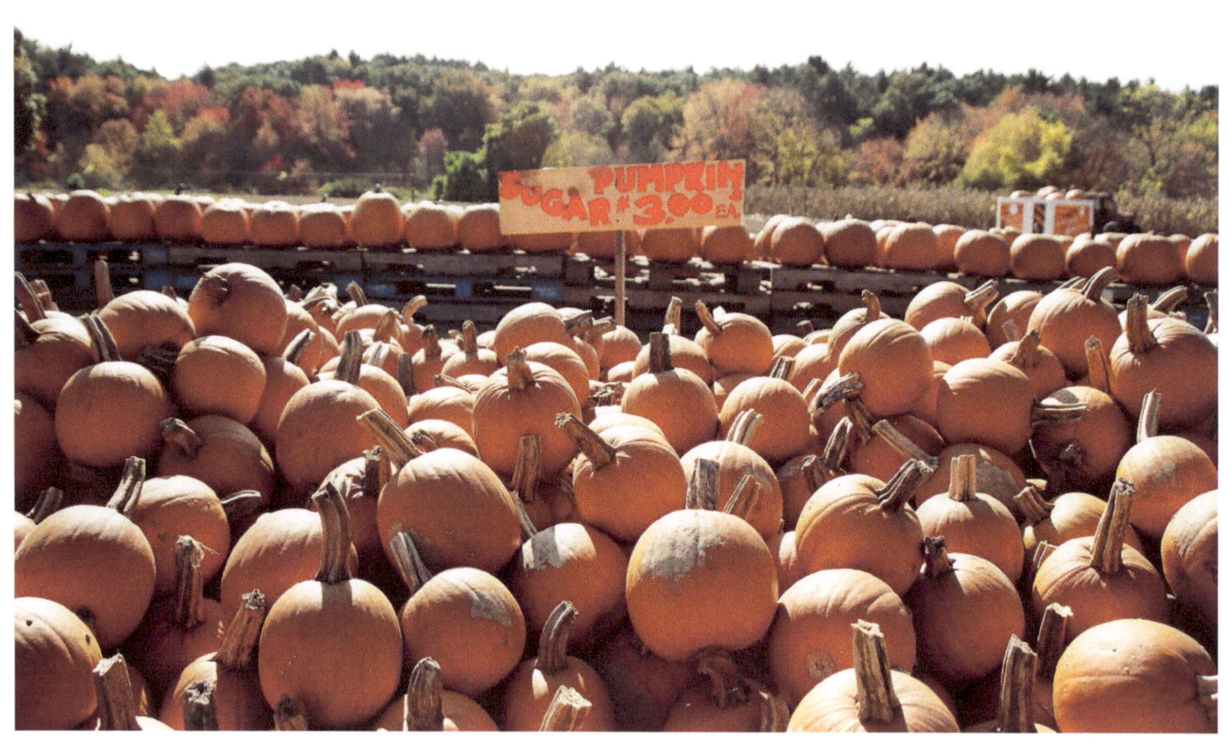

Sudbury, Massachusetts

We forfeit three-fourths of ourselves in order to be like other people.
--Arthur Schopenhauer, 1788 - 1860

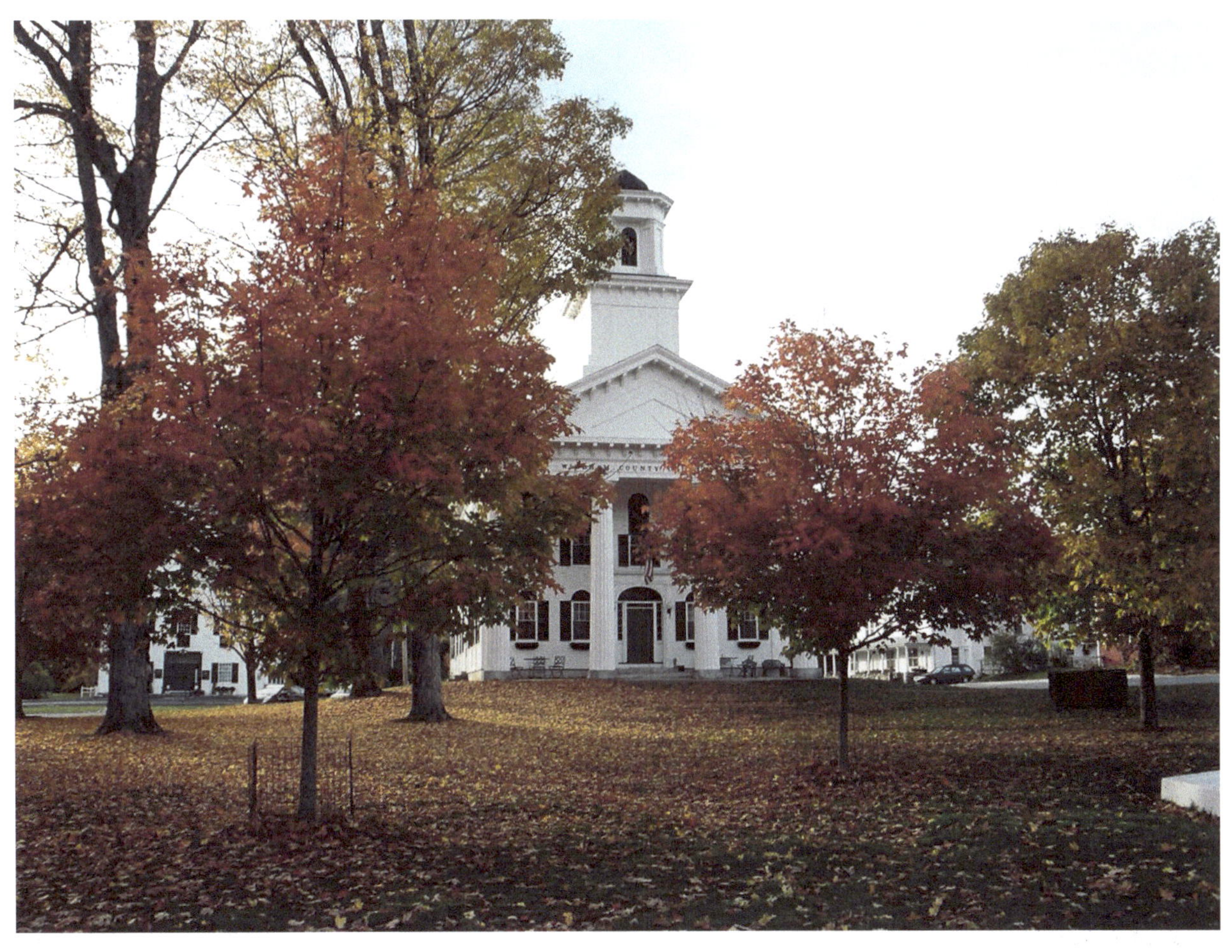

Southern Vermont

I do not accept any absolute formulas for living.
No preconceived code can see ahead to everything that can happen in a man's life.
As we live, we grow and our beliefs change.
--Martin Buber, 1878 - 1965

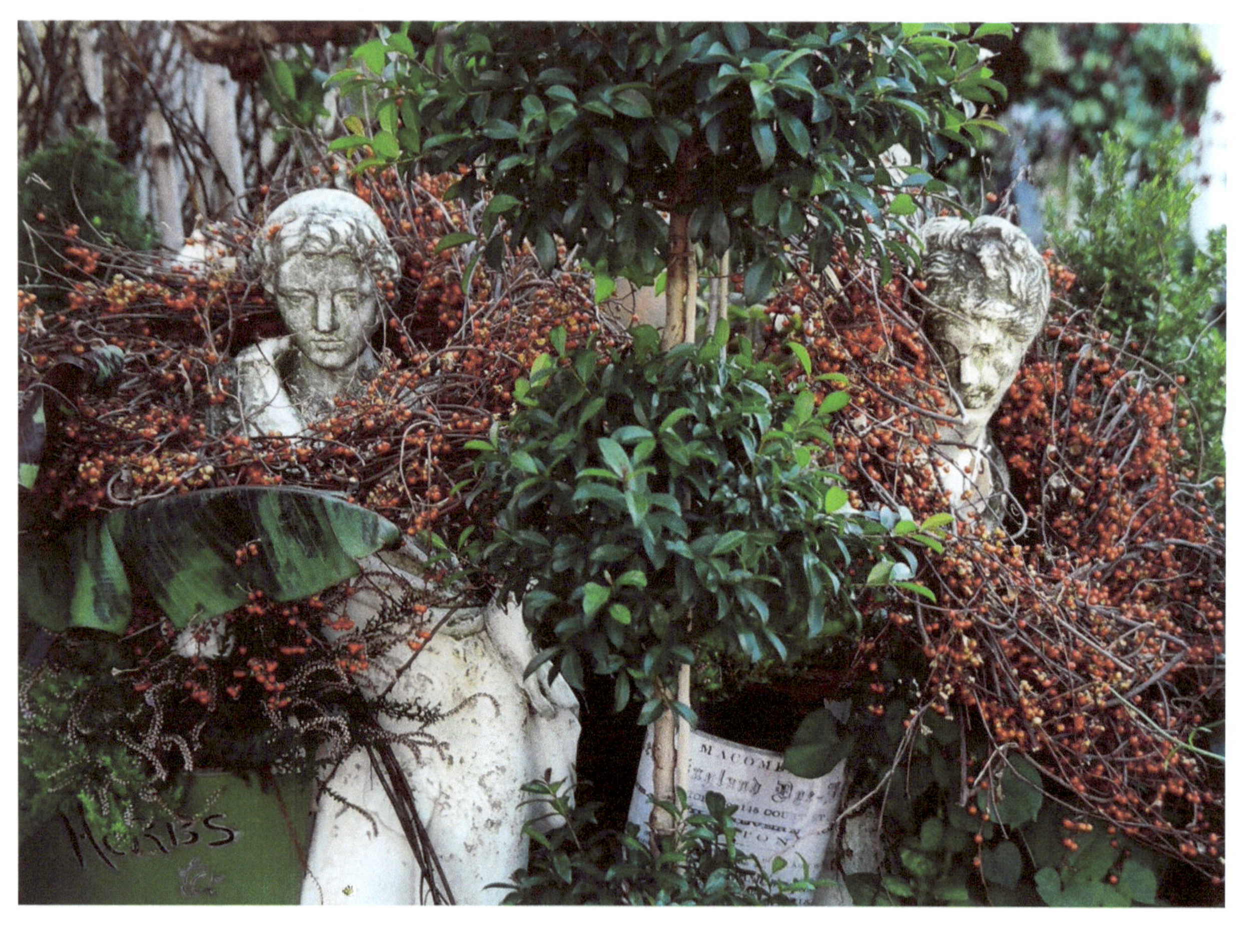

Marblehead, Massachusetts

Why should we all dress after the same fashion?
The frost never paints my windows twice alike.
--Lydia Maria Child, 1802 - 1880

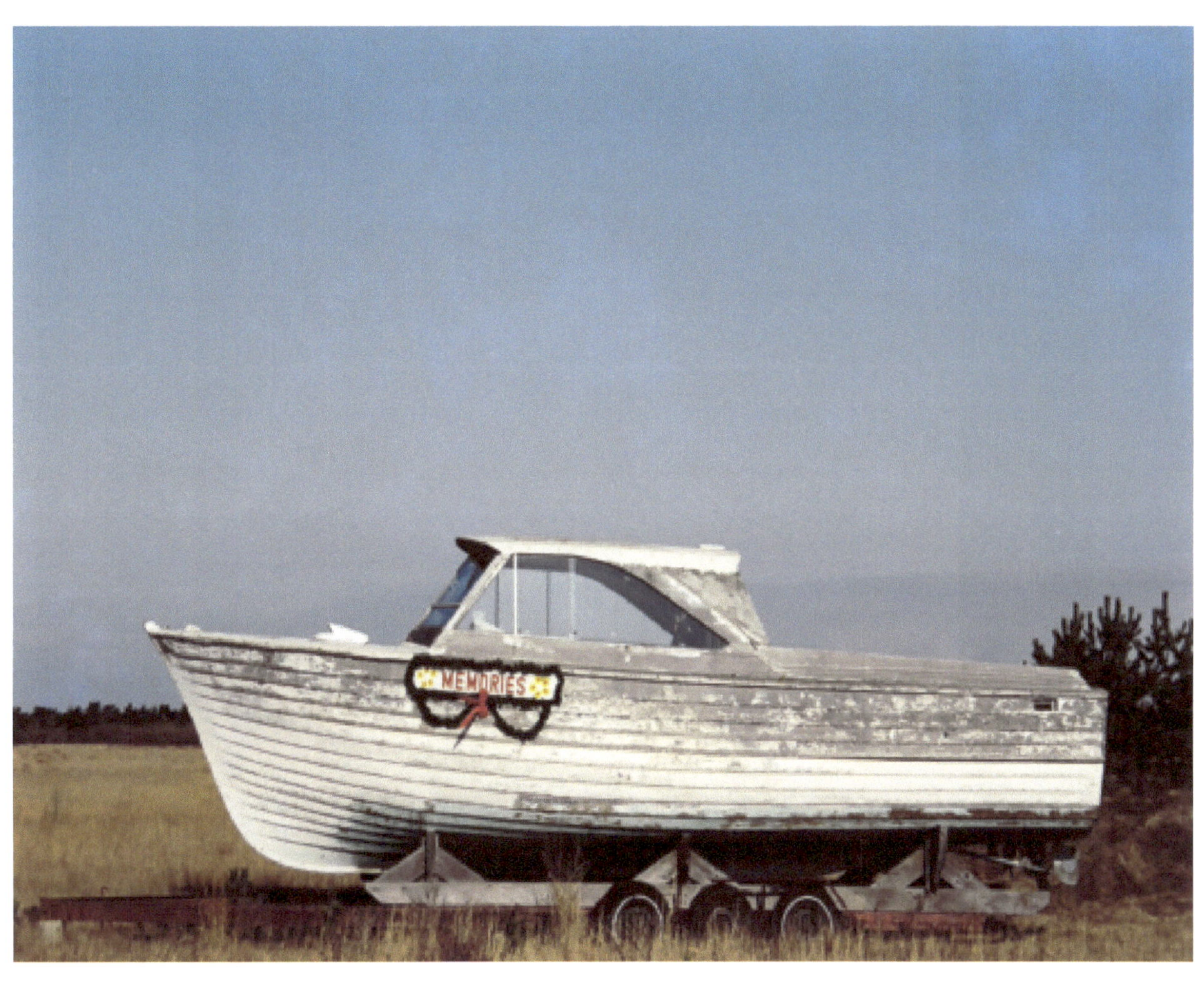

Nantucket, Massachusetts

In the depth of winter,
I finally learned that within me there lay an invincible summer.
--Albert Camus, 1913 - 1960

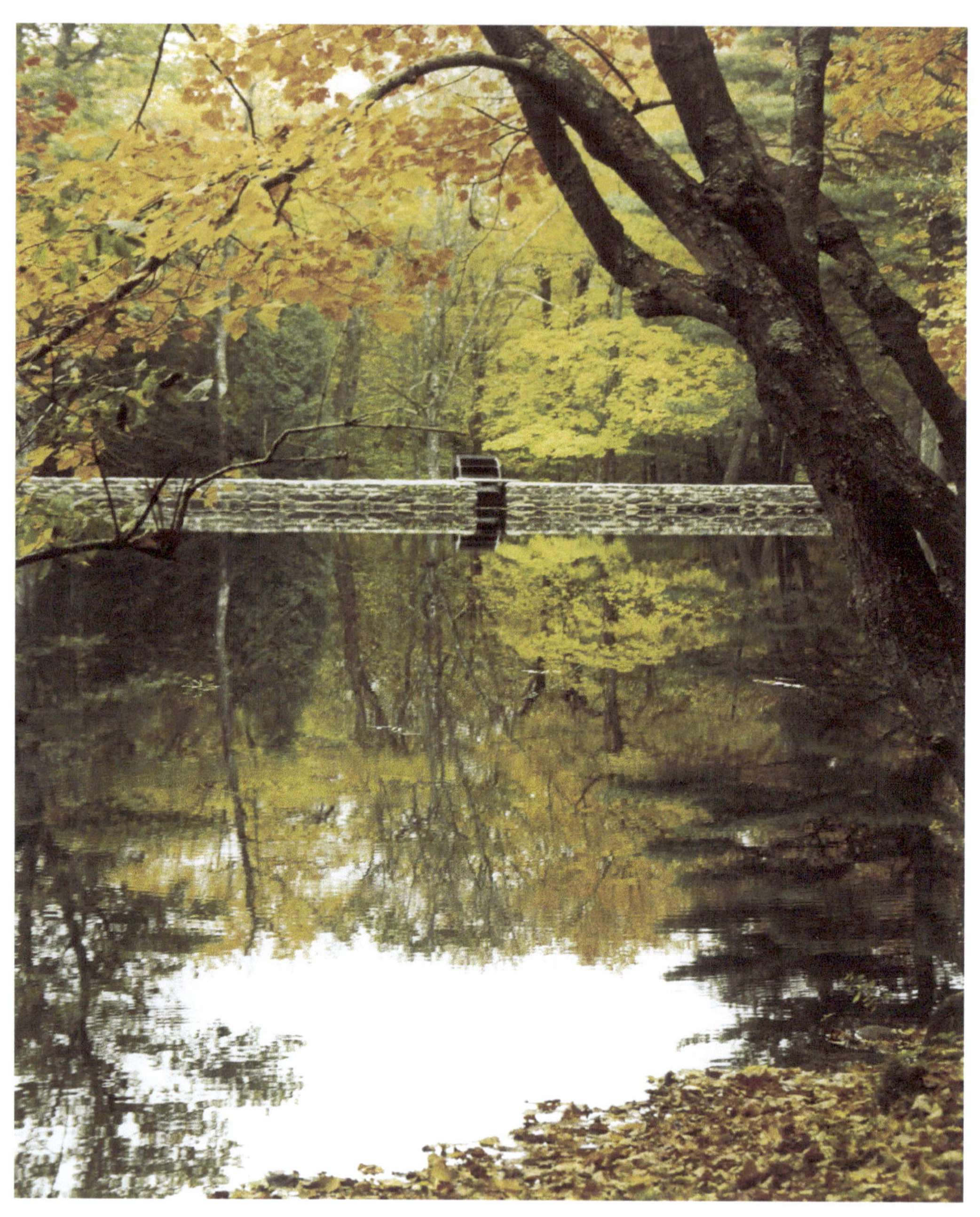

Chatfield Hollow, Connecticut

There seems to be a kind of order in the universe, in the movement of the stars and the turning of the earth and the changing of seasons, and even in the cycle of human life.

--Katherine Anne Porter, 1890 - 1980

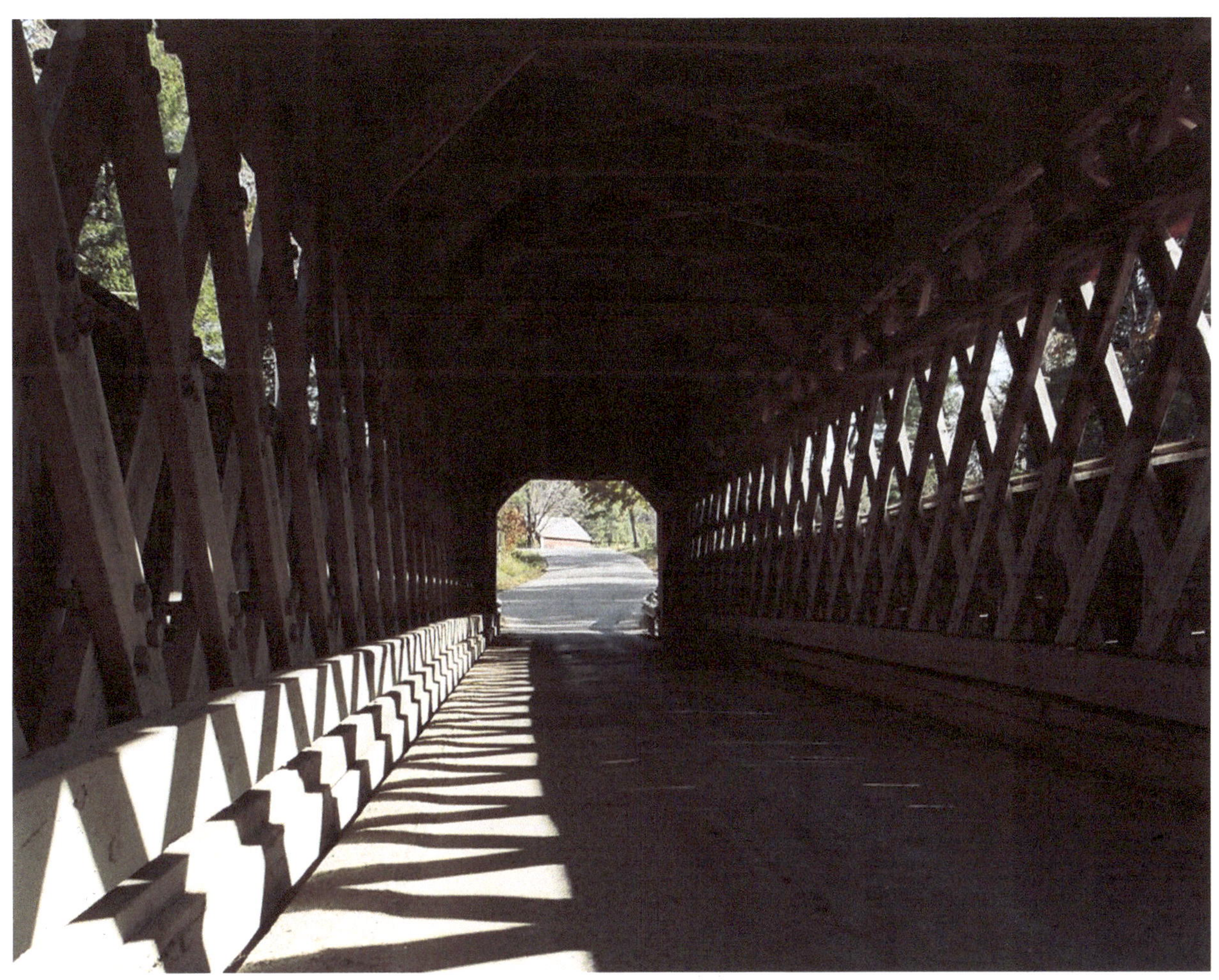

Vermont

I have always been delighted at the prospect of a new day, a fresh try, one more start, with perhaps a bit of magic waiting somewhere behind the morning.

--J.B. Priestly, 1894 - 1984

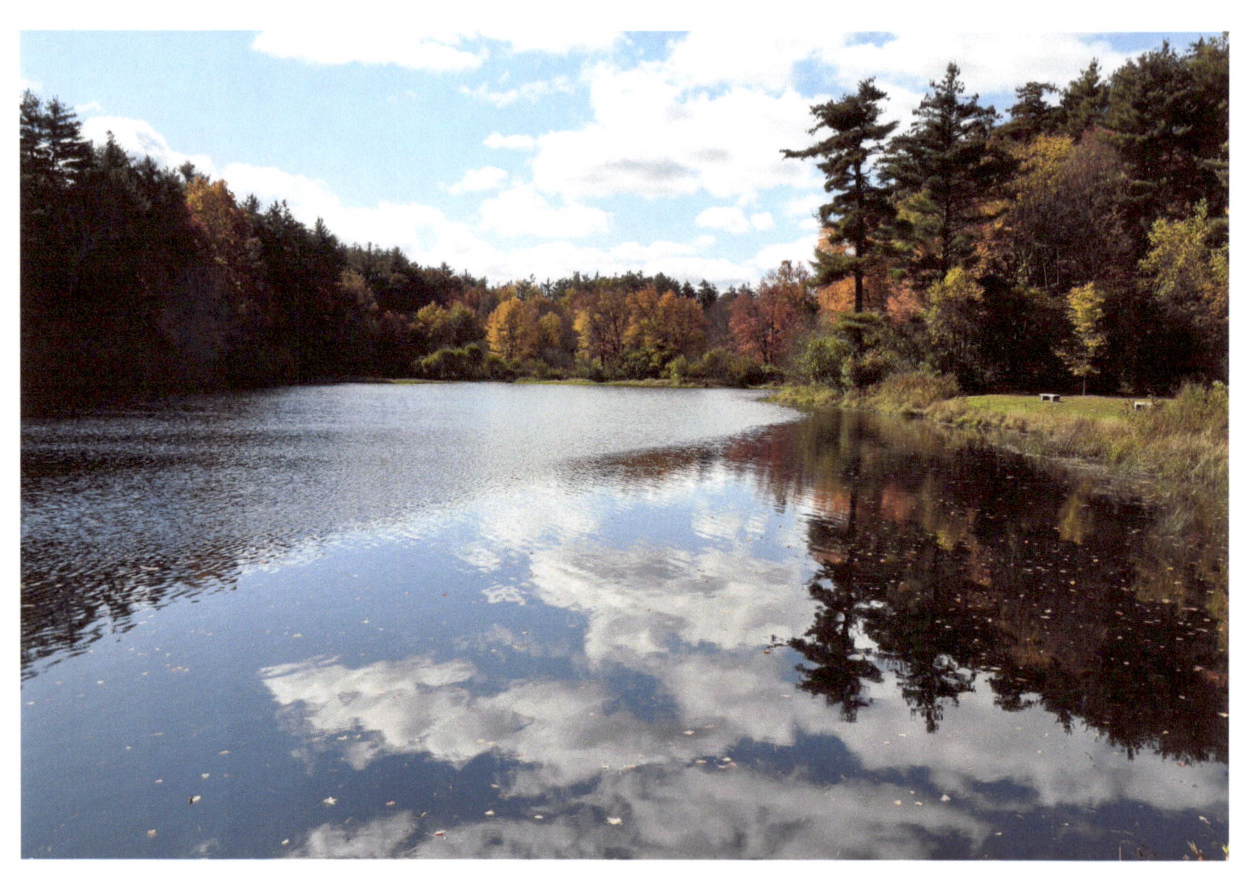

Western Massachusetts

Weather is a great bluffer.
I guess the same is true of our human society --
things can look dark, then a break shows in the clouds, and all is changed.
--E. B. White, 1899 - 1985

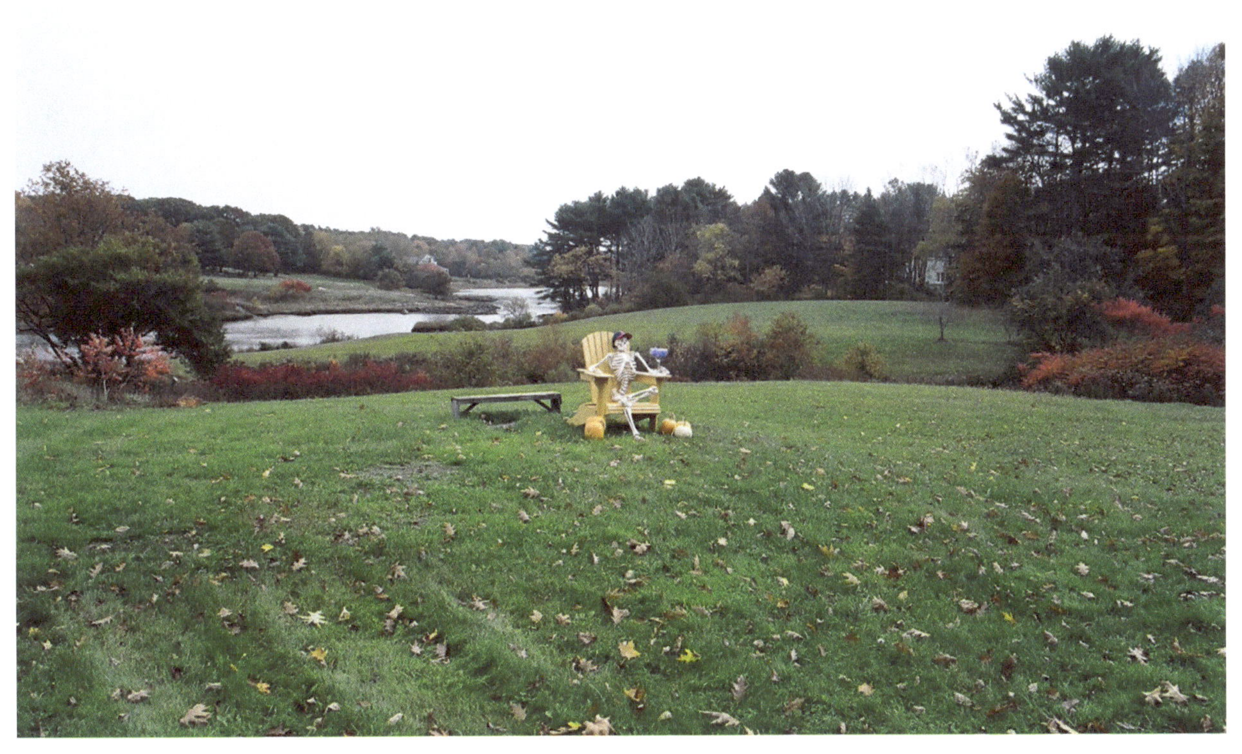

Ogunquit, Maine

If man insisted on always being serious,
and never allowed himself a bit of fun and relaxation,
he would go mad or become unstable without knowing it.
-- Herodotus, 484-430 B.C.

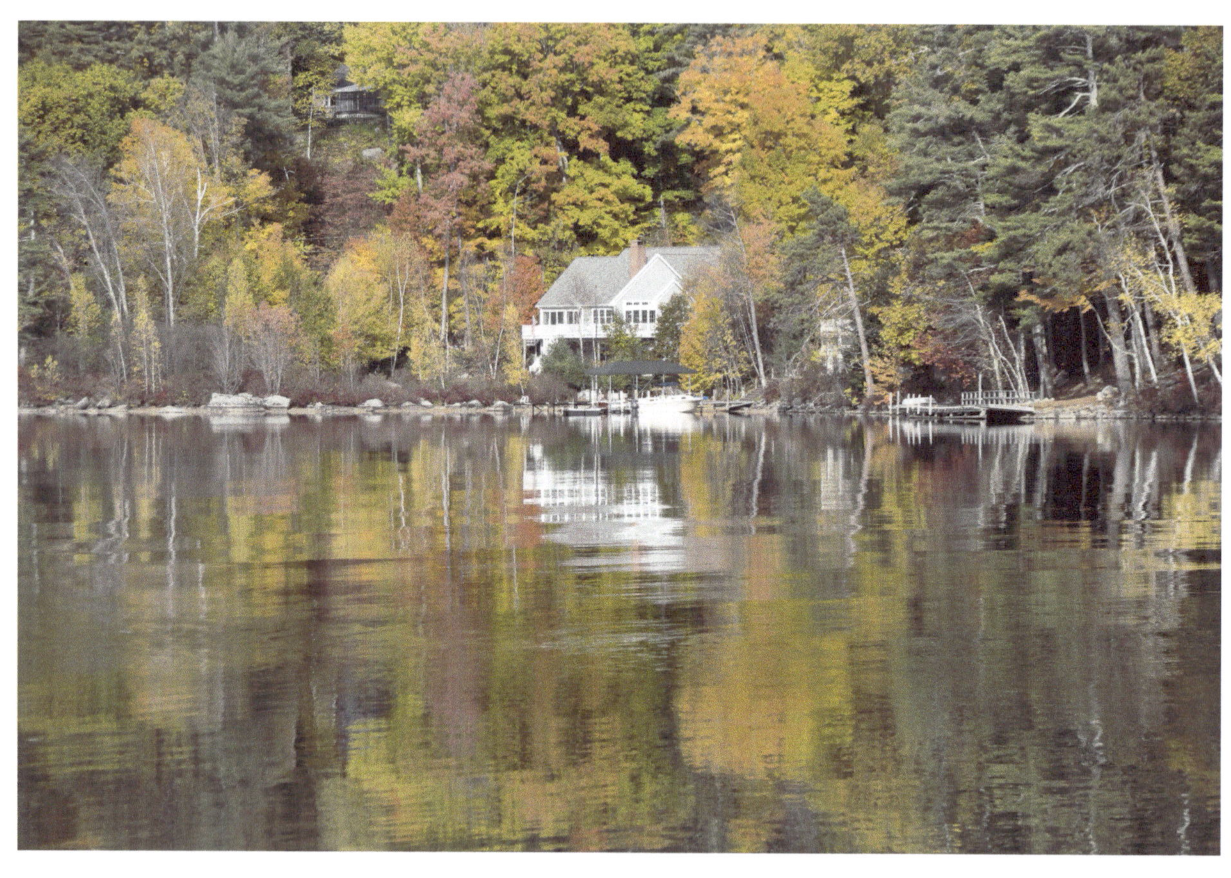

Wolfeboro, New Hampshire

He who chooses the beginning of the road
chooses the place it leads to.
--Harry Emerson Fosdick, 1878 - 1969

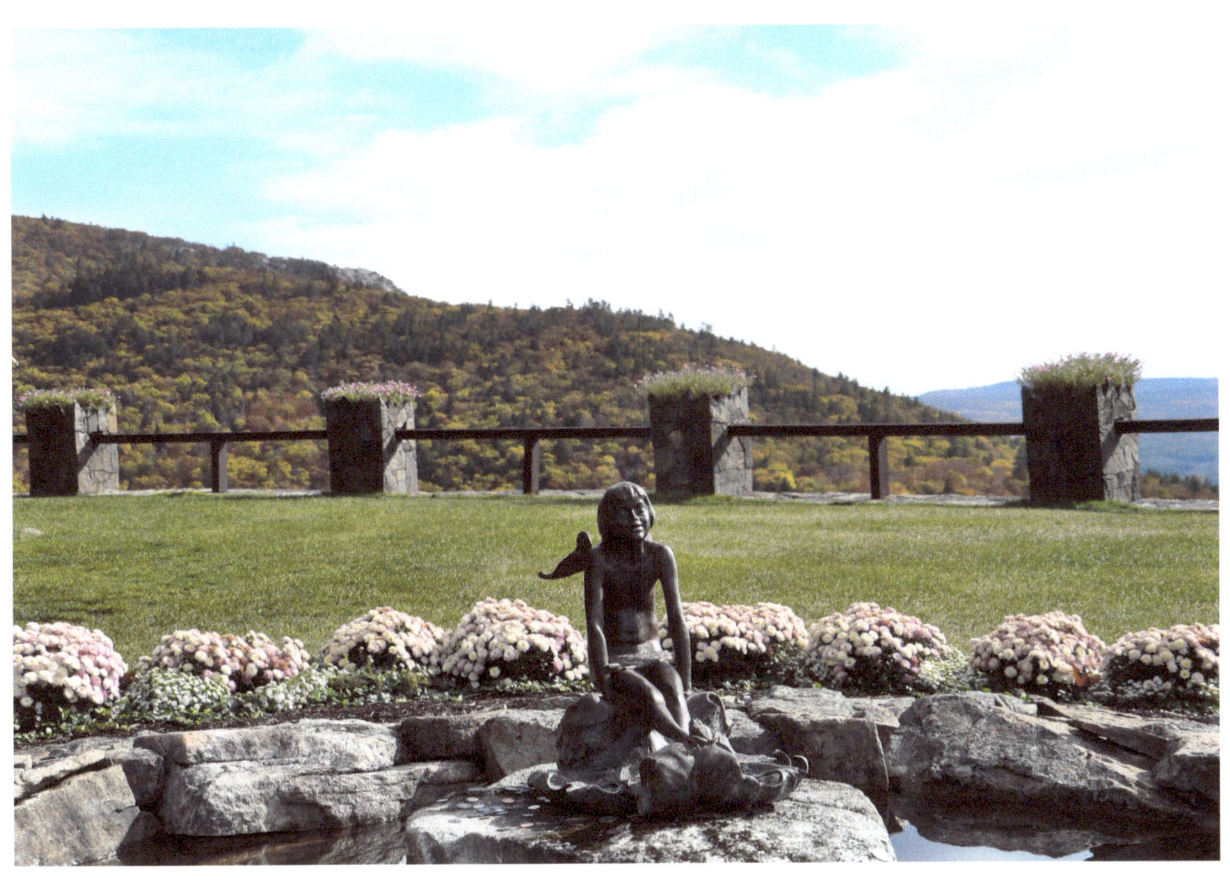

Moultonborough, New Hampshire

Like Confucius of old, I am so absorbed in the wonder of earth
and the life upon it that I cannot think of heaven and the angels.
I have enough for this life.
If there is no other life, then this one has
been enough to make it worth being born, myself a human being.
--Pearl Buck, 1892 - 1973

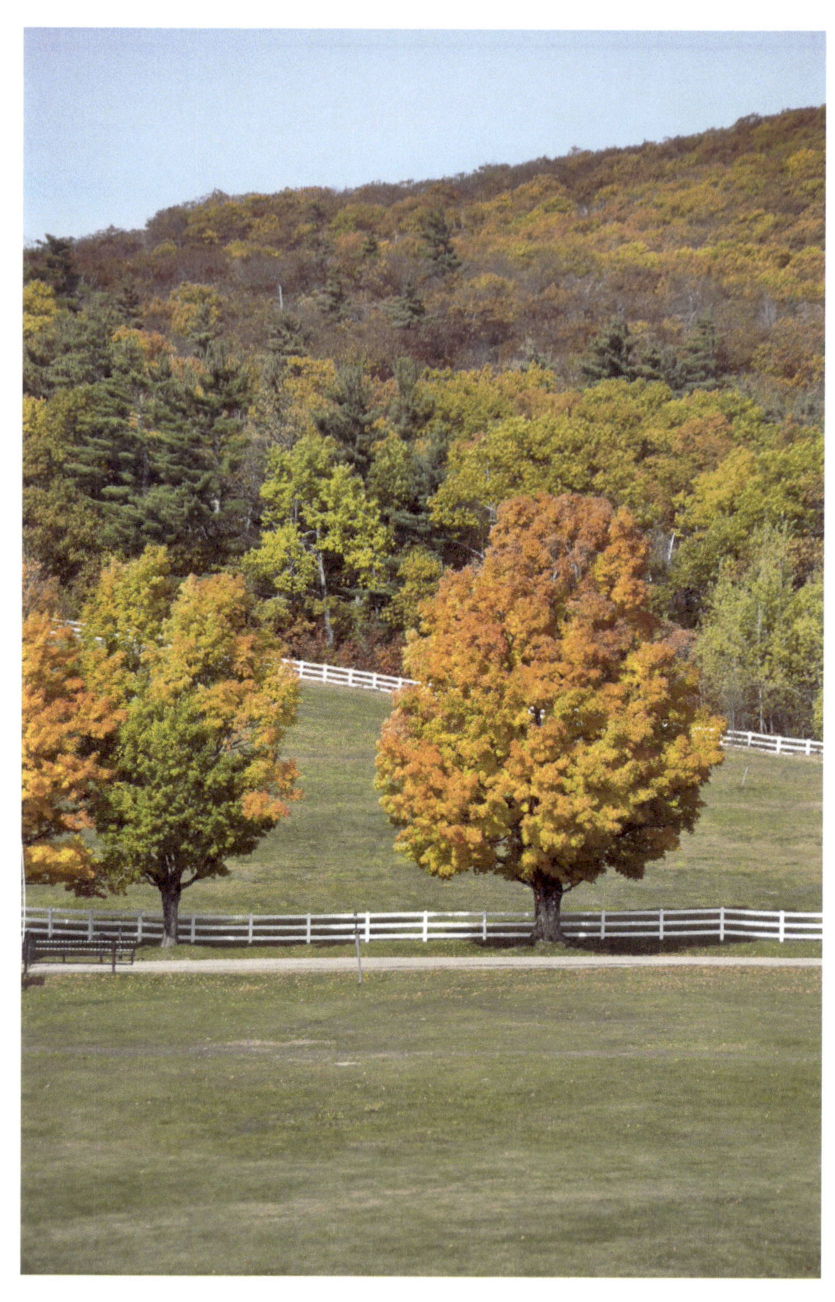

Moultonborough, New Hampshire

Life is always at some turning point.

--Irwin Edman, 1896 - 1954

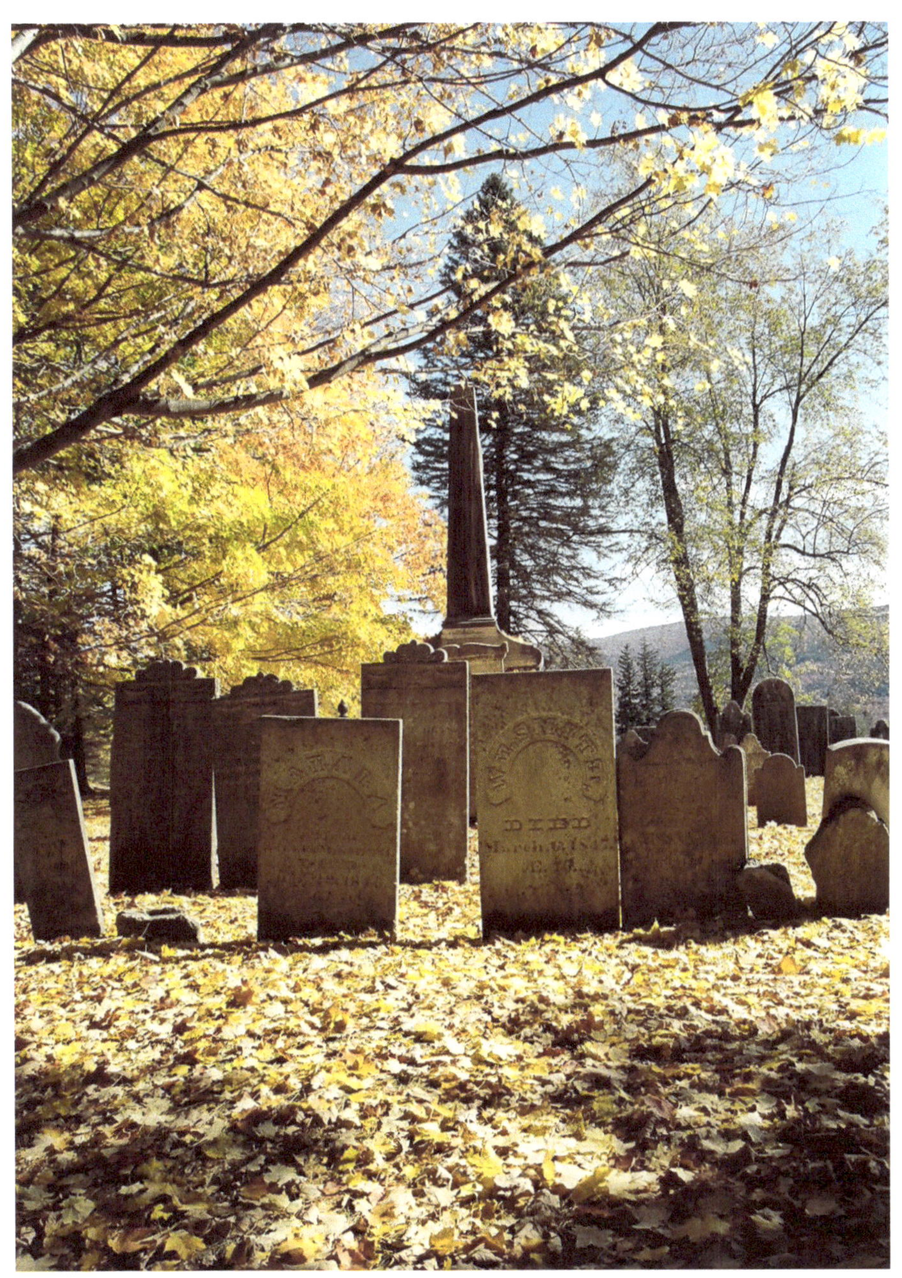

Southern Vermont

Climb the mountains and get their good tidings.
Nature's peace will flow into you as sunshine flows into trees.
The winds will blow their own freshness into you, and the storms their energy,
while cares will drop away from you like the leaves of Autumn.
—John Muir, 1838 - 1914

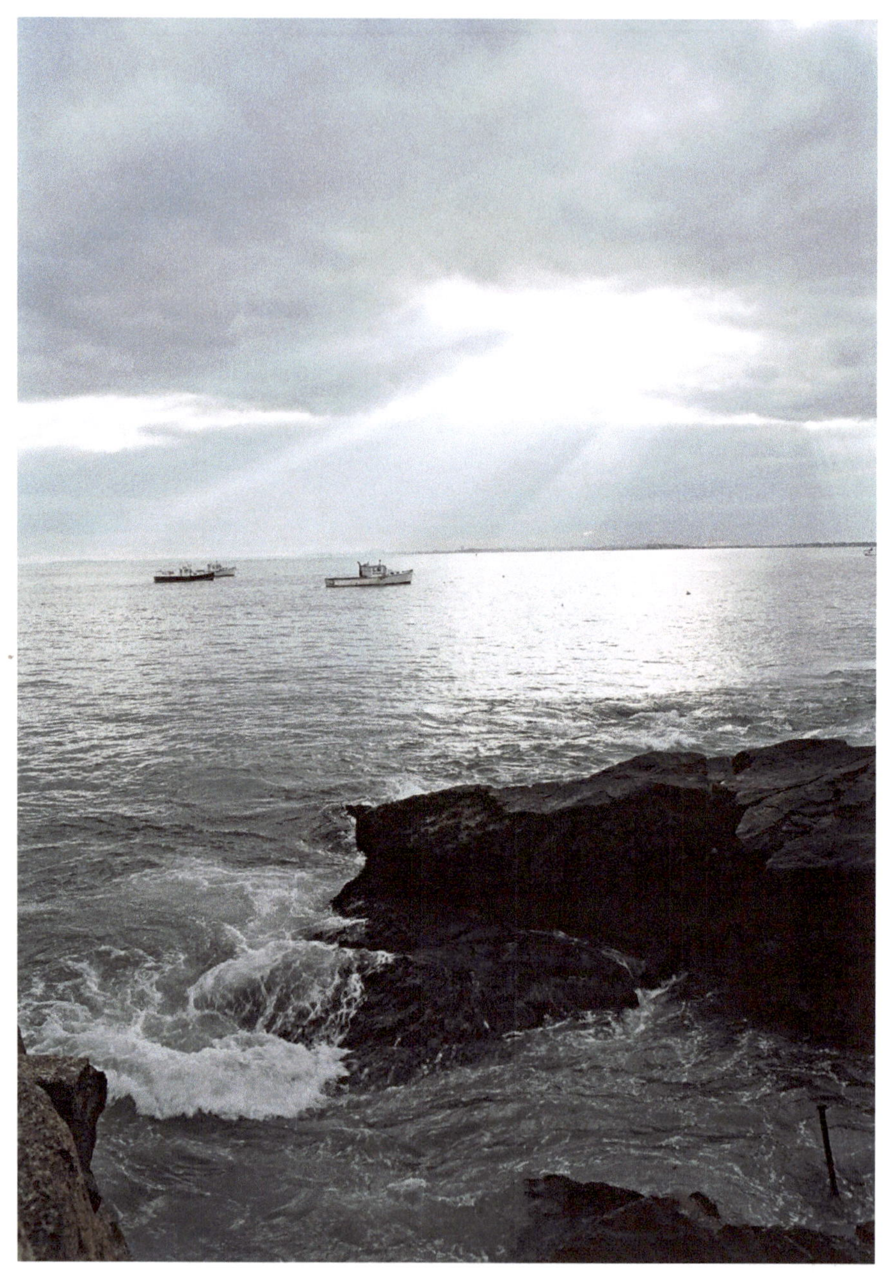

Nahant, Massachusetts

A great attitude does much more than turn on the lights in our worlds;
it seems to magically connect us to all sorts of serendipitous opportunities
that were somehow absent before the change.
--Earl Nightingale, 1921 - 1989

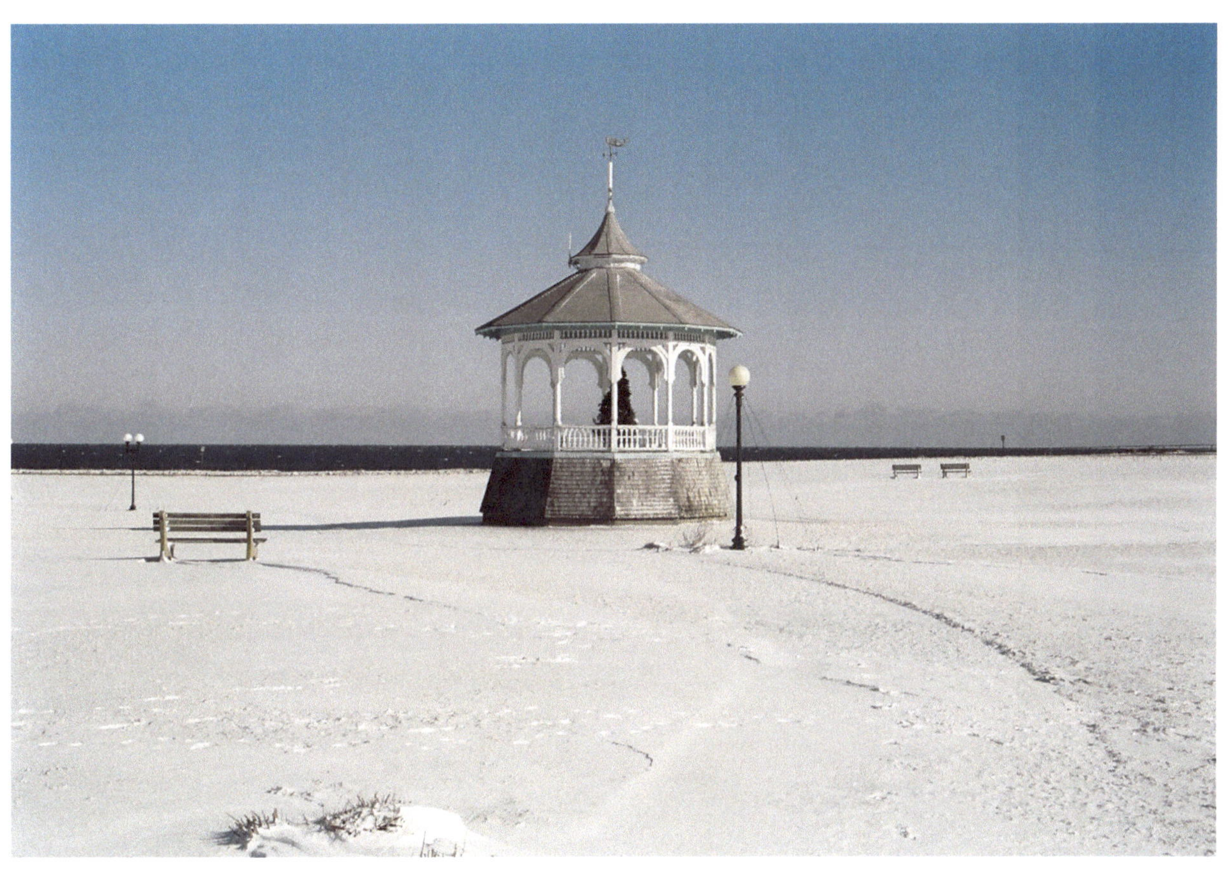

Oak Bluffs, Massachusetts

The first fall of snow is not only an event, it is a magical event.
You go to bed in one kind of world and wake up in another quite different
and if this is not enchantment then where is it to be found?
-- J.B. Priestley, 1894 - 1984

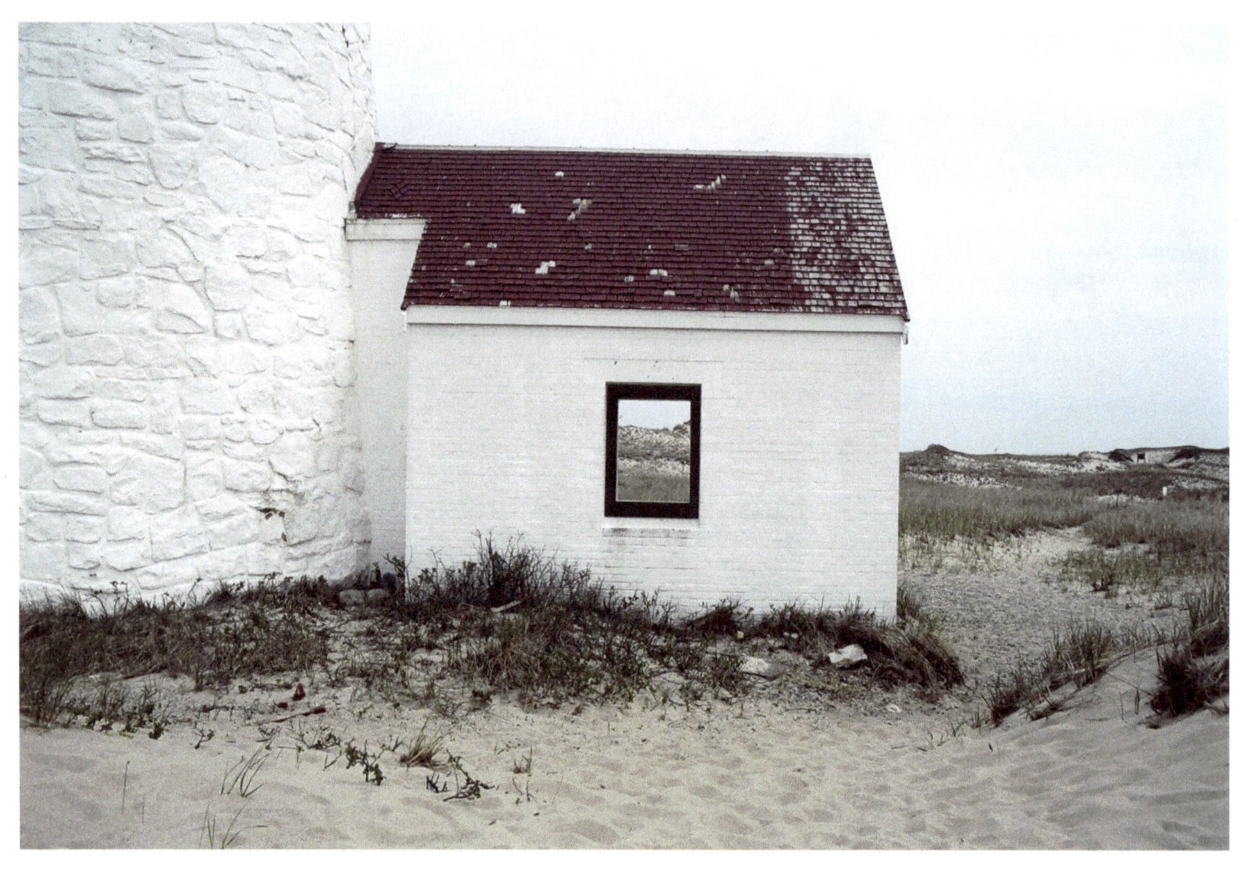

Nantucket, Massachusetts

God dwells wherever man lets Him in.

--Jewish proverb

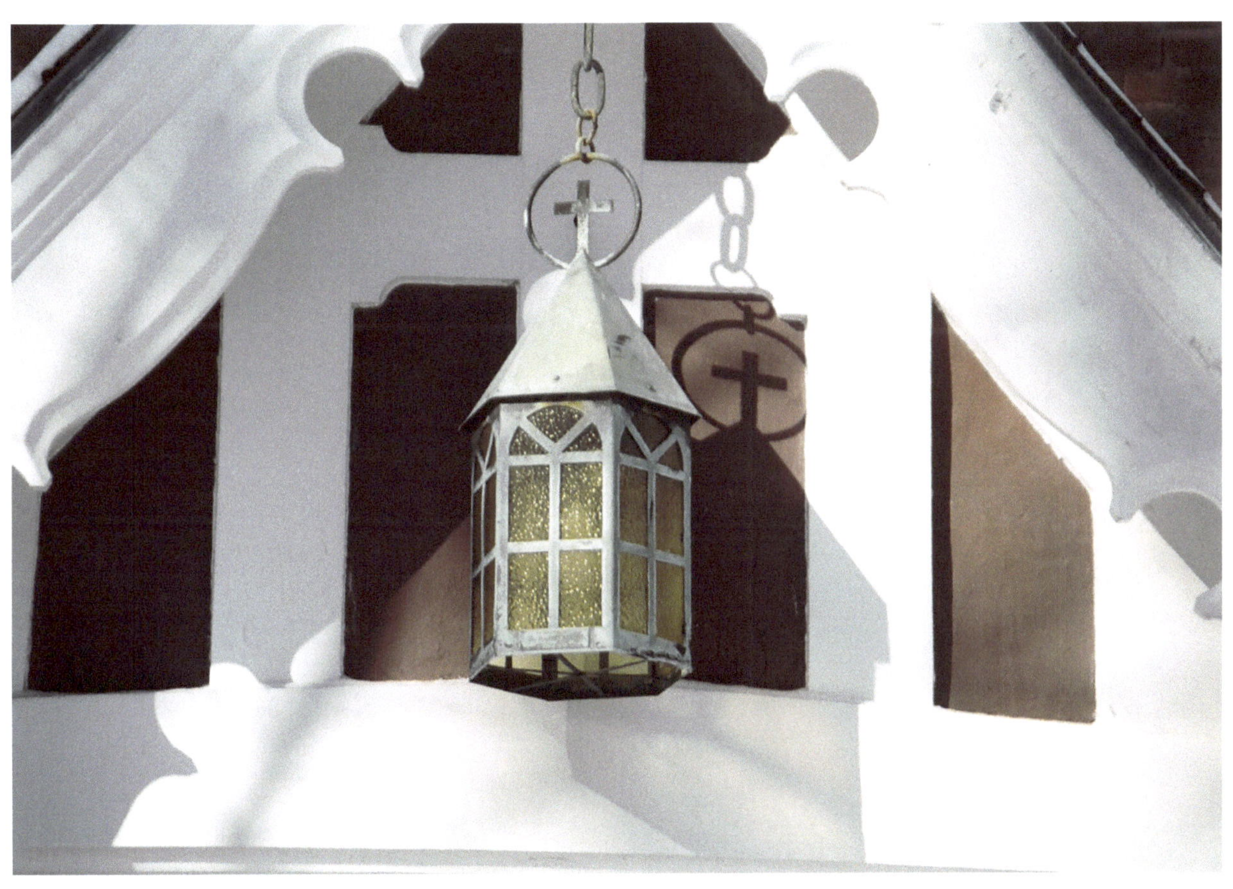

Edgartown, Massachusetts

As far as we can discern, the sole purpose of human existence
is to kindle a light in the darkness of mere being.
--Carl Jung, 1875 - 1961

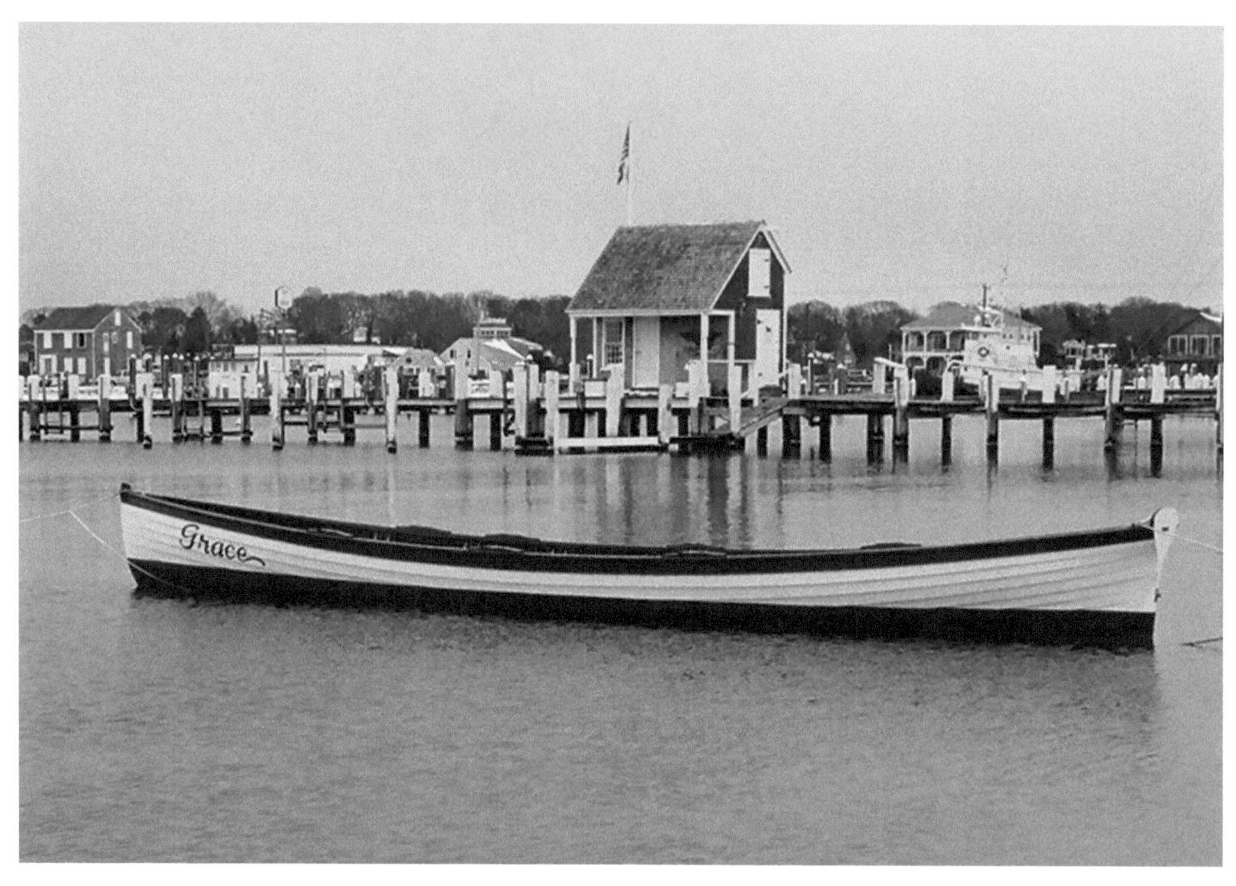

Vineyard Haven, Massachusetts

Accept the place divine providence has found for you.
--Ralph Waldo Emerson, 1803 - 1882

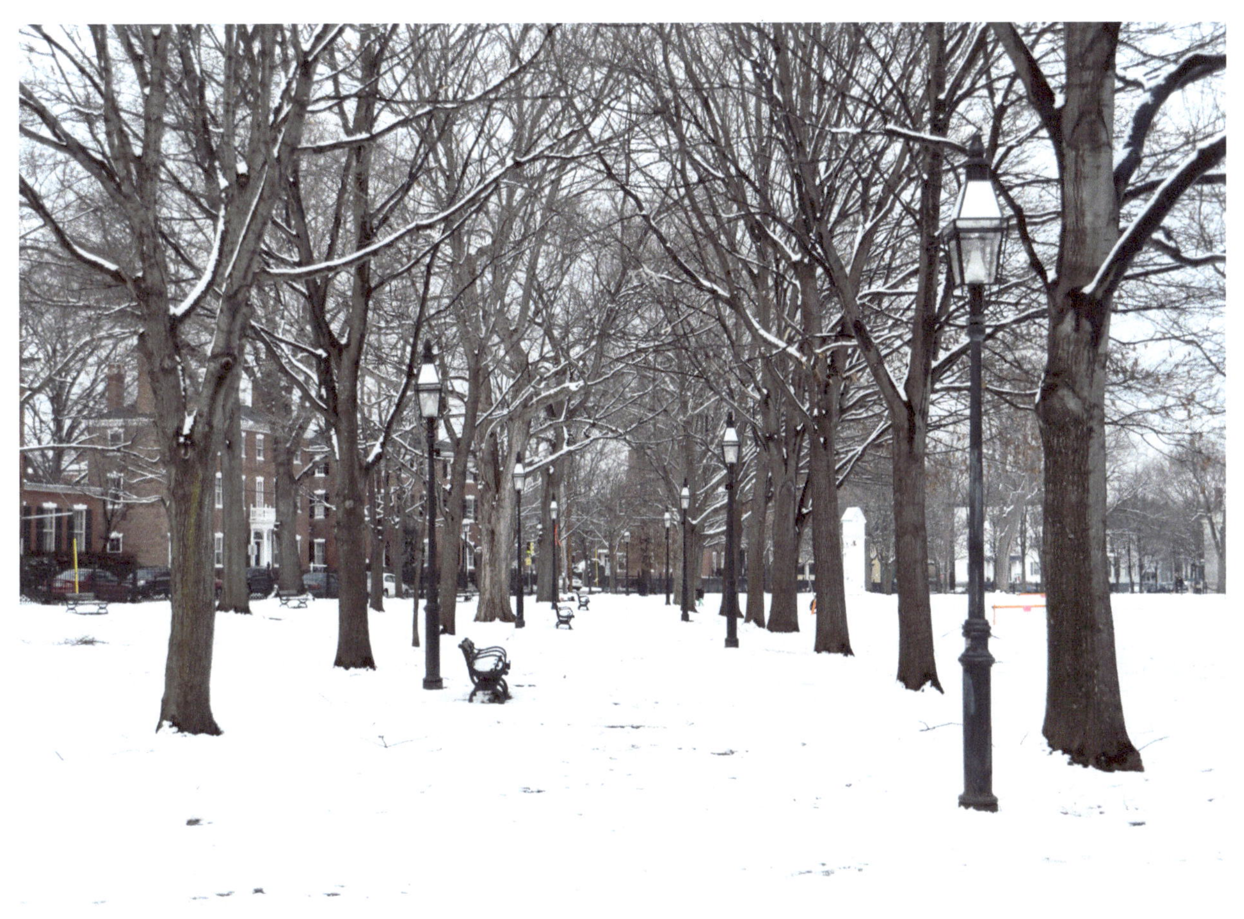

Salem, Massachusetts

It is quite possible to leave your home for a walk in the early morning air
and return a different person--beguiled, enchanted.
--Mary Chase

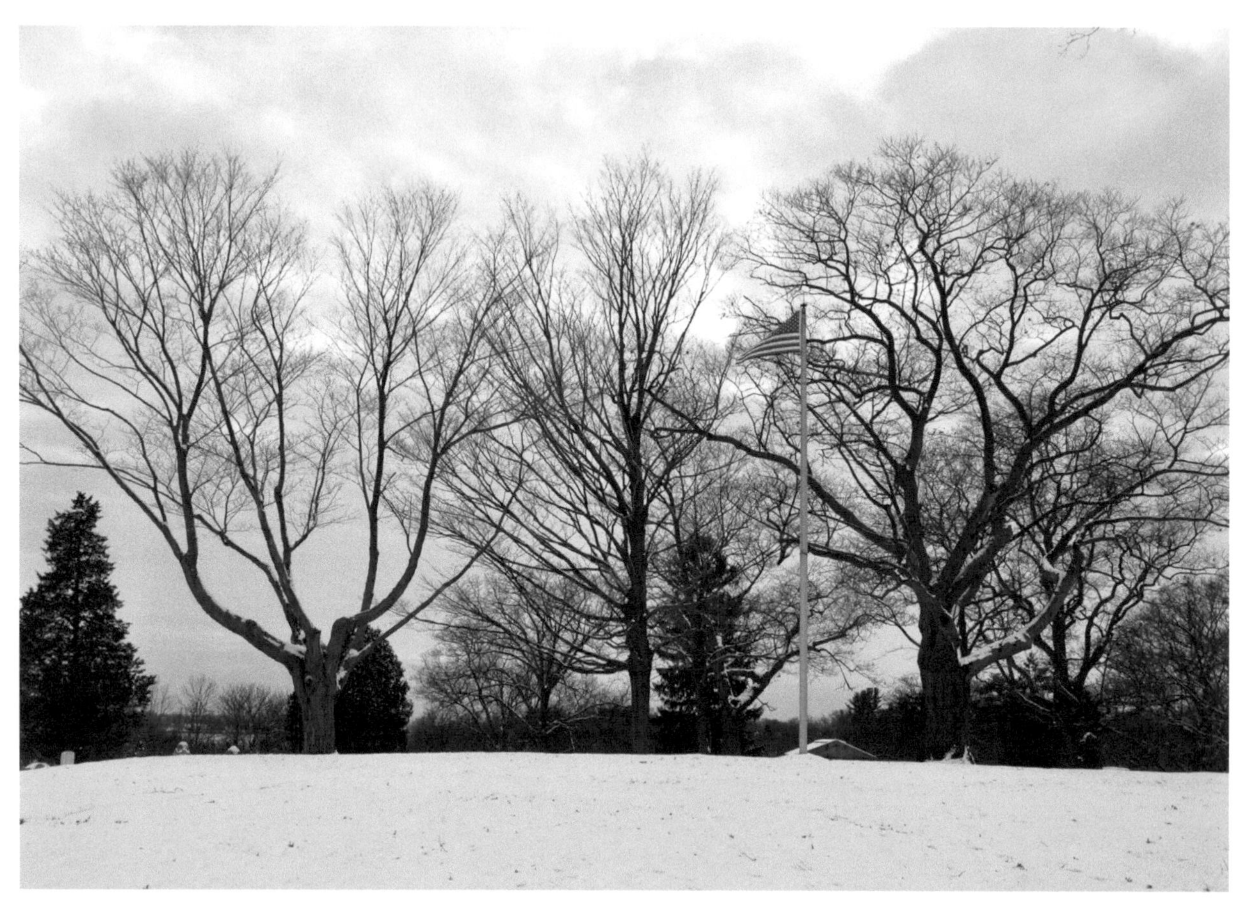

Beverly, Massachusetts

Nature gives to every time and season some beauties of its own;
and from morning to night, as from the cradle to the grave,
it is but a succession of changes so gentle and easy that we can scarcely mark their progress.
--Charles Dickens, 1812 - 1870

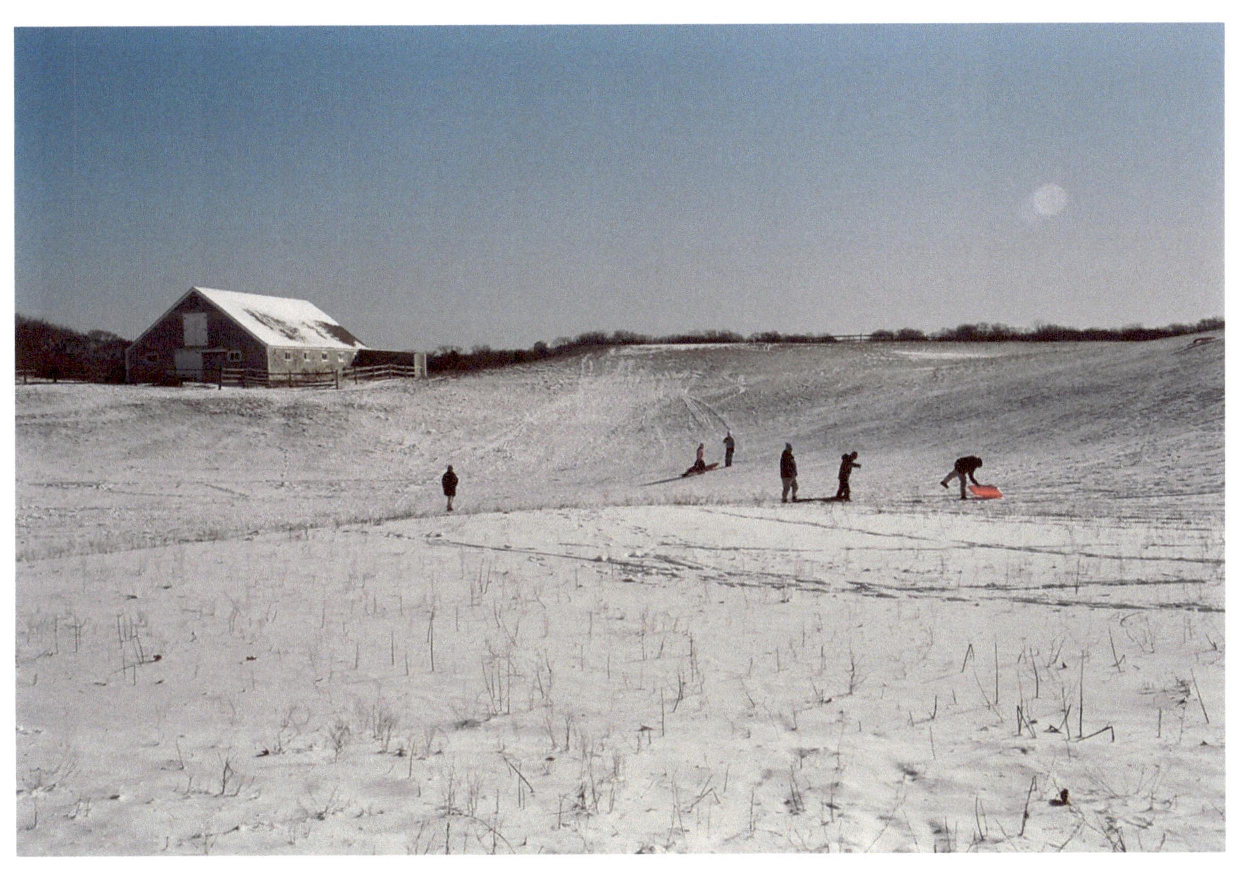

Martha's Vineyard, Massachusetts

When I no longer thrill to the first snow of the season,
I know I'm getting old.
-- Lady Bird Johnson, 1912 - 2007

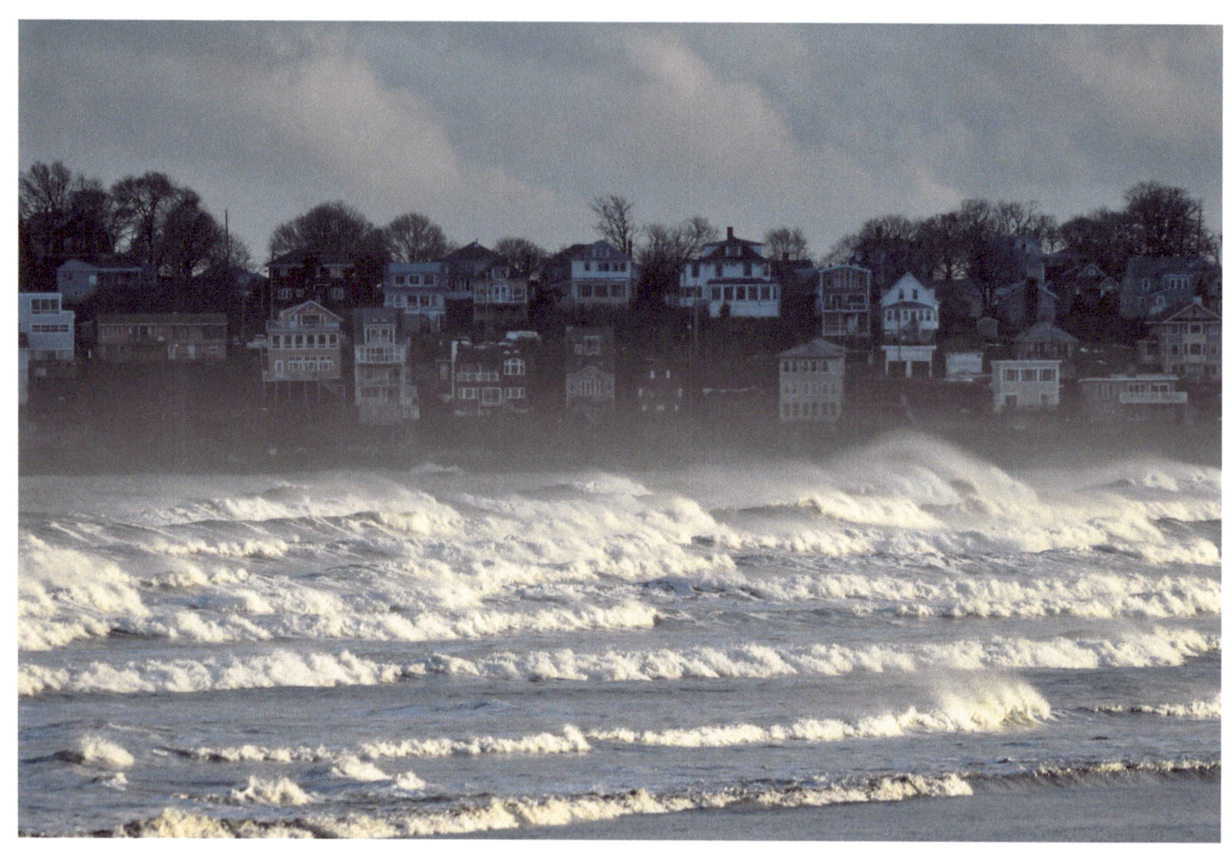

Nahant, Massachusetts

Gaining control of your thoughts is as easy as sitting by the ocean and controlling the waves.
—Michael Lipsey

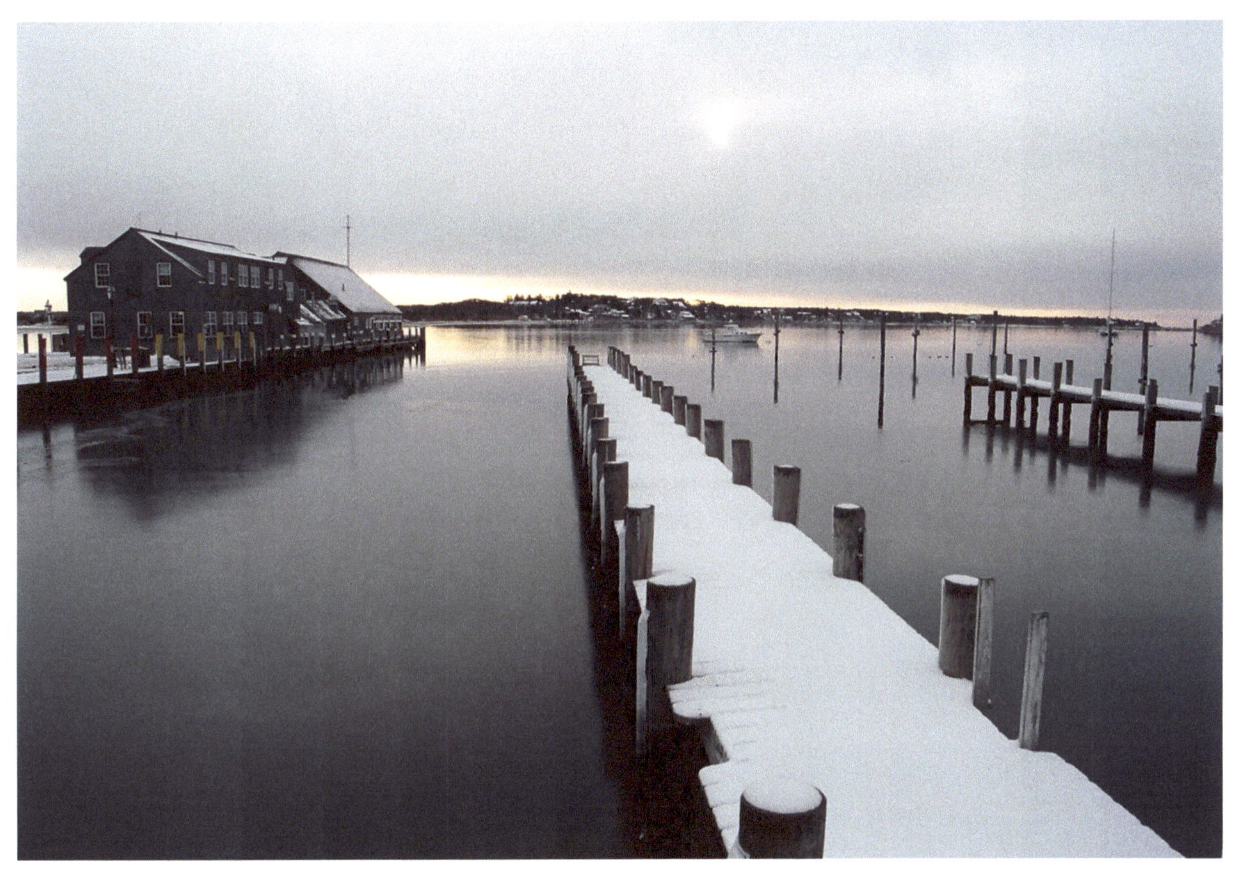

Edgartown, Massachusetts

Nothing can bring you peace but yourself.

--Ralph Waldo Emerson, 1803 - 1882

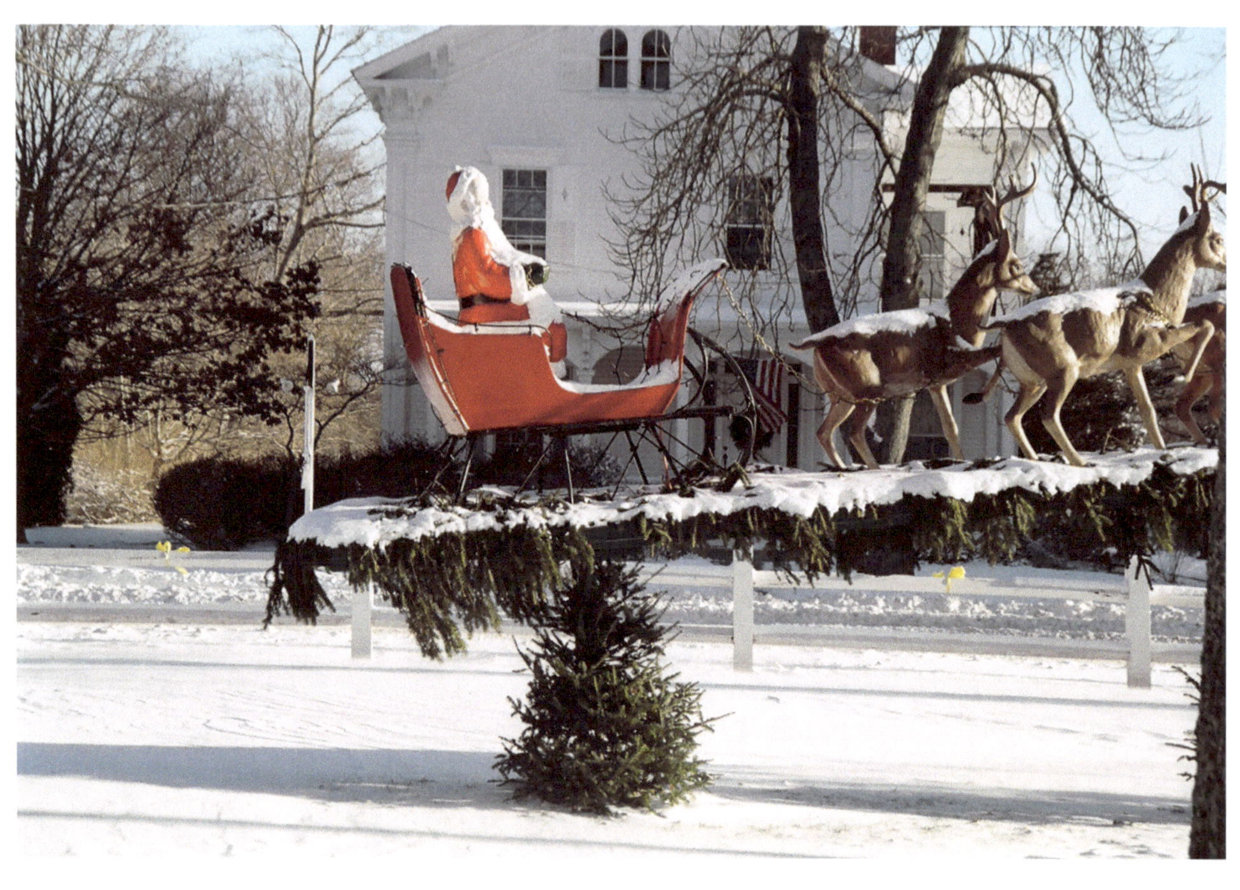

Falmouth, Massachusetts

Believe in love. Believe in magic. Hell, believe in Santa Claus. Believe in others. Believe in yourself. Believe in your dreams. If you don't, who will?

--Jon Bon Jovi, 1962 -

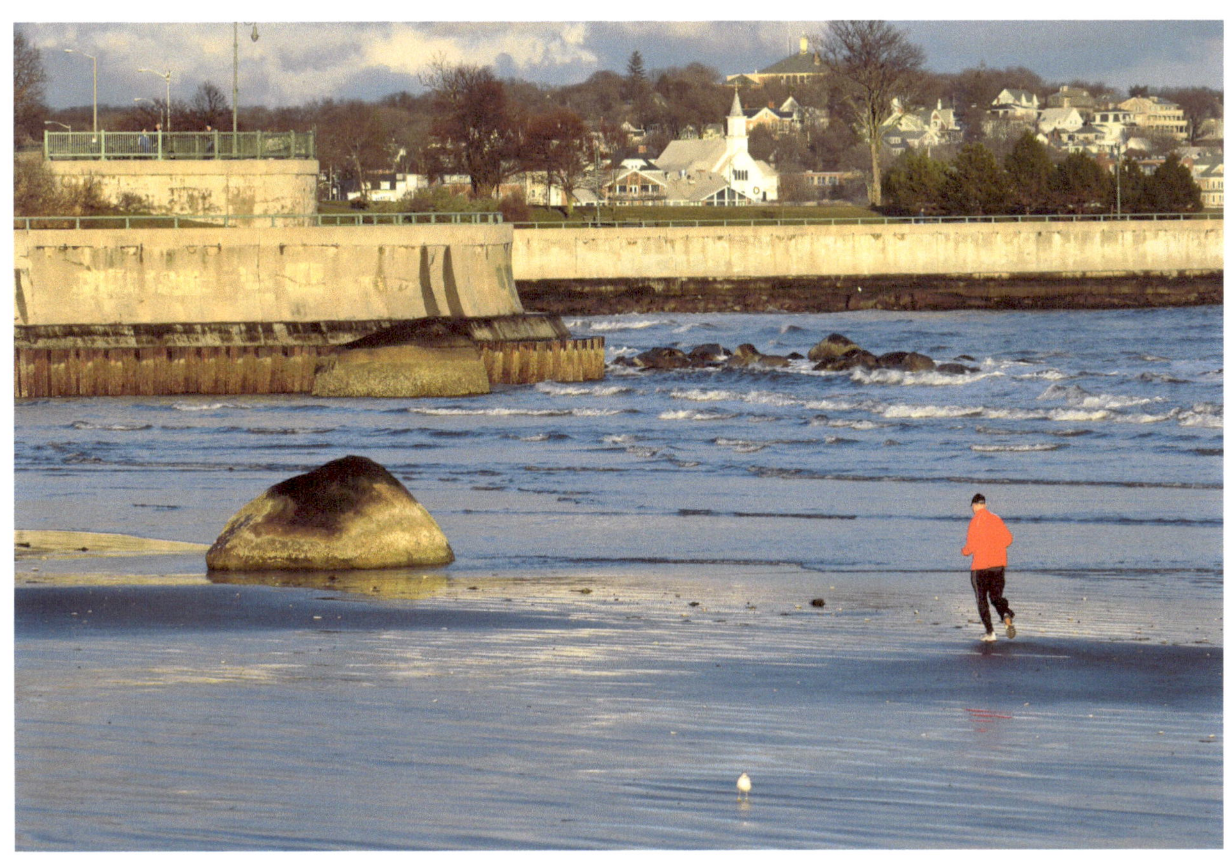

Lynn, Massachusetts

The U.S. Constitution doesn't guarantee happiness, only the pursuit of it.
You have to catch up with it yourself.

-- Benjamin Franklin, 1706 - 1790

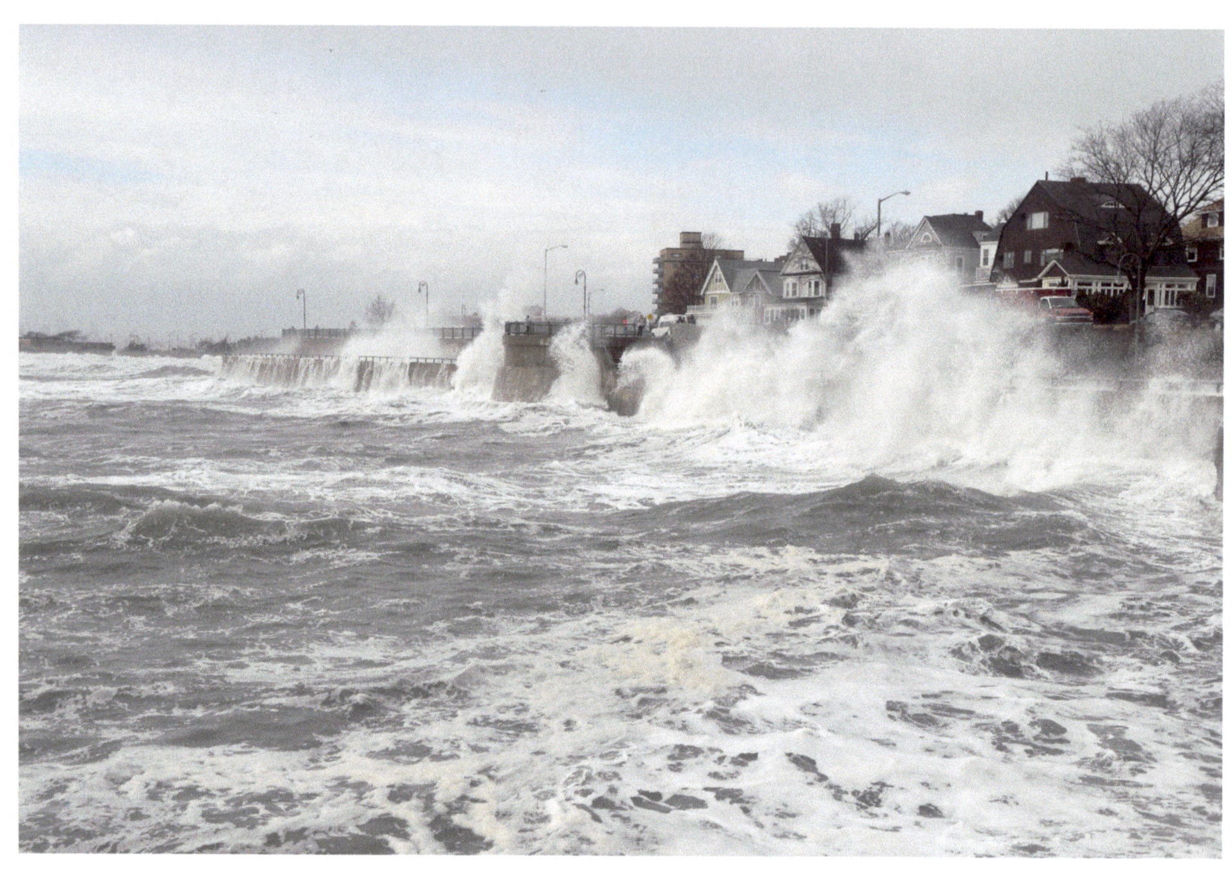

Lynn, Massachusetts

Give wind and tide a chance to change.

--Richard E. Byrd, 1888 - 1957

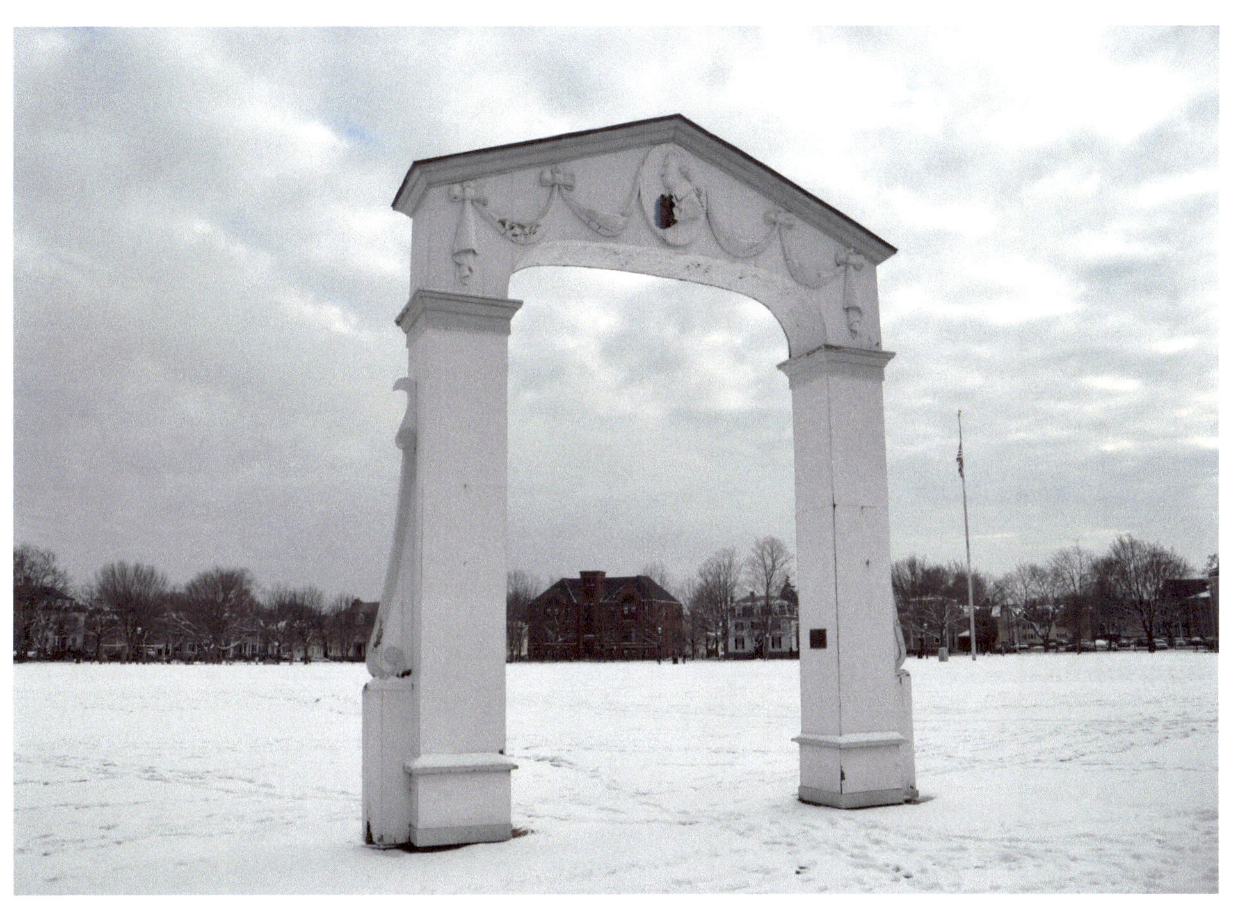

Salem, Massachusetts

All experience is an arch to build upon.

--Henry Brooks Adams, 1838 - 1918

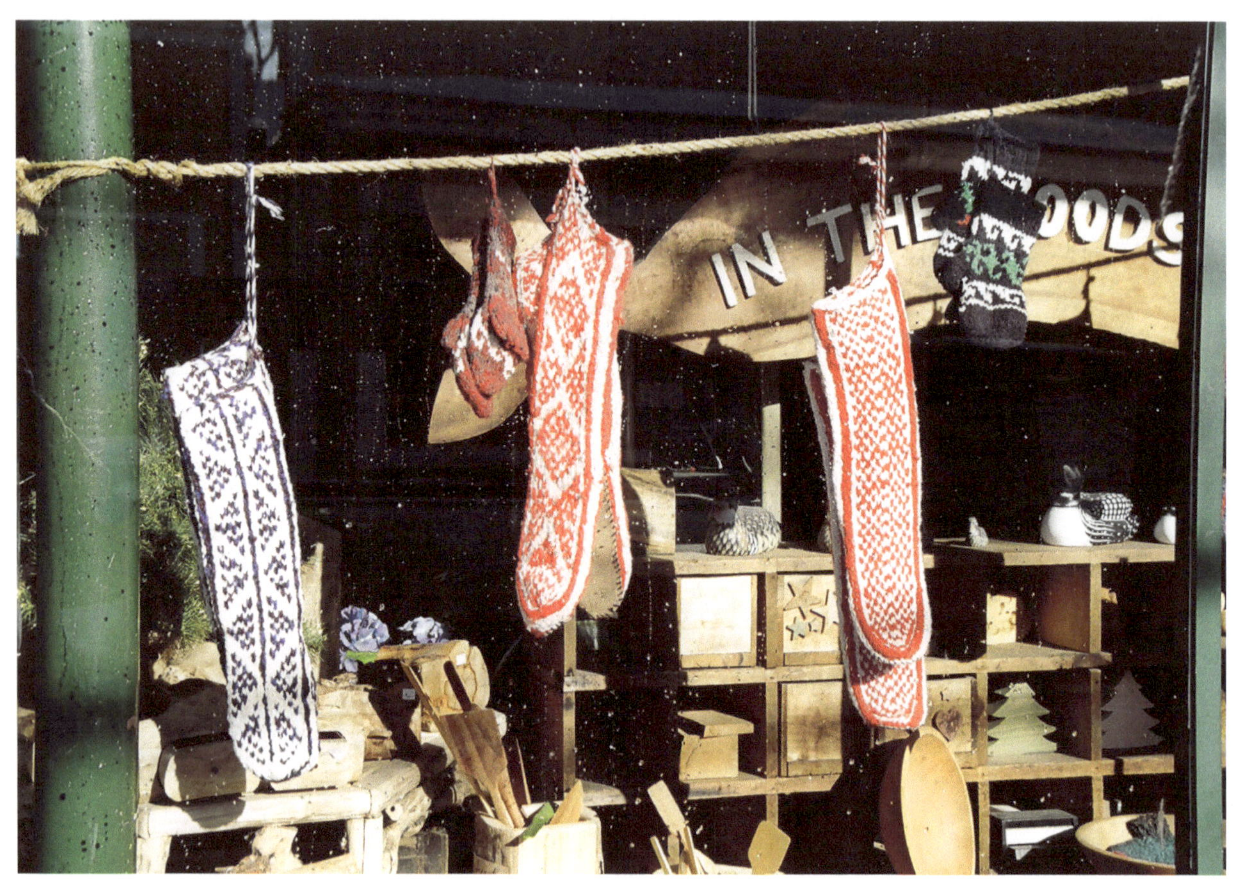

Edgartown, Massachusetts

The good old days are neither better nor worse

than the ones we're living through right now.

--Artie Shaw, 1910 - 2004

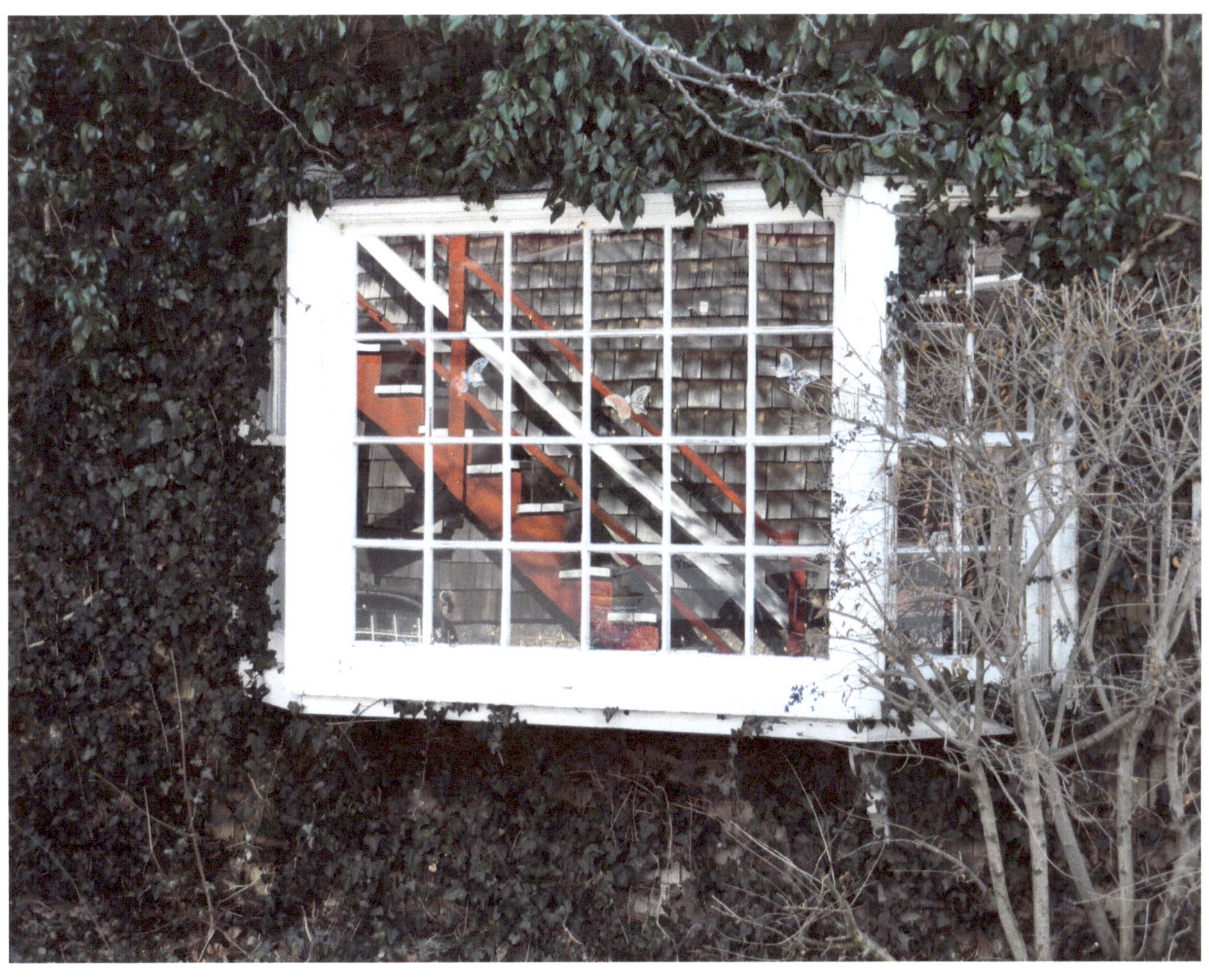

Rockport, Massachusetts

We cannot alter facts but we can alter our ways of looking at them.

--Phyllis Bottome, 1884 - 1963

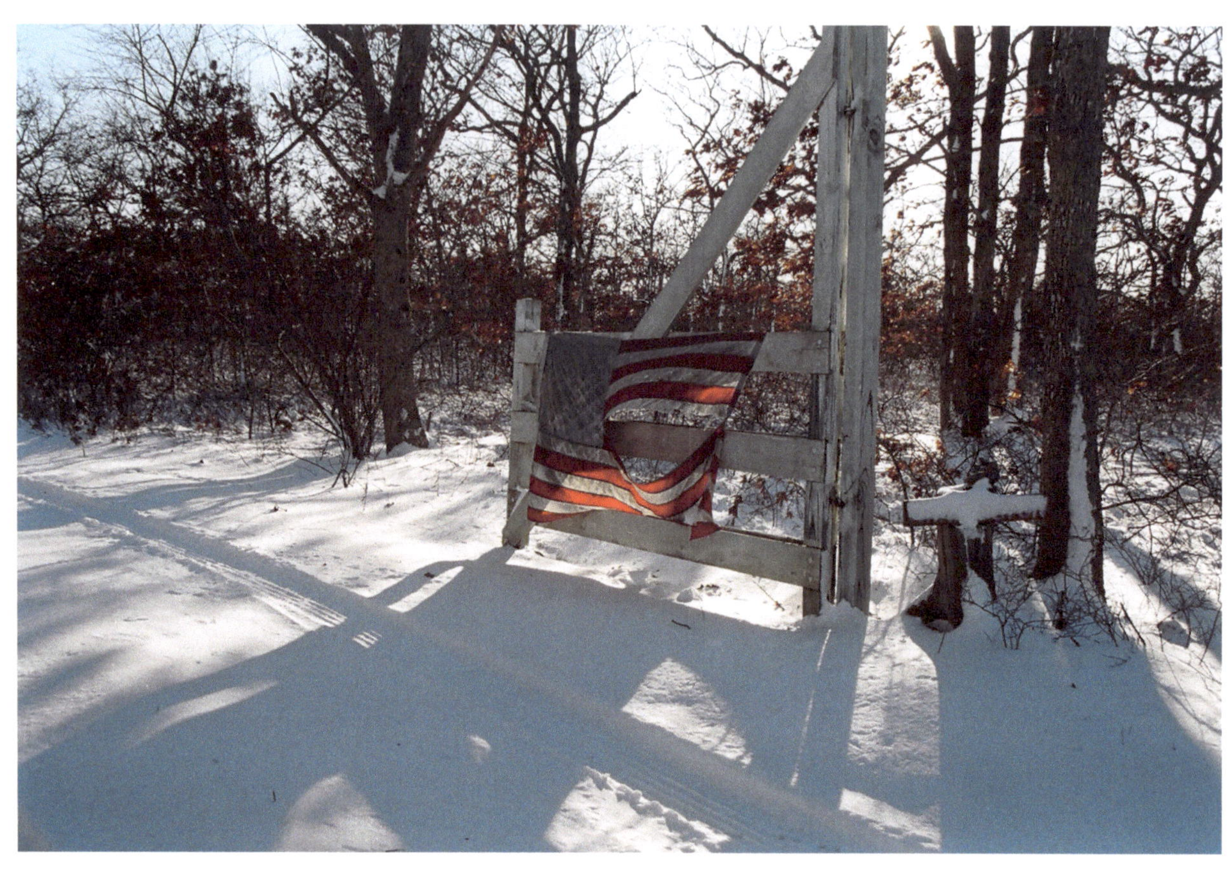

Martha's Vineyard, Massachusetts

The past is but the beginning of a beginning,
and all that is and has been is but the twilight of dawn.
--H.G. Wells, 1866 - 1946

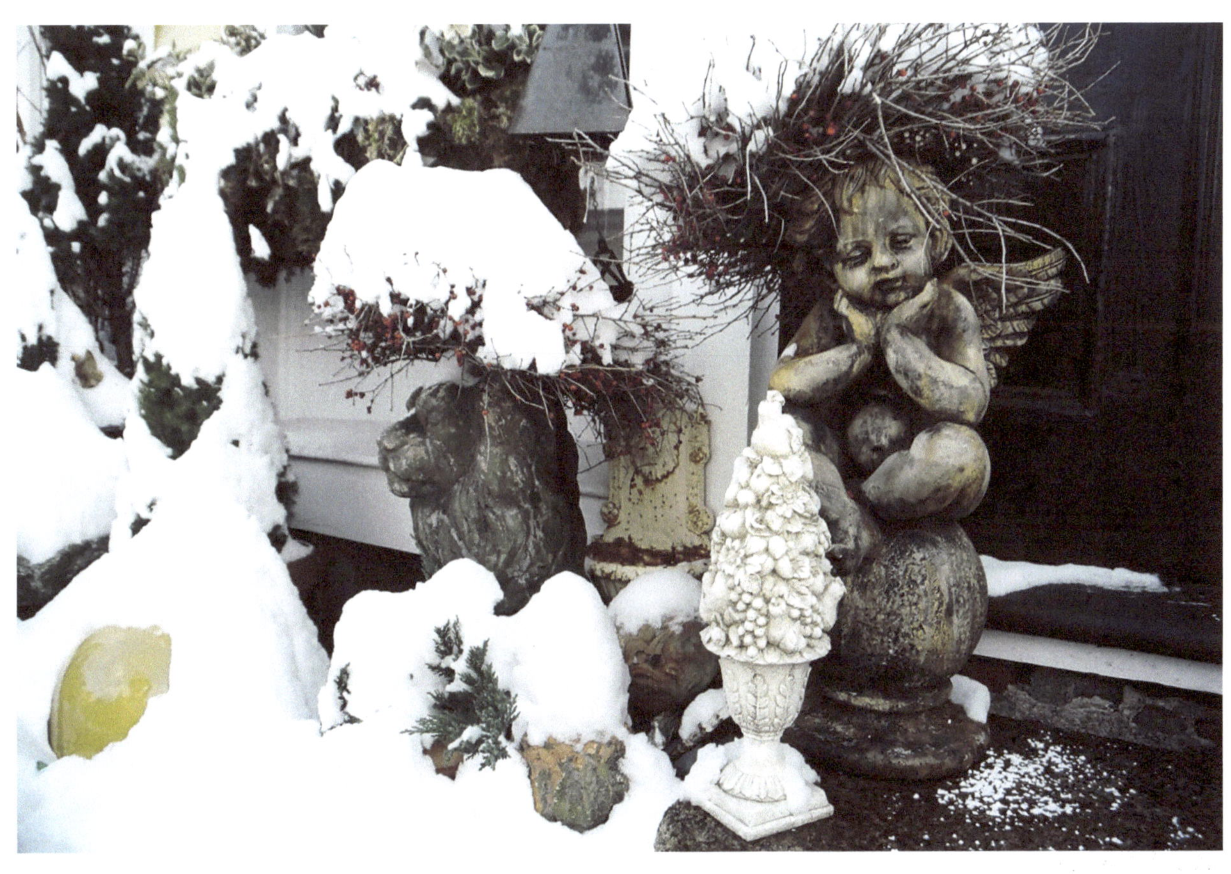

Marblehead, Massachusetts

Angels deliver fate to our doorstep --
and anywhere else it is needed.
--Jessi Lane Adams

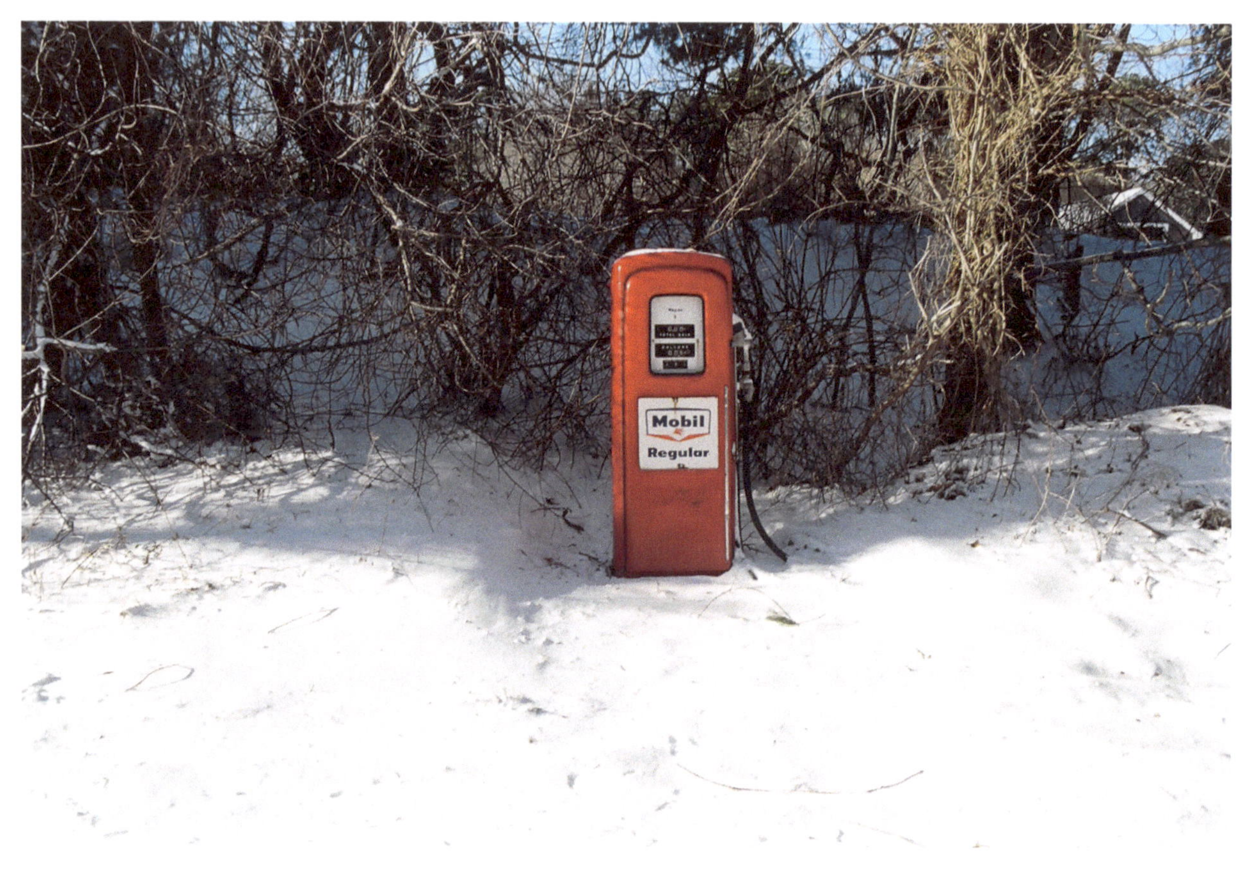

Martha's Vineyard, Massachusetts

Contentment consists not in adding more fuel,
but in taking away some fire.
--Thomas Fuller, 1608 - 1661

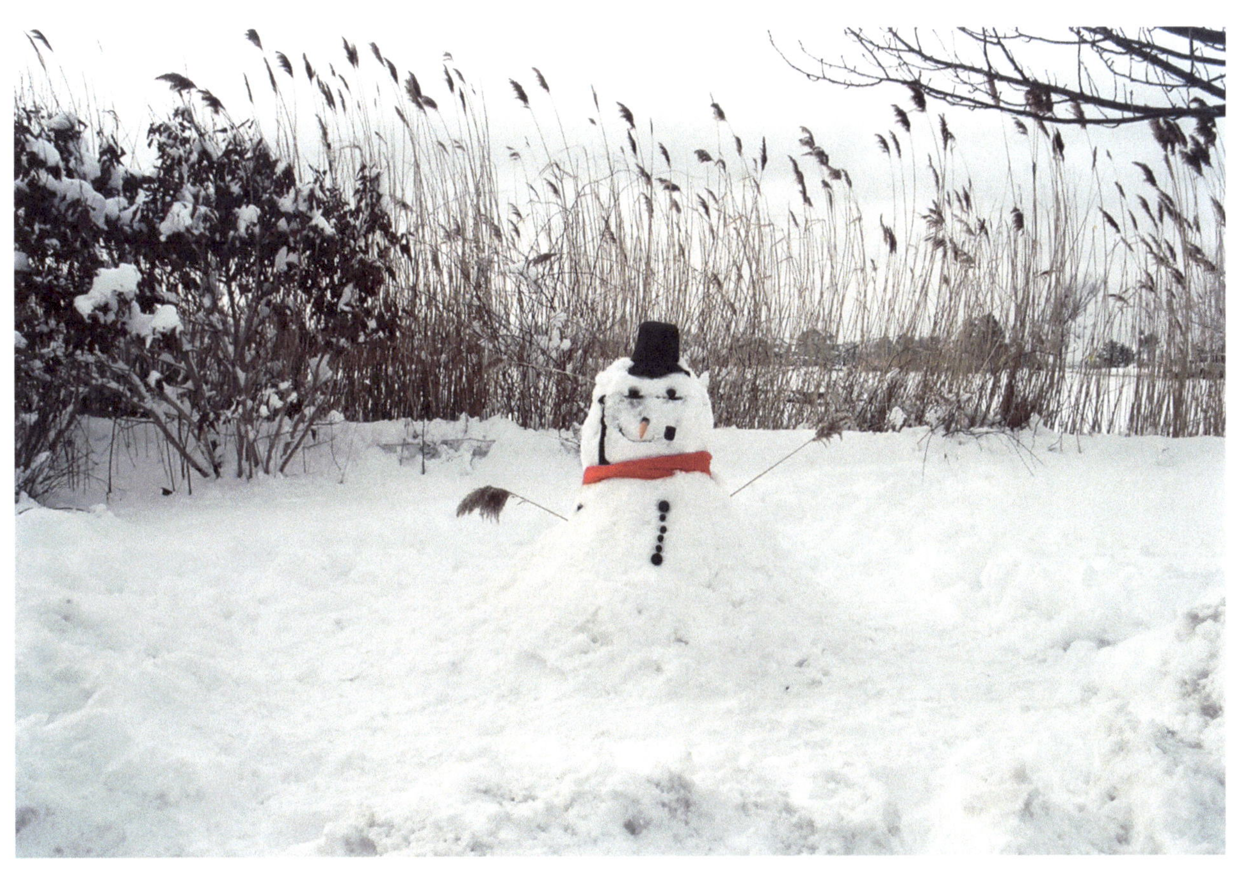

Nahant, Massachusetts

Begin doing what you want to do now. We are not living in eternity.

We have only this moment, sparkling like a star in our hand and melting like a snowflake.

Let us use it before it is too late.

--Marie Beyon Ray

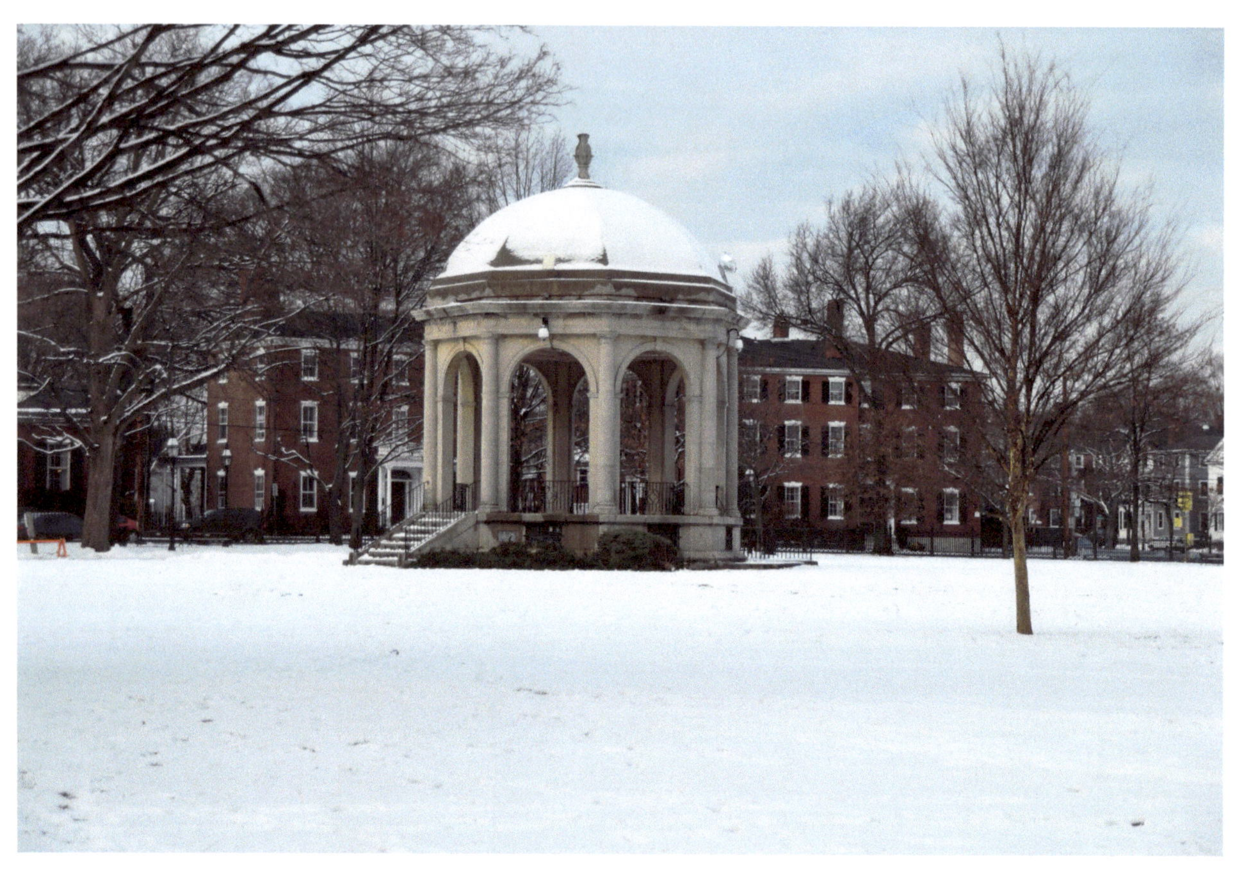

Salem, Massachusetts

Wisdom comes with winters.

--Oscar Wilde, 1854 - 1900

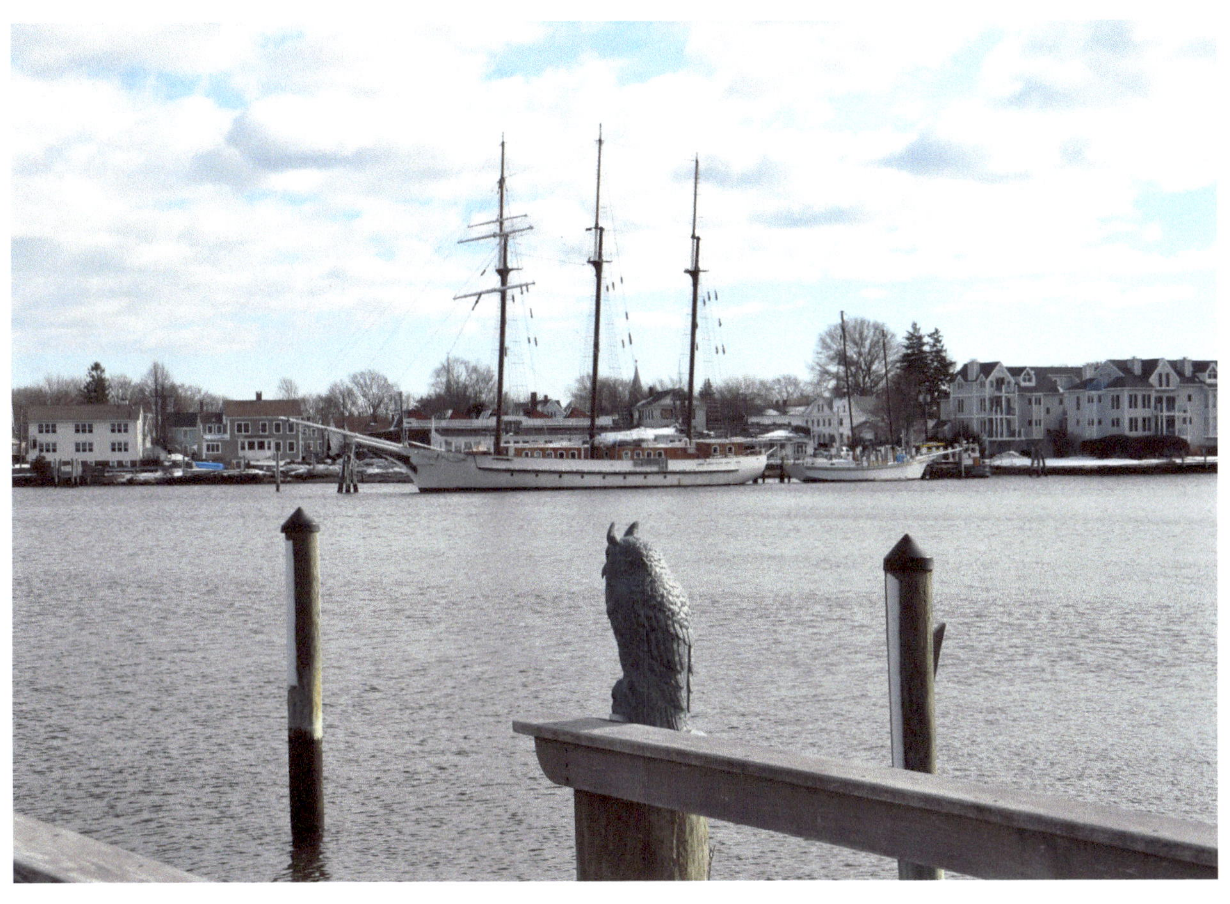

Mystic, Connecticut

A ship in harbor is safe--but that is not what ships are for.

--John A. Shedd, 1859 - 1928

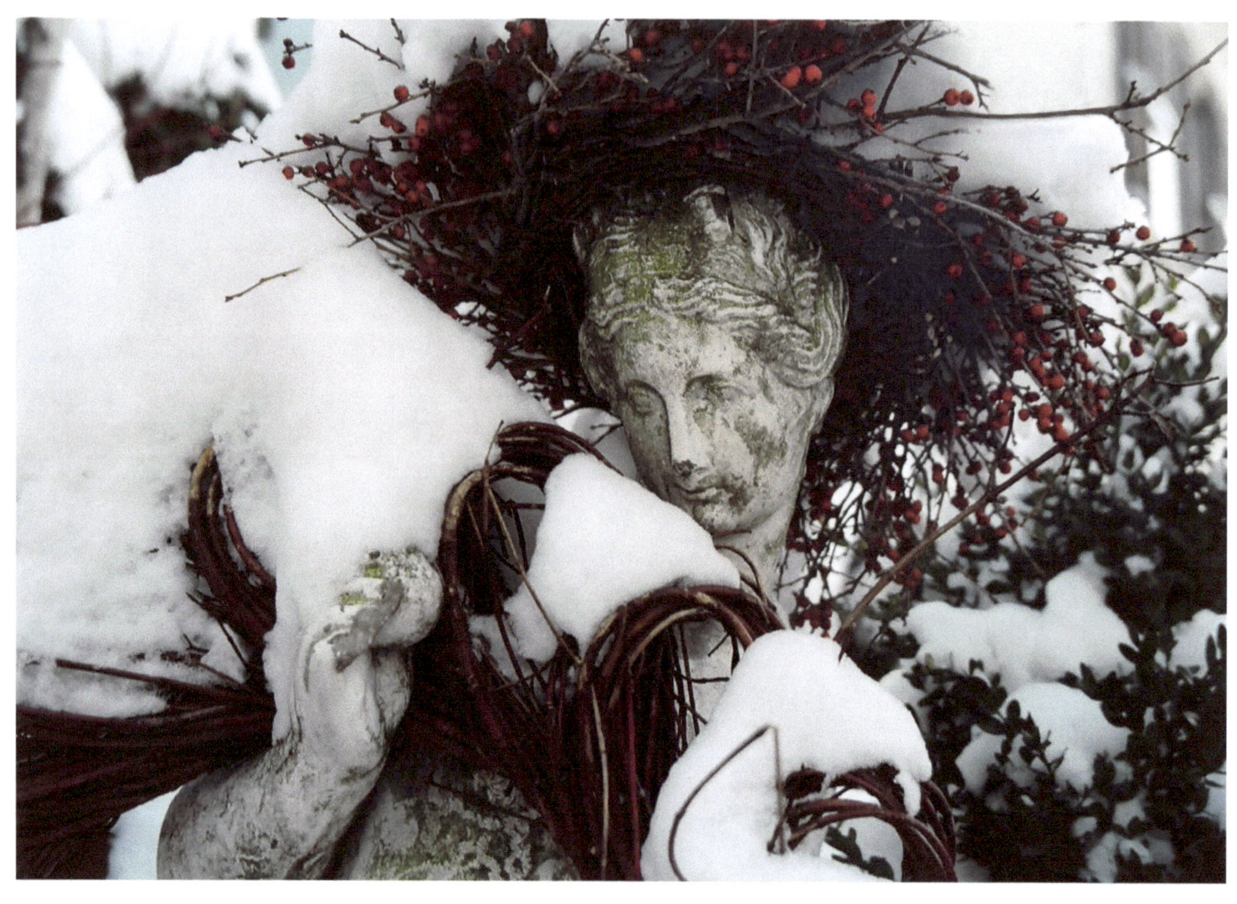

Marblehead, Massachusetts

Life is one long struggle to disinter oneself,
to keep one's head above the accumulations,
the ever deepening layers of objects...
which attempt to cover one over, steadily, almost irresistibly,
like falling snow.
--Rose Macaulay, 1881- 1958

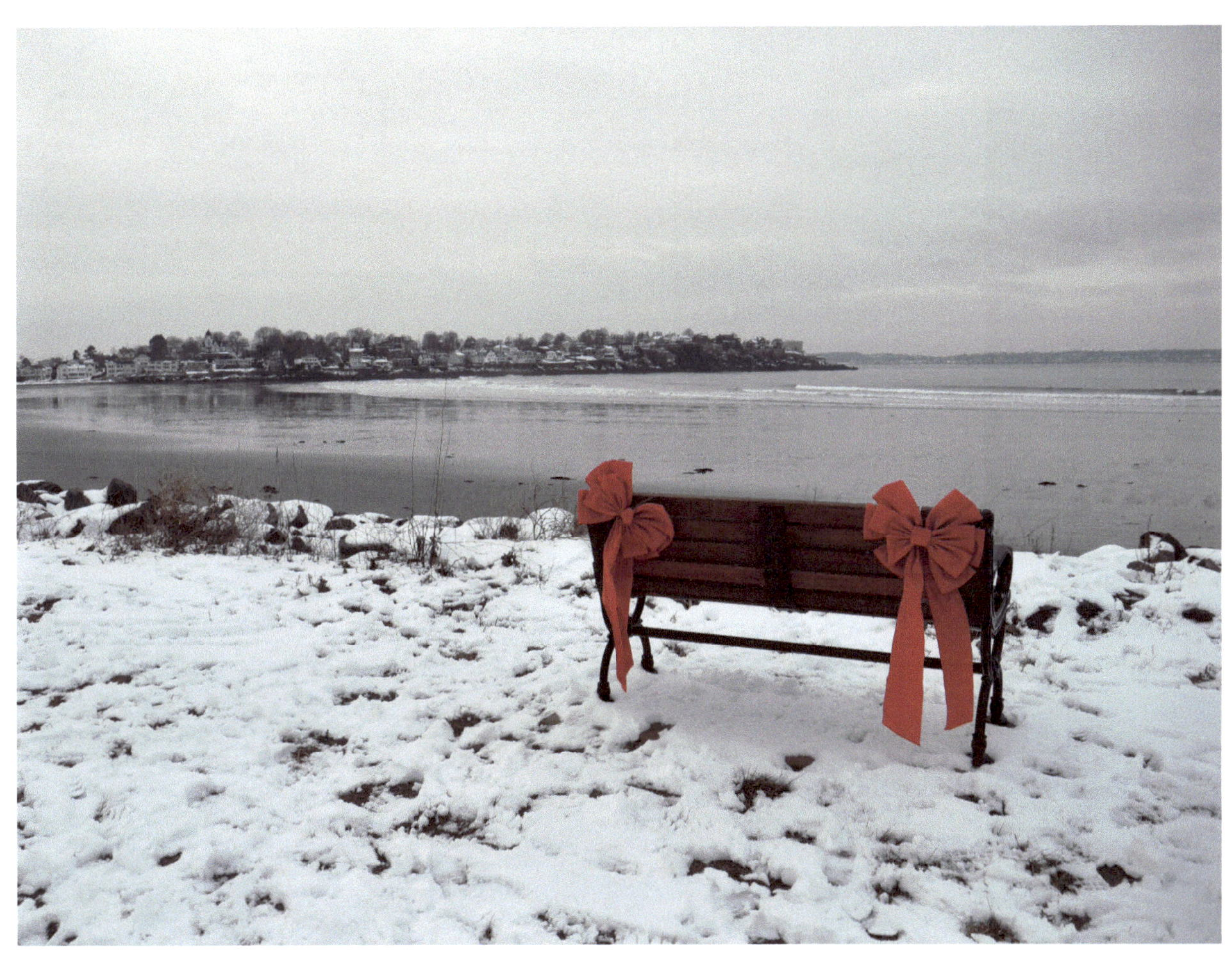

Nahant, Massachusetts

Most human beings have an almost infinite capacity
for taking things for granted.
--Aldous Huxley, 1894 - 1963

Bibliography

Cook, John and Steve Deger and Leslie Ann Gibson,
The Book of Positive Quotations, 2nd edition, Fairview Press, 2007

Dass, Ram, One Liners: A Mini Manual for a Spiritual Life,
Bell Tower, Member of Crown Publishing Group,
a division of Random House, Inc., 2002.

Fox, Emmet, Around the Year with Emmet Fox,
Harper San Franciso, a division of HarperCollins Publishers, 1992.

Ratcliffe, Susan, Little Oxford Dictionary of Quotations, New edition,
Oxford University Press, 2005.

Shanahan, John M., The Most Brilliant Thoughts of All Time (in two lines or less),
Collins, an imprint of HarperCollins Publishers, 2005.

Toliver, Wendy, The Little Giant Encyclopedia of Inspirational Quotes,
Sterling Publishing Co., Inc., 2004.

www.bartleby.com

www.famousquotes.com

www.quotationspage.com

www.quotegarden.com

www.quoteland.com

www.quoteworld.org

www.thinkexist.com

www.worldofquotes.com

www.viewfromthepier.com

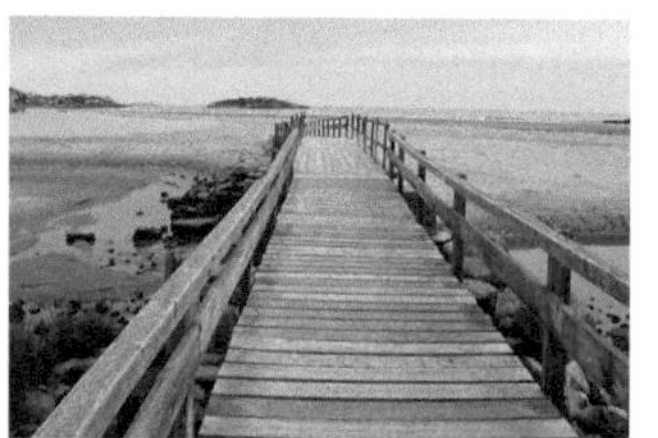

www.viewfromthepier.com

www.ingramcontent.com/pod-product-compliance
Lightning Source LLC
LaVergne TN
LVHW070126110826
845147LV00002B/196

* 9 7 8 0 9 8 2 2 2 0 2 4 5 *